Faulkner and Gender

FAULKNER AND YOKNAPATAWPHA

1994

Faulkner and Gender

FAULKNER AND YOKNAPATAWPHA, 1994

EDITED BY
DONALD M. KARTIGANER
AND
ANN J. ABADIE

UNIVERSITY PRESS OF MISSISSIPPI
JACKSON

99 98 97 96   4 3 2 1

The paper in this book meets the guidelines for permanence and durability of the
Committee on Production Guidelines for Book Longevity of the Council
on Library Resources.

Library of Congress Cataloging-in-Publication Data

Faulkner and Yoknapatawpha Conference (21st : 1994 : University of
Mississippi)
    Faulkner and gender : Faulkner and Yoknapatawpha 1994 / edited by
Donald M. Kartiganer and Ann J. Abadie.
        p.   cm.
    Includes index.
    ISBN 0-87805-921-0 (cloth : alk. paper).—ISBN 0-87805-922-9
(pbk. : alk. paper)
    1. Faulkner, William, 1897–1962—Political and social views—
Congresses.   2. Literature and society—Southern States—
History—20th century—Congresses.   3. Yoknapatawpha County
(Imaginary place)—Congresses.   4. Gender identity in literature—
Congresses.   5. Sex role in literature—Congresses.
I. Kartiganer, Donald M., 1937—   . II. Abadie, Ann J.
PS3511.A86Z783113   1994
813'.52—dc20   96-19048
                                                              CIP

British Library Cataloging-in-Publication data available

Contents

Introduction

*One weekend they took their families to Venice [Califor-
nia], where Zoe and Jill dived and splashed while their
fathers took pictures. In one, Jill was just emerging from
the water. Faulkner looked at it in silence. "It's over very
soon. This is the end of it," he said. "She'll grow into
a woman."*[1]

1

More, perhaps, than any other of the various contextualist
approaches brought to bear on Faulkner's work, the focus on
gender exemplifies the theory of the cultural construction of
reality: the idea that reality is always already shaped according
to a dominant socio/political/ideological order, an order of language. Whatever the nature of an originary, "prediscursive"
realm of anatomical sex, race, genetic or archetypal inheri-
tance—whether it can even be said to exist apart from the
discursive—much recent literary criticism has focused on the
way in which that realm utters itself only through an existing
linguistic system: in the Lacanian terminology, a Symbolic
Order or Law of the Father.

One of the compelling qualities of gender study as a branch
of cultural study is that, owing in large part to the emergence of
feminist criticism, it has convincingly argued the difference
between gender and sex, between what for now we will call the
"acculturated" and the "natural," and consequently the extent
to which gender is the product of an engagement with a social
milieu: the assumption of a style, a set of manners, a stance to
the world, that is less the necessary extension of anatomical sex
than an interpretation of it. One may be born of a particular sex,
but one enacts a gender. It is a role, an impersonation, a
posture—a performance. It is not so much a grounded identity

as a social position, a representation from the repertoire of possibilities within the prevailing linguistic system. Certain gender positions are deemed "marginal," failing to conform to what most gender critics regard as the compulsory heterosexuality and male dominance ordained by that system, but even the marginal takes its cue—and to some extent its particular expression as an outcast speech—from the governing rules of discourse, just as parody borrows, even as it disrupts, a given institution or language.

Consideration of any specific gender role as one of a plurality of options, loosened if not entirely removed from a fixed anatomical ground, opens good fiction—certainly Faulkner's—to a new critical awareness of the variety and richness of character. Despite the presence of a strict hierarchical structure that deems heterosexuality and male hegemony as the only "natural" gender arrangements, Ideal Incarnations of gender, both in society at large and in good fiction, are highly abstract: implicit everywhere as a univocal standard, but never concretely figured. The "straight white bourgeois male," except as the straw man of simplistic class, race, and gender criticism, is missing. Gender "slippage," in other words, seems virtually universal, with every performance failing to some degree to extend seamlessly a "given" sex into actual social practice—every performance, that is, constituting a new interpretation, always awry, both of an immaculate norm and the motley impersonations of a surrounding society.

Among the results of this slippage, a dissonance in gender performance, is a fresh sense of fictional character as a site of multiple, sometimes clashing, personae. Each gender role is a signifier threatening to float free, speaking the reigning discourse, but always with a touch of conscious or unconscious parody. From recognition of the surprising range of gender expression emerges a new critical empathy with those who find themselves occupying the most marginalized positions within the system, as well as with those whose assurance of full membership may become dubious enough to expose them to the most severe psychic constraints—one consequence of which may be outrage at those who have refused such constraints.

The character of Caddy Compson, to cite just one example, in *The Sound and the Fury*—"my heart's darling" for Faulkner and for a good many readers, more recently read as the voiceless, absent woman silenced by a series of male speakers—reveals herself as an extraordinarily eloquent performer of gender possibilities, probably the most varied and certainly the most disruptive in the novel. While playing a maternal role for Benjy and an adoring, submissive sexual role for Dalton Ames, she also adopts a series of "male" roles (some of them, reflecting the overdetermination of gender, coinciding with the "female" roles): taking charge ("we still have to mind me"), being bolder than her brothers in climbing the tree to watch Damuddy's funeral service, preceding the older Quentin in sexual initiation, giving up her daughter to be raised by others while paying child support. As Quentin (enviously?) remembers: "she never was a queen or a fairy she was always a king or a giant or a general."[2]

Out of such a network of gender enactments—none of them more "natural" than another, all of them expressions of complex personality that register variously on Caddy's brothers and on us—may emerge a character less silent than subversive, struggling through multiple roles not so much in search of the "right" one as in commitment to a kind of freedom that no one else in the Compson family dares to recognize or risk: what Judith Butler sees as an act of parody, producing "a fluidity of identities that suggests an openness to resignification and recontextualization."[3]

One of the central debates among feminist critics, which has serious implications for gender critics, has to do with the issue of foundationalism. Originating in the question of whether there is a "woman" apart from the definition of her within the patriarchal order, whether there can be a distinctively "woman's" language to insert within or against the dominant discourse, the issue has expanded into the question of the very ground of gender. Is there a fixed sexual identity which gender interprets, one which, however tenuous the tie between it and actual gender performance, ultimately limits gender, binds it to specific anatomical origins—perhaps measuring it according to some standard of "naturalness"? Or is "woman," indeed "sex" itself, including "man," a product of gender, a creation of the governing discourse that requires certain binary structures (hierarchically valued) in order to justify its own existence? Where, in other words, does gender stop and sex begin?

The most rigorous feminist argument against foundationalism is that by Judith Butler, who employs Michel Foucault's strategy of "genealogy" (at times against Foucault himself) as a way of categorizing even anatomical sex as a "discursive production": "For Foucault, the body is not 'sexed' in any significant sense prior to its determination within a discourse through which it becomes invested with an 'idea' of natural or essential sex. . . . Sexuality is an historically specific organization of power, discourse, bodies, and affectivity. As such, sexuality is understood by Foucault to produce 'sex' as an artificial concept which effectively extends and disguises the power relations responsible for its genesis."[4]

Resisting such notions as a prediscursive Maternal or Mystery identity, or the idea of any language, semiotic or bisexual, that is not itself a cultural construction, Butler insists that the only effective challenge to the cultural order depends upon the rejection of essentialism and the recognition that acculturation is all, that the Symbolic itself has no foundation: "If subversion is possible, it will be a subversion from within the terms of the law, through the possibilities that emerge when the law turns against itself and spawns unexpected permutations of itself. The culturally constructed body will then be liberated, neither to its 'natural' past, nor to its original pleasures, but to an open future of cultural possibilities."[5]

Butler's claim that the myth of foundationalism is itself one of the most powerful constructions of the law, and impossible to bring *against* the law without capitulating to it, is strongly argued. One of the consequences, however—as is frequently the case with a commitment to the supreme power of acculturation—is an inability to account for difference in gender positions, for those who subvert and those who, whatever the inherent slippages, by and large accommodate the law. In the name of consistency and conviction, Butler cannot separate the individual, the "I," from the discourses that construct him or her. Subversion of the law can occur because the "rules governing significance not only restrict, but enable the assertion of alternative domains of cultural intelligibility"; "the injunction *to be* a given gender produces necessary failures, a variety of incoherent configurations that in their multiplicity exceed and defy the injunction by which they are generated." Exceptions, that is, are "enabled," "produced," yet "there is no self that is prior to the convergence or who maintains 'integrity' prior to its entrance into this conflicted cultural field. There is only a taking up of the tools where they lie, where the very 'taking up' is enabled by the tool lying there."[6]

An obvious, if old question remains appropriate. Why do certain people respond to the enabling condition while others do not? Why do some "take up" the tools? The possibility of the parodic revision of the dominant discourse, the gender resourcefulness that can rewrite a role while performing it— these are gestures that suggest an imaginative power, gestures that Faulkner describes throughout his work. They are, in fact, the model of a disruption of convention, of prevailing orders, that is the major quality of that work. The effect, it seems to me, is not of characters "enabled" or "produced"; the discontinuities Caddy risks are available to all the Compsons, but she is the only one to push them to the point of radical subversion. In short, some kind of power—self, will, identity, that learns itself *through* an acculturation whose limits it expands beyond the formerly imaginable—seems at work in both the world and Faulkner's fiction.

And yet the issue may be less momentous for readers of literature than for readers of philosophy. Whether foundational and thus, paradoxically, free of the full limitations of a language system, or wholly constituted by a *"regulated process of repeti-tion,"*[7] Faulkner's grand proliferation of gender acts becomes ultimately a new, splendid source of pleasure and amazement:

> And out of what one sees and hears and out
> Of what one feels, who could have thought to make
> So many selves, so many sensuous worlds,
> As if the air, the mid-day air, was swarming
> With the metaphysical changes that occur,
> Merely in living as and where we live.[8]

2

The thirteen papers presented at the "Faulkner and Gender" Conference fall into two groups: five that are of a fairly general nature, attempting to explore some aspect of Faulkner and gender that pertains to much of the career, followed by eight that focus on specific Faulkner texts. This second group is arranged in the chronological order of the texts discussed.

Doreen Fowler's " 'I want to go home': Faulkner, Gender, and Death" builds upon two of Freud's key texts—"The Uncanny" and *Beyond the Pleasure Principle*—as a way of describing a central duality in Faulkner's portrayal of male characters: "a vacillation between two desires, a desire to keep the self intact and separate from the first other, the mother, and an opposite desire for merger, for a return to the forbidden space of the mother." This divided movement toward, on the one hand, mature, independent adulthood, and, on the other hand, recovery of an original "undifferentiated" union, has, Fowler argues, a biographical grounding in Faulkner's life. Alongside the obvious independence and success of a major writing career there is the fact of Faulkner's protracted adolescence, as well as the lifelong habit of binge drinking that seemed unconsciously designed to reduce him to a state of total dependency—a striking division of behavior and purpose that becomes for Fowler an echo of the fictional conflict: the urge to separate and the urge to return.

Noel Polk begins "Faulkner: The Artist as Cuckold" with a reading of *Absalom, Absalom!* that poses the possibility that the emphasis on race in the novel—especially the concluding argument of Quentin and Shreve that the part blackness of Charles Bon is the reason Henry Sutpen kills him—is a mask concealing issues of sexuality and gender, in particular the fear of cuckoldry: the possibility that Thomas Sutpen discovered not the mixed blood of his Haitian wife, but her premarital sexual betrayal of him. Moving from *Absalom* to an overview of the fiction as well as the life, Polk argues that versions of the cuckold—"the weak husband, the impotent, the voyeur, the pimp"—are a constant imagery in Faulkner, revealing not only a writer who may never have forgiven his wife's initial rejection of him for another man, but illuminating the pathological anxiety of so many of his male characters: "the fear and loathing of women, the shame and filth associated with sexuality, the immutability of desire, and the absolute inextricability of the desire and the shame."

The "Male Homosexual Panic" of John N. Duvall's essay is part of Faulkner's representation of a masculinity in crisis, seeking to define itself at a time of increased awareness of the fluctuations not only of gender but of sexual identity itself. The "panic" emerges as the male need to "police the border between hetero- and homosexuality," a border constituted by, on the one hand, the male desire for the intimacy of homosocial activity, and, on the other hand, the male fear of being regarded as homosexual by "a culture that stigmatizes same sex sexuality." The complexity of that border lies in the fact that "the homo-erotic is embedded in, not opposed to, masculinity," a complexity that Duvall demonstrates in a number of Faulkner's texts, particularly those in which male violence, as in warfare, plays a significant role. The distinctively male action of war in Faulkner contains, Duvall argues, a homoerotic component that devalues "normal" heterosexuality, with the result that "manliness" and heterosexual capacity become opposed qualities. Sexuality, like race and gender in Faulkner, becomes problematic: not a definition but part of an ongoing process, not a stable ground of character but an arena of shifting relations.

Like Duvall's essay, Robert Dale Parker's "Sex and Gender, Feminine and Masculine: Faulkner and the Polymorphous Exchange of Cultural Binaries" addresses the richness and variability of gender identity in Faulkner. Emphasizing the most recent and most extreme approach to the essentialist-culturalist debate on the nature of sex and gender—namely, that which understands both sex *and* gender as culturally constructed—Parker examines some of Faulkner's most complex fictional accounts of females and males oscillating between gender positions. Although he demonstrates how such female characters as Temple Drake and Rosa Coldfield possess a capacity to "vault . . . to the other side of the binary"—largely to protect themselves against rape and patriarchal social oppression—Parker argues that it is Faulkner's male characters who are most anxious about gender transgression, most threatened by the tenuousness of sexual identity. In *The Sound and the Fury* and *Light in August,* as well as in two short stories, Parker explores a number of homoerotic and sexual situations, often inflected by race and forms of triangular desire, which lead less to a definitive position regarding gender roles than to a typically unsettling Faulknerian proliferation of possibility.

In "Maternalizing the Epicene: Faulkner's Paradox of Form and Gender," David Rogers explores the nature and significance of Faulkner's use of the "epicene"—that quality he assigns to such female characters as Cecily Saunders and Temple Drake, but which Rogers expands into a major theme pervading Faulkner's entire corpus, from *Soldiers' Pay* to *The Reivers.* The epicene connotes "sexual uncertainty," which leads to both a "cultural uncertainty" and a "material uncertainty," ultimately emerging as "a sign continually in a state of creative and increasingly immaterial becoming." Focusing on such diverse types as the mulatto, the wanderer, the unwed earth mother, and such characters as Margaret Powers, Dilsey, Lena Grove, and Ratliff, Rogers analyzes the blurring of boundaries and

gender distinctions—of what Alice Jardine refers to as the
"Big Dichotomies"—in order to reveal Faulkner's fiction as the
portrayal of a vast action of continual, dynamic process.

Continuing the emphasis on the "performative nature" of
gender—that is, gender as a cultural construction rather than a
biological given—Minrose Gwin, in "Did Ernest Like Gordon?:
Faulkner's *Mosquitoes* and the Bite of 'Gender Trouble,'"
identifies the early novel as uniquely disruptive, primarily
through its use of parody as a means of "denaturalizing" heterosexuality—subverting its traditional status as precultural origin,
variations from which are always perversions. Ernest Talliaferro
is not only a possible member of a "queer group" that serves to
confer normality on the "straight" one; his attempts at heterosexual engagement become a parody of such engagement, the
effect of which, as Judith Butler has emphasized, is to dramatize
the synthetic nature of sexuality itself: "the very notion of an
original." Particularly striking in Gwin's essay is her discussion
of passages excluded from the novel (probably by the publisher)
that extended that parody to what was apparently an unaccept-
able degree.

Faulkner's susceptibility to some of his culture's current
attitudes regarding homosexuality becomes for James Polchin,
in "Selling a Novel: Faulkner's *Sanctuary* as a Psychosexual
Text," an often ignored key to the popularity of that novel among
both contemporary reviewers and readers. In the characters
of Popeye and Horace Faulkner creates "two veiled cases of
homosexuality," the first an example of the psychopathy and
criminality commonly assumed to be linked to homosexuality,
the second a case of repressed homosexuality. Despite their
overt positions on opposite sides of the law and professional
respectability, Horace and Popeye, according to Polchin, mirror
each other as "the feminized, unnatural man," one of whom is
eventually destroyed by society, while the other is returned to
his conventional, domesticated, heterosexual role.

The struggle for control and definition of female identity—the
struggle to determine gender—becomes for Michael Lahey the

central drama of Faulkner's comparatively neglected short story
"There Was a Queen." According to Lahey, Narcissa Sartoris
(the widow of Bayard from *Flags in the Dust*) is torn between
public and private female identities, the first a largely Sartoris-
male creation (although represented in the story by Aunt Jenny
and Elnora), the second, a female one, which the first recognizes
but refuses to validate. The focus of these opposed identities is
the erotic letters which Narcissa received from Byron Snopes in
Flags, and which now, twelve years later, have fallen into the
hands of an unscrupulous FBI agent. Narcissa is at once shocked
by the letters—and at the prospect of their being made public—
and fascinated by them; offended at Byron's epistolary attempts
to create for himself her erotic identity, and yet also tempted to
regard the letters as an opportunity for her own erotic liberation.
Narcissa's situation becomes for Lahey a representation of a
fundamental Southern debate over what is "appropriate" to
female gender.

In her study of chapter 5 in *Absalom, Absalom!*, Andrea
Dimino demonstrates how the blurring of gender becomes part
of the narrative strategy of the novel. Distinguishing between
the Miss Rosa of chapter 1 and the narrator of the centrally
placed, almost entirely italicized chapter 5, Dimino argues that
the second "Miss Rosa" is a new voice in the text, an "expansion
and blurring" of the first, which transforms Quentin Compson
from a passive witness to the Sutpen history into its chief
reinterpreter. The narrator of chapter 5 is a melding of voices,
questioning chronology and causality: the "decorous ordering"
of the rigid systems of social and narrative convention. She is
"not superseded by the subsequent narrative that Quentin and
Shreve create," but rather enacts the breakthrough that makes
it possible.

In "Faulkner's 'Greek Amphora Priestess': Verbena and Violence in *The Unvanquished*," Patricia Yaeger examines the
female body as simultaneously an entry point of history and a
site of gender definition and oppression—specifically the body
of Drusilla Hawk Sartoris, whose shifting physical identity be-

comes a virtual "somatic battlefield for the race and class struggles" that go on just beneath the surface of the novel. The conflict of *The Unvanquished*, saving it from its tendency toward sentimentality and melodrama, is rooted, on the one hand, in its awareness of the limited choices of Southern women—"Drusilla's desire for a life of significant action"—as well as of the "vast and capacious humanity" of African Americans, and, on the other hand, the displacement of that awareness by its utopian portrayal of the emergence of the New Southern male hero, Bayard Sartoris. Faulkner's resort to comic trivialization of African American voting rights and the reduction of Drusilla to hysteria seriously mutes, yet does not wholly silence, his realization that an emergent New South has not yet dealt with the problems so prominent in the Old.

For Deborah Clarke, in "Gender, War, and Cross-Dressing in *The Unvanquished*," Faulkner's Civil War novel—in its primary attention to the home front rather than the battle fields—describes the essential breakdown of gender, as well as generational and racial, categories. Women, African Americans, and children, in the havoc of war, find themselves in a "cross-dresser's dream," free to violate those binary (and necessarily hierarchical) divisions which normally reduce them to subservient status. The deep irony, of course, is that their sole purpose is ultimately to restore the very system against which they are rebelling. With the end of the war, that system reasserts itself, particularly in the case of Ringo, who has momentarily supplanted Bayard as Granny Millard's chief partner in trading with the Yankees. The complex and controversial exception is Drusilla, the formerly cross-dressed soldier, who, Clarke argues, mounts a new and even greater threat to the binary system by playing her reassumed feminine role "with a vengeance," revealing the inadequacy of "male" discourse, ultimately becoming "so powerfully feminine as to seem masculine."

In "Faulkner Unplugged: Abortopoesis and *The Wild Palms*" Joseph Urgo examines the implications for gender and the attempt of Harry Wilbourne and Charlotte Rittenmeyer to "unplug" themselves from their traditional sources of power: Harry from his career as a physician, Charlotte from her role as a mother. The man's escape from a patriarchically inspired profession, his violation of social convention, has a quality of characteristic American male individualism and freedom, signalling "life and vitality," whereas the woman's comparable gesture of autonomy suggests death, infanticide, suicide. Remarkably prescient of our current "Age of Abortion," *The Wild Palms* enacts abortion as plot, as narrative strategy, and as a prevailing imagery, complicating the issue always with the question of gender and its role in our "quest for creative freedom, individual license, and autonomy."

In "Mister: The Drama of Black Manhood in Faulkner and Morrison," Philip M. Weinstein points to the problematic condition of the African American male figure, whose right of "unfettered identity" depends on an assumption of manhood explicitly denied the slave and implicitly the freedman. Emphasizing the role of property ownership—since Locke the key element in the recognition of the free man—he explores the crisis of characters such as Paul D and Lucas Beauchamp, who cannot claim to own even themselves or cannot demand the respect (signified by the address "Mister") that will allow them the status of "fully individuated human beings within the social order." Ultimately, Weinstein suggests an important distinction between the two writers, namely, that Faulkner remains largely within the codes of "mastery" and "difference"—whatever the racial situation—while Morrison pursues a concept of mutuality, a possibility of knowing the "self through transferential investment in others."

Donald M. Kartiganer
The University of Mississippi
Oxford, Mississippi

NOTES

1. Joseph Blotner, *Faulkner: A Biography,* One-Volume Edition (New York: Random House, 1984), 459.

2. William Faulkner, *The Sound and the Fury* (New York: Vintage International, 1990), 74, 173.

3. Judith Butler, *Gender Trouble: Feminism and the Subversion of Identity* (New York: Routledge, 1990), 138.

4. Ibid., 92.

5. Ibid., 93.

6. Ibid., 145.

7. Ibid.

8. Wallace Stevens, "Esthetique du Mal," *The Collected Poems of Wallace Stevens* (New York: Alfred A. Knopf, 1964), 326.

A Note on the Conference

The Twenty-first Annual Faulkner and Yoknapatawpha Conference sponsored by the University of Mississippi in Oxford took place July 31–August 6, 1994, with nearly three hundred of the author's admirers from around the world in attendance. The thirteen lectures presented at the conference are collected in this volume. Brief mention is made here of other activities that took place during the week.

The conference opened with a reception hosted by the University Museums and an exhibition of paintings by the Mississippi artist John McCrady (1911–1968), whose painting, *Political Rally*, was the illustration for the conference poster and program. The Museums staff also organized a *Find the Faulkner/ Name the Novel* puzzle exhibit. At the opening session Acting Vice Chancellor Gerald Walton welcomed participants, and William Ferris, Director of the Center for the Study of Southern Culture, presented the 1994 Eudora Welty Awards in Creative Writing to Matthew F. Gill of Hattiesburg and Paige Porter of Clinton. The awards are selected annually through a competition held in high schools throughout Mississippi. Following the presentation was *Voices from Yoknapatawpha*, readings of passages from Faulkner's fiction selected and arranged by former conference director Evans Harrington.

Conference participants then gathered at Faulkner's home, Rowan Oak, for the announcement of the winner of the fifth Faux Faulkner write-alike contest, sponsored by American Airlines' *American Way* magazine, Yoknapatawpha Press and its *Faulkner Newsletter*, and the University of Mississippi. John H. Ostdick, editor of *American Way*, joined Dean Faulkner Wells, organizer of the contest, in congratulating Samuel Tumey, a lawyer from Liberty, Mississippi, for his winning parody:

"Quentin and Shreve on Football." After a buffet supper, held on the lawn of Dr. and Mrs. M. B. Howorth, Jr., and sponsored by *American Way*, Patricia Yaeger delivered the opening lecture and Square Books hosted a party.

Monday's program consisted of four lectures and the presentation "Knowing William Faulkner," during which J. M. Faulkner presented slides and stories of his famous uncle. Other highlights of the conference included a panel discussion by local residents—Howard Duvall, Mildred Murray Hopkins, Chester A. McLarty, and Patricia Young—moderated by M. C. Falkner, another of the writer's nephews; "Teaching Faulkner" sessions conducted by visiting scholars James B. Carothers, Robert W. Hamblin, Arlie Herron, and Charles A. Peek; a reading by Oxford writer Larry Brown; and bus tours of North Mississippi and the Delta. Social highlights were a party at Tyler Place hosted by Ruthie and Chuck Noyes, Sarah and Allie Smith, and Colby Kullman; a walk through Bailey's Woods and a picnic at Rowan Oak; and the closing party at Ammadelle, home of Mrs. John Tatum and her family.

The conference planners are grateful to all the individuals and organizations who support the Faulkner and Yoknapatawpha Conference annually. In addition to those mentioned above, we wish to thank Mrs. Jack Cofield, Dr. William E. Strickland, Mr. Richard Howorth of Square Books, Mr. James Rice of Holiday Inn/Oxford, the City of Oxford, and the Oxford Tourism Council.

Faulkner and Gender

FAULKNER AND YOKNAPATAWPHA

1994

"I want to go home": Faulkner, Gender, and Death

Doreen Fowler

In the Appendix to *The Sound and the Fury*, as though an afterthought to the novel, in prose as richly evocative as any in literature, Faulkner describes Quentin Compson's love of death:

> But who loved death above all, who loved only death, loved and lived in a deliberate and almost perverted anticipation of death, as a lover loves and deliberately refrains from the waiting willing friendly tender incredible body of his beloved, until he can no longer bear not the refraining but the restraint, and so flings, hurls himself, relinquishing, drowning.[1]

The woman Quentin desires is death: or, perhaps more accurately, the death Quentin desires is a woman. Sex and death commingle in Faulkner's prose, as if death and sex shared some deep, secret commonality.

Faulkner is far from alone in urging a correspondence between sex and death. This equivalence is found in widely divergent cultures. The French phrase for sexual orgasm, for example, is *petit mort*, little death. And the Elizabethans commonly used the phrase "to die" as a synonym for sexual intercourse. And what, after all, is rape but an attempt to sexually annihilate the female other? In Faulkner, sex and death become very nearly interchangeable. When Quentin asks Caddy about Dalton Ames, "Caddy you hate him dont you?," she replies, "yes I hate him I would die for him Ive already died for him I die for him over and over again everytime this goes."[2] Caddy's answer is cryptic, mystifying, unless we understand that, for her, sex is a kind of dying. Of course, to most of us, sex and death seem quite discriminable. And yet the insistent pairing of sex and death in all literatures argues some buried psychic correspondence. To locate that correspondence, I turn now to Freud's essay on "The Uncanny."

In this essay, Freud begins by distinguishing the uncanny from that which incites fear generally. He argues that within the larger category of general fear there exists a particular kind of eeriness that attaches to certain objects, situations, or events. This particular eeriness Freud labels the uncanny. "Uncanny" is of course the English translation of Freud's German word. The German term is *unheimlich,* literally unhomelike, a word with resonances that the English translation lacks. The inequivalence of the two words becomes markedly apparent as Freud proceeds to examine "uncanniness" by a two-pronged attack. First he explores the etymology of the word; then he considers a number of situations that produce an uncanny feeling, seeking to locate in the objects that frighten us the impetus for the fear.

Freud's linguistic study of the word *"unheimlich"* produces an interesting finding, namely, that the word "homelike" contains among its many shades of meaning one which coincides with its opposite, "un-homelike." Strangely enough, that which means comfortable or familiar also comes to mean that which is alien. This oddity comes about because *heimlich* has two meanings—it means both familiar and also hidden or concealed; and the second meaning of the word evolved until it finally denoted the unfamiliar. Having made this discovery, Freud asks us to bear it in mind, hinting that this paradoxical merging of opposites will be called into play later in his analysis. He then ponders a number of instances of the uncanny, leaving until last the one that appears to be most germane. Possibly he is saving the best until last; more probably he is repressing this example, hoping to bury it at the end. Freud concludes his examination of uncanniness by citing this case:

> It often happens that neurotic men declare that they feel there is something uncanny about the female genital organs. This *unheim-*

lich place, however, is the entrance to the former *Heim* [home] of all human beings, to the place where each one of us lived once upon a time and in the beginning. There is a joking saying that "Love is home-sickness"; and whenever a man dreams of a place or a country and says to himself, while he is dreaming: "this place is familiar to me, I've been here before," we may interpret the place as being his mother's genitals or her body. In this case too, then, the *unheimlich* is what was once *heimlich,* familiar; the prefix *"un"* ["un"] is the token of repression.[3]

The answer Freud was seeking was at hand from the beginning. As if, at some subliminal level, he always knew the answer, it was at hand in the name he proposed for the class of fear he was investigating, in the name, *"unheimlich."* The English translation, "uncanny," obscures the meaning that the German word lays bare, for what is *"unheimlich,"* unhomelike, is the home we repress, that is, the original home, the womb. Our first home, the place of origin that enclosed us before birth, inspires a feeling of unease, a feeling of the *unheimlich.* The womb is both homelike, comfortable and familiar, and unhome-like, fearfully alien, because origin implies end, because the darkness of preexistence seems to image eerily the darkness of nonexistence, because the mother who gives us life must also be she who takes it away. Thus *heimlich* and *unheimlich* converge because that which is familiar to us is also frightening; and sex seems to prefigure death because, for the male partner, sexual intercourse can appear to figure a return to the womb, a return to what was before life began.

In "The Uncanny," Freud, whose theories are male- and father-centered, comes as close as he ever does to uncovering a troubling image buried deep in the unconscious, an image of womb as tomb. However, in another influential essay, which was written at approximately the same time as "The Uncanny," he invokes death as a return to an original state. In "Beyond the Pleasure Principle," Freud puts forth his most controversial theory: he deduces the existence of a death instinct. He proposes that at some indeterminate point in time external forces accidentally awakened life in lifeless matter. Because the instincts are regressive by nature, Freud states, their goal is always to return to an earlier condition: this means that the organism seeks a return to the beginning, to an original inanimate condition. Freud formulates this return this way:

> This final goal of all organic striving can be stated too. It would be counter to the conservative nature of instinct if the goal of life were a state never hitherto reached. It must rather be an ancient starting point, which the living being left long ago, and to which it harks back again by all the circuitous paths of development. If we may assume as an experience admitting of no exception that everything living dies from causes within itself, and returns to the inorganic, we can only say *"The goal of all life is death,"* and, casting back, *"the inanimate was there before the animate."*[4]

Freud's theory makes no reference to motherhood, but his proposition that death is a return to the origin disturbingly conjures the figure of the mother. Death, he tells us, is a return to "an ancient starting point, which the living being left long ago." The place we left long ago, the starting point that lurks repressed in our psyches, is the maternal womb. Freud's theory that our lives are circular, that we return in the end to the beginning, would seem to be consistent with a distressing psychic and cultural association of the mother with death.

Lacan is a Freudian revisionist, and his rewriting of Freud foregrounds a psychic projection of death onto the mother. In Lacanian theory, separation from the mother constitutes identity. According to Lacan, in the beginning, that is, in the womb and in the first months of life, the child exists in an imaginary dyadic relation with the mother in which there is no difference and no self. To distinguish a separate self, to distinguish self from other, there must be an absence. That absence is created by splitting from the maternal body. In obedience to the Law of the Father, symbolized by the phallus, we separate from the mother, who becomes the first other. Her exclusion makes possible identity, meaning, and culture. After this rupture, for the rest of our lives, we feel a lack within us, and we spend our lives hunting for substitutes to cover over the gap left by her absence; but, if we attempt to fill the gap, we are gathered back into the whole from which we came.[5]

Faulkner's novel *As I Lay Dying* can be read as an extended illustration of Lacanian theory. Lacan holds that for there to be separate existence the mother's body must be banished. All of *As I Lay Dying* is an attempt to bury the body of the dead mother. In this novel, burying Addie resonates metaphorically, as Faulkner uses the image of burial to outwardly sign a psychic repression of the mother. Repression, the desire to erase the mother's presence, is really the issue here, for the family members not only bury Addie after she dies, they also secretly wish for her death as she lies dying, as if her death will somehow empower them. For example, as Jewel watches Cash labor over Addie's coffin, he says, "Good God do you want to see her in it";[6] and Darl, who intuits Dewey Dell's desire to go to Jefferson for an abortion, says, "You want her to die so you can get to town: is that it?"[7] Jewel's grief-driven outburst and Darl's mysterious intuitive powers break through to the unconscious, uncovering a perverse desire for the mother's absence. Read in Lacanian terms, this hidden, guilty desire is to be expected, for, according to Lacan, only by repressing the mother can we fully come into our own as separate, conscious selves. This theory also makes sense of Vardaman's riddling cry, "My mother is a fish."[8] Vardaman equates his mother with the fish he killed and they all ate as a way of expressing his ill-defined sense that their mother is somehow their sacrificial victim, that *they* are the vultures who feed on her corpse. At every level, the novel dramatizes the Lacanian position that by erasing the mother we come into being. Only by burying Addie can the family members assume their places in a patriarchal order. Now Anse can get his new teeth and a wife, a substitute for the banished mother; now, as Tull's daughters are quick to observe, Addie's sons can also seek wives; now they can get to town, symbol of Lacan's Symbolic order, the world of language and culture.

If we read *As I Lay Dying* through Lacan, as an extended

reenactment of the separation from the mother that constitutes
selfhood, we should note that Faulkner also inscribes in this
novel Addie's protest against maternal repression. If the family
is intent on burying Addie's body, Addie is equally intent on
refusing to be buried. Her request to be interred in Jefferson
defers her burial, permitting her to force herself onto their
conscious minds, as she surfaces in the flood and erupts out of
the burning barn. Addie is the mother who refuses death.[9]

If in *As I Lay Dying* Faulkner inscribes separation from the
mother's body as the price of admission into patriarchal culture,
in most of his novels he observes a vacillation between two
desires, a desire to keep the self intact and separate from the
first other, the mother, and an opposite desire for merger and
return. An instructive example of this ambivalence is Goodhue
Coldfield's death in *Absalom, Absalom!*

The circumstances of Rosa's father's death are most peculiar
and have often been misread by critics. Goodhue Coldfield nails
himself into an attic room after his store is broken into by
Confederate soldiers. Reading this passage, some critics have
concluded that he is hiding in the attic, seeking to evade military
service.[10] But Rosa's father is not a coward. Rather, he is
responding to a violation of his borders. When the Confederate
soldiers loot his store, they violate his boundaries; more, these
boundaries are transgressed not by the enemy, but by his
countrymen, as if there were no difference between friend and
foe. He responds by trying to shore up the self. He retreats to
the attic room and nails himself shut in it, trying to keep the
self intact and the other out. At the same time, however, the
form that his retrenchment takes betrays a conflicting desire for
dissolution and absorption. Mr. Coldfield shuts himself up in a
small, enclosed, dark space, and in that space he is totally
dependent on his daughter, a mother-substitute, for his continued existence. By an elaborate system of pulleys, Rosa channels
food to her father; this intricate food-bearing system markedly
resembles another—the intricate web of veins and arteries that
relays nourishment to the fetus in the womb of the mother.

Mr. Coldfield's chosen confinement metaphorically recreates a return to the womb; and, when he starves himself to death in the attic room, with plates of untouched food beside him, his suicide consummates his ambivalent desires for separation and return. On the one hand, by refusing to accept the sustenance hoisted to him by his daughter, he symbolically rejects maternal nurture. On the other, in death, he succumbs to a desire for absorption.

With unsettling regularity, death is imaged in Faulkner's fiction as both a denied and desired return to the origin. In *Absalom, Absalom!*, Henry Sutpen kills Charles Bon to prevent a return to an original undifferentiated state, that is, he kills Bon to prevent his black brother from marrying his white sister, to prevent both incest, a reversion to the womb, and a levelling of black-white difference. Yet, after killing Bon to stop this return, Henry himself returns to the mother. After he shoots Bon, Henry disappears, and the next time he is seen, he is dying in a small, dark, upper room of the Sutpen house, nursed by a surrogate mother, his older sister, Clytie. Figuratively, Henry has returned to the womb. As Henry tells Quentin, he has come home to die. Death is a homecoming, a return to the place of origin.

And Henry, we remember, is ushered into death by a mother figure, by Clytie. At one level, Clytie is trying to save Henry. Clytie thinks the ambulance that turns into their drive is the long awaited Law coming to take Henry away for killing Bon. She sets fire to the house to save Henry from hanging. That at least appears to be her conscious intention, the intention as-cribed to her by Quentin and Shreve. At another level, how-ever, Clytie's incineration of herself, Henry, and Sutpen's house may be driven by a desire she is not consciously aware of, a buried, unrecognized desire for revenge; for, when she burns down the house with herself and Henry in it, she is slaying Bon's murderer and reducing to ashes the symbol of Sutpen's dream. Albeit unconsciously, Clytie plays the role of avenger

and, more than this, since she acts as mother to both Bon's son
and grandson, she is the mother avenger.

Everywhere in *Absalom, Absalom!* we observe a deep ambivalence toward women. Consider, for example, the case of
Thomas Sutpen. Sutpen's stated ambition is to establish a
posterity, to beget sons who will carry his name forward into
succeeding generations. It does not take a psychoanalyst to read
into this consciously avowed purpose a desire to overcome
death. In fact, all of Sutpen's life's work expresses this desire.
He devotes his life to the pursuit of tokens of his immortality:
the house, the land, the family, the outsized marble grave
marker. And this same desire to defeat death inspires Sutpen's
scarcely veiled misogyny. In a novel filled with barred passages,
Sutpen repeatedly shuts out women. He sets aside his first wife;
he drives Rosa away with his crude sexual proposition; he
dismisses Milly, comparing her unfavorably to his horse, all
with the same purpose: in his quest to escape death, Sutpen
seeks to elude women, to extricate himself from a dark commin-
gling that may seem to foreshadow the ultimate darkness.

Sutpen, then, denies women as he denies death. And yet
even Sutpen betrays signs of an opposite desire to return to the
matrix. Sutpen shows traces of a death wish when, toward the
end of his life, he repeatedly drinks himself unconscious. This
unconscious state simulates death. It is Sutpen's way of flirting
with nonexistence, and, predictably, this courting of death takes
the form of a return. When Sutpen is unconscious and helpless,
he is carried home to Judith, the daughter surrogate for the
mother, who opens the door and takes him in. Each time
Sutpen's limp body is brought home to Judith, it prefigures his
death, until the last time, when Sutpen is carried home dead.
For Thomas Sutpen, as for so many others—Goodhue Coldfield,
Henry Sutpen, Charles Bon, and Bon's son—death is a homecoming.

Thus far I have traced in Faulkner's fiction an image out of
the unconscious, an image of death as a return to the original
place. But this unconscious image is inscribed not only in

Faulkner's novels; it figures also in his life, and even more remarkably, in his death. The same demons that spurred him to write his great novels also drove him to bizarre practices, practices that sometimes endangered his life as they enacted a return.

To begin with, Faulkner often exhibited regressive tendencies.[11] For instance, his childhood years of dependency seem to have been unduly prolonged; except for a few short trips, he lived with his parents, dependent on them both for economic and emotional support, until he married at the age of thirty-two. Moreover, Faulkner looked like an adolescent until he was almost thirty. His face was narrow and immature, and, in addition, he was small and terribly thin: at twenty-one he weighed only 113 pounds. But Faulkner not only looked like a boy well past adolescence, he also behaved like one. For example, when, in 1918, at the age of twenty-one, he lived apart from his mother for the first time, he wrote to her daily or every other day, and his letters, filled with boyish requests for food, clothing, and news from home, betray a painful homesickness. "Momsey," he writes to his mother, "I couldn't live here at all but for your letters. I love you darling."[12]

Other instances of a latent desire in Faulkner to return to childhood could be cited. For example, when he came home from the war, people in Oxford expected him to find a wife and take up a profession; instead they saw him playing games in the streets of Oxford with ten-year-olds, his brother Dean and Dean's friends. Even when Faulkner left home temporarily and visited New Orleans, he seemed merely to exchange one family for another, for in New Orleans he lived like a son with Sherwood and Elizabeth Prall Anderson, whom he cast in the role of surrogate parents.

These regressive tendencies are the outward manifestation of a residual desire to resume the infant's relation with the mother. In fact, in certain rather bizarre ways, Faulkner seemed sometimes to seek to infantilize himself. I refer to Faulkner's curious drinking practices. In the eyes of at least one witness, Faulkner's

manner of drinking conjured the image of a baby nursing. The
observer's response is interesting enough to be quoted in full.
On one occasion, in 1921, a young would-be poet, James
Feibleman, observed Faulkner drinking in the offices of *The
Double Dealer*. While other writers sat in chairs talking and
drinking, Faulkner sat silently in a corner on the floor—in spite
of an empty chair beside him—drinking out of a whiskey bottle.
Feibleman was struck by the way Faulkner drank from the
bottle: Faulkner, he said, held the bottle "near his head and
tipped [it] into his mouth from time to time," giving "the
impression more of nursing than of drinking."[13] I mention
Feibleman's observation as a way of leading up to a discussion
of Faulkner's notorious binge drinking, for Faulkner's epic
drunkennesses, when read for their symbolic significance, reveal the meaning that Feibleman covertly alludes to; they reveal
a desire to return.

Faulkner could and did drink socially. He also, if he chose,
could abstain from drinking altogether. But on certain occasions,
he quite deliberately would choose to binge drink. This binge
drinking was a means to an end; it was a vehicle Faulkner used
to regress. This rather large claim is, I think, supported by
the often repressed details of Faulkner's drinking bouts. For
instance, when Faulkner drank to get drunk, he retired to his
bed, wearing either pajamas, or just a pajama top or bottom, or
nothing. In bed, he would drink until he passed out. When he
came to, he would drink himself unconscious again. This cycle
would be repeated, for days, sometimes weeks, until he chose
to stop or until he was hospitalized. By means of this protracted
drinking Faulkner rendered himself completely helpless. During and after a bout, he would have to be nursed like an infant.
He would be spoon-fed food and fluids. Sometimes he would
soil himself in bed and have to be changed. During these
periods of dependency, in his early years and sometimes even
after his marriage, it was his mother who nursed him. In fact,
observing the way Faulkner's excessive drinking earned him his
mother's undivided attention, John Faulkner often opined that

his brother feigned drunkenness so as to be waited on by their mother.[14] While John was wrong about one thing—Faulkner's drunkenness was altogether genuine—he may have been right about another. He may have accurately guessed the unconscious aim of Faulkner's binges. At least part of Faulkner's purpose in drinking in this most peculiar way may have been to return to an exclusive relation with his mother. Certainly the desire for an exclusive relation with the mother or her representative figures prominently in Faulkner's novels: Quentin Compson falsely confesses to incest with Caddy to "isolate [her] out of the loud world," he says, "so that it would have to flee us of necessity."[15] Similarly, a furious Jewel Bundren, faced with the imminent loss of his mother, turns to violence to express his desire for sole possession of Addie: "It would just be me and her on a high hill and me rolling the rocks down the hill at their faces, picking them up and throwing them down the hill faces and teeth and all by God until she was quiet and not that goddamn adze going One lick less. One lick less and we could be quiet."[16]

By binge drinking, then, Faulkner symbolized a return to a former, forbidden relation with the mother, a return often invoked in his fiction. And, in his life as in his fiction, this desire for a maternal reunion is experienced as a death wish. The convergence of a desire to die with a desire to return is perhaps nowhere more strikingly illustrated than in Faulkner's drinking bouts, for at the same time as his excessive drinking infantilized him it also endangered his life. By consuming such large quantities of alcohol, Faulkner may well have killed himself. With good reason, Frederick Karl calls these drinking binges "virtually acts of self-destruction,"[17] for, when Faulkner drank himself unconscious, his brain activity was reduced, and his blood pressure, heart rate, and respiration were depressed; in effect, he was taking a step toward a coma, from which he might never have awakened. Thus Faulkner's drinking, which satisfied a desire to regress, might well have taken him all the way back, to the darkness before there was a William Faulkner.

To say the least, Faulkner's drinking was bizarre, but even more bizarre is a tactic adopted by Faulkner's mother, Miss Maud, to curb her son's drinking, a tactic that was meant to save him but which might have killed him. Miss Maud hated her son's drinking, as she had hated her husband's, and she came up with a seemingly clever ploy to trick her son into sobriety when a bout had begun. When Faulkner had taken to his bed and drunk himself unconscious, Miss Maud would dose him with sleeping pills.[18] She did this with the best of intentions. Her purpose was to prevent continued drinking by keeping him asleep. What of course Miss Maud did not know, since it was not widely known at that time, is that she could have killed him. The mixing of barbiturates and alcohol is deadly. By administering sleeping pills to a man who had recently consumed one or more fifths of bourbon, Miss Maud could have caused Faulkner to die of a drug overdose.

Most likely, Miss Maud never knew that she had endangered her son's life. But Faulkner certainly knew. He knew his mother gave him sleeping pills while he lay unconscious, and he knew the dangers of mixing alcohol with drugs. The profound irony of Miss Maud's well-meant act would not be lost on him. And this irony makes its way into his fiction. In *Requiem for a Nun,* Nancy Mannigoe, nurse to Temple Drake's children, decides that the only way she can save the child Temple is about to abandon is by smothering her to death. In *Absalom Absalom!,* Clytie, meaning to save Henry, sends him to his death. Faulkner's fiction is peopled with maternal figures who, with the best of intentions, threaten death.

I turn now to the strange circumstances of Faulkner's death, which, by some quirk of fate, can be read as yet another reenactment of a figurative return to the origin. The events surrounding Faulkner's death are well known. Faulkner died of a heart attack at Wright's sanitarium in Byhalia, Mississippi, in the early morning hours of July 6, 1962. He had begun drinking a day or so earlier, and on the fifth of July, early in the drinking cycle, he consented to be taken to the small private hospital.

His nephew, Jim Faulkner, and his wife, Estelle, checked him in at 6 p.m. and stayed with him until 10 p.m. At 2 a.m. Estelle was awakened by a phone call. Faulkner was dead. These are the facts as reported in Blotner's two-volume biography published in 1974. The account is repeated, virtually unchanged, in his one-volume edition, published ten years later. All subsequent biographers have essentially repeated the facts as reported by Blotner, as if there were no more to be known about Faulkner's death. And so certainly it seemed. In 1985, for example, Joseph Blotner consulted Dr. Wright again for an article he was writing entitled "Faulkner's Last Days." Blotner records Wright's rather curt reply: "Dr. Wright said that he had provided all the information that was available when Blotner interviewed him in November 1966 and that there was nothing new to be learned about Faulkner's admission to the hospital or his death there of a heart attack on 6 July, shortly after midnight."[19] Despite Dr. Wright's rather summary dismissal, recently new details about Faulkner's last moments have emerged. In the March 1992 issue of *Southern Living*, in a brief and largely overlooked essay entitled "Brother Will's Passing," Jim Faulkner has retold the story of Faulkner's death, and has added some intriguing details that, for one reason or another, did not make their way into Blotner's biography. Jim Faulkner's account would certainly seem to take precedence over Blotner's. Faulkner's nephew had first-hand knowledge of the events he describes. He was among the last to see Faulkner alive and was among the first to arrive at the scene after Faulkner expired. The details of Faulkner's death were reported to him by Dr. Wright and by the attending nurse within hours after the event. By contrast, Joseph Blotner interviewed Dr. Wright in 1966, four years later, and Blotner never spoke with the nurse who, curiously, refused Blotner's request for an interview.[20]

I propose now to compare two texts, two versions of the death of William Faulkner, Joseph Blotner's and Jim Faulkner's. First, I quote from the 1974 edition of Blotner's biography:

Faulkner had been resting quietly. A few minutes after half past one, he stirred and then sat up on the side of his bed. Before the nurse could reach him he groaned and fell over. Within five minutes Dr. Wright was there, but he could detect no pulse or heartbeat. He applied external heart massage for forty-five minutes without results. He tried mouth-to-mouth resuscitation, again with no results. It had been a coronary occlusion. There was nothing more he could do. William Faulkner was gone. [21]

In the one-volume edition of Blotner's biography issued in 1984, this text is repeated verbatim with one difference. In the later edition, Blotner omits the sentence, "It had been a coronary occlusion," and instead writes, some paragraphs later, that "Dr. Wright called it a coronary occlusion," [22] sounding a note of uncertainty. I turn now to Jim Faulkner's reconstruction of these same moments in his 1992 essay. According to Faulkner's nephew, who got his information from Dr. Wright and his nurse in the early morning hours of July 6, 1962, Faulkner died this way:

The nurse was in Brother Will's room shortly after midnight. He sat up while she gave him a shot. Then he put his right hand over his heart, groaned, and lay back down. The nurse called Dr. Wright, and he got to him in about five minutes. He worked with Brother Will for nearly an hour, but he couldn't bring him back. [23]

In Blotner's account, there is a significant omission: the woman is omitted. The nurse who figures so prominently in Faulkner's nephew's narration is unaccountably missing from Blotner's. Even more surprisingly, the injection the nurse administered immediately prior to Faulkner's death is absent from Blotner's version. Consider for a moment this shot. Almost certainly the nurse injected Faulkner with a sedative. What else would a nurse be giving a patient in the middle of the night but something to help him sleep? Moreover, elsewhere in his biography Blotner writes that it was standard practice at the Byhalia clinic to administer "a mild sedative when the patient was admitted" and then to "switch to something stronger" thereafter. [24] Sedatives, barbiturates, were commonly prescribed at that time to control withdrawal symptoms in recovering alcoholics. If indeed it was a sedative that the nurse gave him, then an eerie repetition took place just before Faulkner died, as the nurse reenacted Maud Faulkner's practice of dosing her son with sleeping pills as he lay in a drunken stupor.

We will never know with certainty the cause of Faulkner's death. Most likely, Faulkner died of a heart attack, as his death certificate states. The injection the nurse gave him, despite its proximity to Faulkner's death, most probably did not provoke his death. Faulkner was checked into the hospital at 6 p.m. He had consumed no alcohol, or small monitored quantities of it, since that time. Given that there were not high concentrations of alcohol in his blood at the time the sedative was administered, it is unlikely it could harm him. That said, however, the injection takes on importance because of its absence from Blotner's text. It is a fact that was withheld. Presumably, when Blotner interviewed Dr. Wright in 1966, the doctor sought to expunge this information from the record. Interestingly, Dr. Wright did not lie outright to Blotner. He merely censored his narration. The nurse who administered the shot, we recall, refused Blotner's request for an interview outright. She chose not to speak at all, repressing not a part, but all of the experience.

"Facts," Faulkner wrote in *Requiem for a Nun*, are "rubble dross";[25] they have little to do with truth. And, as Faulkner demonstrated past doubt in *Absalom, Absalom!*, it is impossible ever to reconstruct a factually accurate model of a past event, for the witnesses' reports are always subjective, censored, and self-serving, like Dr. Wright's account of Faulkner's last moments. For this reason, I am not so much concerned with the historical truth of Faulkner's death, which we can never know, as I am with the metaphorical significance of his passing, for, metaphorically, Faulkner's death was of a piece with his life and with his fiction.

Metaphorically, the nurse who is missing from Blotner's account is a mother figure. By his severe and protracted drinking, Faulkner made himself as helplessly dependent as an infant and put his life in the hands of a mother figure. When Faulkner first started his binge drinking and for many years thereafter, it was his mother who saw him through these bouts, sitting by his bedside night and day, caring for him, keeping him alive. In later years, a series of mother substitutes, both women and men, played Maud Faulkner's role. The nurse who attended Faulkner at Wright's sanitarium, who sat up through the night just outside his door while he slept,[26] was the last in a long series of mother substitutions. This last time, like so many times before, all that stood between William Faulkner and death was the figure of a mother. It was as if Faulkner were ceaselessly driven to evoke death in the form of a return to the origin until finally events conformed to his unconscious image.

As he was leaving Rowan Oak on the evening of July 5, 1962, as he was half-carried, half-dragged out of the house to go to the Byhalia sanitarium, Faulkner was led through the kitchen. There he passed the cook, Chrissie Price. She saw something in Faulkner's face, in his demeanor, that moved her to speak to him. "Mr. Bill," she said, "do you want to go to the hospital?" Speaking plaintively and with surprising clarity, Faulkner replied, "I want to go home, Chrissie." The family members who heard him dismissed his reply, since Faulkner *was* at home. He was out of his head, they thought; he was making no sense.[27] But Faulkner was not speaking literally, he was speaking metaphorically.

NOTES

1. "Appendix: The Compsons," *The Portable Faulkner*, ed. Malcolm Cowley (New York: The Viking Press, 1946), 710.

2. *The Sound and the Fury* (New York: Vintage International, 1990), 151.

3. "The Uncanny," *The Standard Edition of the Complete Psychological Works of Freud*, trans. James Strachey, 24 vols. (London: Hogarth Press, 1955), 17:245.

4. *Beyond the Pleasure Principle* (New York: Boni and Liveright, 1920), 47.

5. This account of Lacan is necessarily highly condensed and makes only passing reference to the important role of the Law of the Father or phallus in identity formation. For a fuller treatment of these Lacanian themes, see Jacques Lacan, *Ecrits: A Selection*, trans. Alan Sheridan (New York: Norton, 1977), 281–89. See also James M. Mellard, *Using Lacan: Reading Fiction* (Urbana: University of Illinois Press, 1991), 1–68; and

Robert Con Davis, "Critical Introduction: The Discovery of the Father," *The Fictional Father: Lacanian Readings of the Text*, ed. Robert Con Davis (Amherst: University of Massachusetts Press, 1981), 1–26.

6. *As I Lay Dying* (New York: Vintage International, 1990), 14.

7. Ibid., 39–40.

8. Ibid., 84.

9. For a detailed discussion of Lacanian themes in *As I Lay Dying*, see my essay, "Matricide and the Mother's Revenge: *As I Lay Dying*," *Faulkner Journal* 4 (Fall 1988/Spring 1989): 113–25.

10. See, for example, John T. Matthews, *The Play of Faulkner's Language* (Ithaca: Cornell University Press, 1982), 133.

11. In her impressive foray into psychobiography, Judith Wittenberg notes Faulkner's regressive tendencies. See *The Transfiguration of Biography* (Lincoln: University of Nebraska Press, 1979), 9–35.

12. *Thinking of Home: William Faulkner's Letters to His Mother and Father, 1918–1925*, ed. James G. Watson (New York: Norton, 1992), 53.

13. Joseph Blotner, *Faulkner: A Biography* (New York: Random House, 1974), 1:33.

14. For this account of Faulkner's binge drinking, I draw on three sources: a personal interview with Joan Williams, August 5, 1990; a personal interview with Jim Faulkner, February 4, 1991; and Blotner, 1:717–21.

15. *The Sound and the Fury*, 220.

16. *As I Lay Dying*, 15.

17. Frederick R. Karl, *William Faulkner: American Writer* (New York: Weidenfeld and Nicholson, 1989), 347.

18. Ibid., 348.

19. Joseph Blotner and Chester A. McLarty, M.D., "Faulkner's Last Days," *American Literature* 57 (December, 1985): 648–49.

20. Jim Faulkner, Personal interview, February 4, 1991.

21. *Faulkner: A Biography* (1974), 2: 1838.

22. Joseph Blotner, *Faulkner: A Biography*, One-Volume Edition (New York: Random House, 1984), 714.

23. Jim Faulkner, *Southern Living Magazine* (March 1992), 109.

24. *Faulkner: A Biography* (1974), 1: 721.

25. *Requiem for a Nun* (New York: Random House, 1950), 261.

26. *Faulkner: A Biography* (1974) 2: 1837.

27. Ibid., 2: 1836. See also "Faulkner's Last Days," 648.

Faulkner: The Artist as Cuckold

NOEL POLK

In order to believe that Thomas Sutpen rejects Charles Bon because he has black blood, you have to do a good deal of fancy footwork around some significant obstacles. First, you have to believe that Sutpen is far more race-conscious than he proves himself to be in any other place in the novel. Second, you have to believe that Bon at birth had physical characteristics—skin pigmentation, hair texture, lip thickness: something—that identified him as black, but which disappeared as he got older so that he could enroll at the University of Mississippi and pass as white all of his life. Third, if you believe that Sutpen was worried about dynasty, traditional problems of primogeniture, you have to overlook the Mississippi law that forbade a black son to inherit a father's estate.

Nevertheless, Bon's "blackness" overwhelms discussion of *Absalom, Absalom!* because it provides the novel's character-narrators, after many trials and errors, with a motive that allows them to explain why Henry Sutpen kills Charles Bon at the gates of Sutpen's Hundred. But Quentin and Shreve posit Bon's blackness *very* late, toward the end of chapter 8, in the scene in which Sutpen summons Henry to his tent on the eve of battle and informs him about Bon's racial heritage.[1] Sutpen's revelation provides a focus, a release, a renewed energy for the narrative quagmire they have been in; from this moment, however, the narrative becomes a sort of endgame: from here, all is inevitable. The scene at the gate of Sutpen's Hundred toward which the narrative has been moving becomes, finally, unstoppable: the novel relaxes from its hems and haws, its stops and starts, its proffered and then rejected explanations. In three pages from this point, Charles Bon is dead: Henry has kilt him dead as a beef.

But Sutpen's revelation asks a major question that the boys, in their headlong rush toward climax, simply beg. Why should the strong, imperious, even demonic father give the responsibility for stopping an incestuous and miscegenous union to the son? Why not stop it either by killing Bon himself or whisking Judith away to a nunnery, say, since obviously just forbidding the marriage is not going to work? The answer, I think, lies first in the fact that Quentin and Shreve know already that Henry and not Sutpen kills Bon, and their narration must move toward that act, which is the narrative nub of the entire novel. Moreover, and more importantly, Sutpen's relegation of that responsibility to his son reaffirms to the reader how specifically *Absalom* is a son's story and not a father's. *Absalom* insists throughout that the source of its narration is also its focus: thus the responsibility that this fictionally created father hands to this fictionally created son is very much at the center of *Absalom*'s many layers of meaning. What finally pushes Henry over the edge in this scene is not any affirmation that blood may not marry blood, but that black blood may not mingle with white: the ultimate white horror is not just Thomas Sutpen's ace in the hole, but Quentin's and Shreve's as well.

We should be suspicious of the suddenness and the sufficiency with which the race card provides a turning point for the boys' narration. Of course, it's been a long cold night in the Harvard dorm, and they may simply want to get to bed. But in a novel which questions *everything*, it is very curious that they do not question *anything* in this scene. They simply accept the race card as the one piece of acceptable information that allows their Hamlet-hero Henry finally to act. I repeat: in this reading, incest, by itself, is not enough. Race replaces incest as the key concern; indeed, the narrators specifically pare incest away from the terms of the climactic confrontation: *"So it's the miscegenation, not the incest, which you cant bear"* (285), Bon taunts Henry: I'm not your brother, he continues: *"I'm the nigger that's going to sleep with your sister"* (286).

Sutpen's race card, then, overwhelms both *Absalom*'s narrators and its critics. For the most part, even critics who have pursued other themes—history, culture, gender, language, and narrative theory, for example—have accepted race's centrality to *Absalom*, and Bon's black blood has become the still point around which the world of *Absalom* and its critics turns. I insist, however, that Sutpen's race card is better understood as Quentin's and Shreve's thematic ace in the hole, offered so late in the narrative not because other explanations for Henry's murder of Bon would not do but rather because the other explanations are rife with issues that Quentin and Shreve do not want to deal with directly. Thus, I propose race becomes, in *Absalom* and in Faulkner generally, a mask for very serious matters of sexuality and gender.

Indeed, to question Bon's black blood requires us also to question Sutpen's reasons for putting away his Haitian wife, reasons which readers have always and consistently assumed to be that that wife was part negro, and that her blackness was the fact she and her family deliberately kept from him. But nowhere in anything Sutpen is reported as saying is there any justification for accepting this as fact. The only "evidence" of Bon's racial makeup is in the novel's Chronology, which bears a very problematic relationship to the novel proper.[2] But Quentin and Shreve do not have access to that chronology: they know only what they hear or make up.

Our most direct evidence about Sutpen's Haiti days comes from the story Sutpen tells General Compson in the intervals between their chase of the escaped French architect. Nothing he says about his wife and child has to do with race; the only thing approaching a reason for putting them away has to do with his virginity: "On this night I am speaking of (and until my first marriage, I might add) I was still a virgin. You will probably not believe that, and if I were to try to explain it you would disbelieve me more than ever. So I will only say that that too was a part of the design which I had in my mind" (200). I'm much less astonished to believe that he was a virgin than to discover that his virginity was a part of his much discussed "design," and I'm forced to ask: if *his* virginity was an important part of his design, how much *more* important to that design—to the design, to his sense of himself as a man—would be the virginity of the woman he chose as wife? I would, then, like to argue that the reason Thomas Sutpen puts away his Haitian family has nothing to do with Negro blood, but with his belated discovery, after the birth of the baby, of his wife's previous marriage and/or previous sexual experience.

Others have suggested this possibility,[3] but dismiss it as quickly as they raise it, in order to get back to race as the novel's defining issue. But it is worth considerably more than a passing glance, both for the possibilities it raises for understanding the novel differently, and for the ways in which it allows us a new understanding of *Absalom*'s place in one of the larger arcs of Faulkner's career.

If Sutpen rejects the Haitian wife because she did not come to him as a virgin, we may ask several new questions, and perhaps offer different answers to questions we have asked for the nearly sixty years of this novel's life. We may first suppose that Bon was either not Sutpen's son, or at least that he feared that Bon was not his, feared that he would then be raising someone else's child as his own. Thus the novel raises not just legal and cultural questions of primogeniture, which we regularly discuss, but also, and perhaps more importantly, assumptions residing historically in the male psyche about every male's "right" to his own virgin; more of this shortly. Second, if we accept Sutpen's betrayal in Haiti as a sexual one, we may better understand why he is so hell-bent on marrying Ellen Coldfield, the daughter of the most righteous Methodist steward in Jefferson: where else than in such a "righteous," repressive home could he have more hopes of finding the virgin of his design? Third, if we accept that Bon might not be a Sutpen at all, black or white, or that Sutpen fears that he is not, we open the way to question what other issues besides bigamy or incest or concubinage or race may have energized the infamous Christmas Eve in the Sutpen parlor. Perhaps Sutpen simply doesn't like this foppish young man. Perhaps Judith has asked her father to send him away. Perhaps Sutpen discovered something in New Orleans other than Bon's background. Perhaps, perhaps, perhaps.

Perhaps Bon and Henry confess to or in some way display a homosexual relationship; that would certainly be enough for Sutpen to reject Bon and for Henry to reject Sutpen. Other narrators have insinuated as much; throughout, Quentin's father has given us—and Quentin—an effeminate and foppish Bon, a Henry dazzled by the sophisticated cosmopolite. In one oft-noted passage he articulates a very specific sense of the triangulation among the principles, which works equally well for both *The Sound and the Fury* and *Absalom, Absalom!*:

> In fact, perhaps this is the pure and perfect incest: the brother realising that the sister's virginity must be destroyed in order to have existed at all, taking that virginity in the person of the brother-in-law, the man whom he would be if he could become, metamorphose into, the lover, the husband; by whom he would be despoiled, choose for despoiler, if he could become, metamorphose into the sister, the mistress, the bride. (77)

Both *Absalom* and *The Sound and the Fury* hint broadly and unsubtly about the homoerotic tension between Quentin and Shreve; the triangle comprised of Bon, Henry, and Judith specifically replicates, in a slightly more obvious manner,[4] that triangle made up of Quentin, Caddy, and Dalton Ames in the earlier novel. And it is very much worth noting that none of the narrators in *Absalom*, least of all Quentin, proposes that Henry kills Bon for the same reason that Quentin wants to kill Dalton Ames, though it would seem a natural: not to prevent incest or miscegenation, but to preserve that part of family honor resident in his sister's maidenhead or, to put it another way, just to control his sister's body, to try to contain Judith's sexuality, as other Faulkner males have done. I believe that we have not explored this possibility because we have heretofore, in *Absalom*, been so completely caught up in race and that our collective failure, as Faulkner readers, to face the gender problematics of *Absalom* stems from the same collective need to evade the issue as Quentin and Shreve evince: that is; for Faulknerians, race is easier to deal with than gender.

I'd like to push this meditation upon *Absalom* just a bit further in order to ground this magnificent novel in the complex of Oedipal relationships that seem to me central to Faulkner.[5] Thomas Sutpen's curious and fatal relationship with Wash Jones supplies us with all the evidence we need. Briefly, Wash Jones is a surrogate replication of Thomas Sutpen's worthless white trash father, the author of all the chaos and misery of Sutpen's early years in the Virginia/West Virginia mountains, which he describes to General Compson so vividly, even if with such detachment. It is a childhood completely consonant with other childhoods in the Faulkner of this period, including Rosa Coldfield's: Sutpen's childhood is a living hell of instability, alcoholism, and paternal ruthlessness (178–96).

In my reading of his conflict with Wash Jones, Sutpen has now gained ascendancy over his own father, an ascendancy powerfully symbolized by the reversal of their positions: he the rich planter in the hammock, his surrogate father the servant who brings the jug, admires him unconditionally, and does exactly what Sutpen tells him. If Wash Jones is Sutpen's father, it follows that the unfortunate Milly, Wash's granddaughter, is Sutpen's surrogate sister, their union and their child incestuous. It is perfectly appropriate, in this Freudian schema, that Wash kills Sutpen with that rusty scythe. Provoked, Wash transforms himself not merely into Father Time, as this scene has nearly always been read, but into the avenging, punishing father; the scythe is his castrating knife. What more appropriate punishment, in Faulkner as in Freud, for the crime of incest? Sutpen both commits the incest that Quentin cannot commit *and* forces his own father to punish him—which Quentin tries but also fails to do. In Quentin's reconstruction of *Absalom*'s narrative, then, *both* Sutpen and Bon perform the very acts that in *The Sound and the Fury* he, Quentin, cannot. Thus *Absalom, Absalom!* is, among other things, Quentin's fantasy of masculinity in which he simultaneously enacts the preservation of his sister's honor and the destruction of the darker impulses toward incest and homoeroticism that he cannot face.

I've begun with this little disquisition on *Absalom,* a well-known text, by way of introducing a theme in Faulkner as constant as words, a theme charged with significant layers of meaning throughout his art and perhaps in his life. To be brief, the cuckold is a major player in Faulkner's fiction, a figure who recurs time and again in a wide variety of formulations: the weak husband, the impotent, the voyeur, the pimp. The obsessive frequency in the fiction of the cuckold and the triangular rela-tionships created by cuckoldry suggests that they are a high priority in Faulkner's fictional enterprise. An astonishing amount of the fiction directly explores the variety of ways in which men deal with the real or imagined sexual lives of wives or partners which they cannot, or fear they cannot, control. Thomas Sutpen's "design" is but one manifestation of Faulkner's career-long preoccupation with the problems of female sexuali-ty's relationship to the economy of male desire. In Sutpen's case, as in many others in Faulkner, male desire requires control not just of a female's sexual present and future, but of her sexual history as well.

I'd like to argue that the fourteenth way of looking at this very complex blackbird lies in the lens provided by *Absalom*'s implied double triangle—Quentin-Caddy-Dalton; Henry-Judith-Bon—triangles replicated throughout Faulkner's fiction, trian-gles rife with all sorts of homo- and hetero-erotic implications for the characters and, as we shall see, perhaps for the author. This triangle of desire is specifically Oedipal and is, I think, more important to Faulkner's fiction, by a long shot, than race. Consider that only four of Faulkner's novels—*Light in August, Absalom, Absalom!, Go Down, Moses,* and *Intruder in the Dust*—and that at most three of well over a hundred short

stories—"Sunset," "That Evening Sun," and "Dry September"—are in any way chiefly "about" race, and you will have
some sense of how relatively little of his work Faulkner invested
in race-consciousness. On the other hand, gender problematics
drip from nearly every line he ever wrote, and it seems to me
very clear that even *Light in August, Absalom, Go Down,
Moses,* and "Dry September" are in fact more centrally concerned with gender than with race. Race has also, I suspect,
provided a mask for the mostly white male or male-identified
women critics who have worked on Faulkner; it must be easier
to deal with race than with gender, whose problems are much
closer, much harder to find a language for, because we are much
more intimately complicit with the repressive structures of
gender hierarchy. Race is a mask for gender throughout
Faulkner.

Aside from Freud, the most useful contexts for thinking about
these Faulknerian concerns are those provided by René Girard,
who frames a theory of desire in *Deceit, Desire, and the Novel;*
Eve Kosofsky Sedgwick, who expands upon and provides a
brilliant new context for Girard's ideas in *Between Men;* and
Tony Tanner, also to a certain extent building from Girard, who
deals with cuckoldry in *Adultery and the Novel.*[6] Girard proposes that desire is always triangular, that it is never original or
spontaneous, and that it therefore always involves a mediator:
we can only desire what somebody else desires first. Moreover,
in the triangle of desire the most important relationship is that
between the subject and the mediator, *not* that between the
subject and the object, and varying degrees of tension in the
triangle are directly tied to the distance between the subject
and the mediator and to the obstacles that the mediator puts in
the way of the subject's merging with either the mediator or the
object. Tony Tanner's articulation of this phenomenon is acute
and specific: "Since desire, which is always involved in some
way with the sense of incompletion, is an essential source of
action in any social structure, which by its very nature tends
toward a self-perpetuating stasis, it is necessarily a central topic

of all literature. Desire in action reveals itself as energy, and energy encountering structure is the paradigmatic tension of much of our literature" (87).

I do not know of a more complete or conscious illustration of this triangle at work than in Faulkner's wonderfully funny short story of 1942, a deliberate Faulknerian frolicking in Freudian fields, "A Courtship." In "A Courtship," David Hogganbeck and Ikkemotubbe become competitors for the hand of a Eula Varner-like maiden who has no name but merely a designation as "Herman Basket's Sister." They eventually engage in a race, having agreed that whoever wins the race gets the girl; Herman Basket's Sister, who is not consulted in any of their arrangements, appears indifferent. They race, naked, 130 miles to a ceremonial cave, an ominously vaginal "black hole" where "boys from among all the People would go . . . to prove if they had the courage to become men."[7] But the victory is not just to the swiftest. In a typical Faulknerian complication, the first one to arrive must enter the cave and shoot a pistol: if the cave does not collapse on him, he wins; if it does, of course, he loses a good deal more than Herman Basket's sister. But the two do not race as fierce competitors out to win the maiden's hand at all cost; indeed, during the course of the race they bond completely with each other, and by race's end they are both thinking of "that damned sister of Herman Basket's" (CS 376), who, being the presumed object of their mutual desire, has gotten them into their complicated situation. Subject and mediator merge.

Ikkemotubbe gets to the cave first, enters, and fires: "*Aihee. It comes*" (CS 377), he thinks, as he hears the cave rumble down on him. David Hogganbeck, outside, hears the rumble too, and fearing for Ikkemotubbe, thrusts himself half-way into the cave's vaginal opening and supports it on his back while Ikkemotubbe crawls under him and out. But he cannot back out, and seems stuck there; Ikkemotubbe contemplates his friend's "buttocks and legs pink in the sunrise" (CS 377) while he decides what to do. He first gets a long pole and thrusts it into the cave, to try to pry the roof off of David Hogganbeck's back. When that doesn't work, he grasps David Hogganbeck "by the meat" (*CS* 377) and pulls him backward to safety, as the cave collapses. They have thus shared the same orifice and given birth to each other; they are each other's brother and father. Even while enacting a ritualistic macho competition for the woman's hand, they have rescued each other from the feminine; clearly the athletic competition is a thin, veritably gossamer veil for homo-erotic or at least homosocial elements in their friendship. They prefer each other's company; they do not really want Herman Basket's Sister, indeed, they fear that very primal cave, but feel compelled by their culture to compete for her, to dare and conquer "it," anyway.

Back home, they discover that while they were racing, Herman Basket's sister has married an artist, a harmonica player named Log-in-the-Creek. David Hogganbeck and Ikkemotubbe console each other, while the narrator projects forward a bit to Ikkemotubbe's future: he gives up love, and begins to desire power instead; his mediator becomes the slaveholding civilization of the United States, and he learns how to kill "anything . . . which happened to stand between [him] and what he wanted" (*CS* 379).

One of the staple assumptions of American literary study is that Faulkner drew heavily on his own family and region for a good deal of his fiction. We know in great detail the extent to which he exploited family legends about the old cunnel and the young cunnel, how Oxford became Jefferson and Ben Wasson and/or Phil Stone became Horace Benbow, and how Faulkner transmuted all these relatively external and more or less docu-mentable materials into his art. More recent work, especially since the publication of Joseph Blotner's massive biography in 1974 (although there was plenty of it before that time), has been interested in Faulkner's internal life, in the kinds of things we can learn about Faulkner's mind from his works, and about his works from his mind. This is a perilous enterprise: in my work on Faulkner and Freud, for example, I have generally taken the coward's way out by using Freud as a source, as others have taken the Bible, Homer, and other works of literature and philosophy as sources. There are in Faulkner innumerable scenes, tableaux, characters, and situations which fit various important Freudian paradigms in seemingly indisputable ways; what to do when we find in Faulkner's life, especially in his relationships to women, the same kinds of scenes, characters, and situations that fit those same Freudian paradigms in precisely the same seemingly indisputable ways? Does such a triangulation from Faulkner to Freud to Work support Freud's suggestion that writers write in order to deal with their neuroses? Does the fact that Faulkner's mother resembles in a few external and apparently superficial ways many of the mothers and grandmothers in the fiction suggest that under the surface of a seemingly absolute devotion to her there was a great deal of hostility? Are such correspondences coincidental? Numerous critics now argue that they are not coincidental, though I am not so sure. It would be very easy, I think, to make too much of certain of these correspondences, and equally easy not to make enough.

I cannot speak very directly here about Faulkner's fictional *intentions*, much less dare to psychoanalyze him through any documents he left us. But I believe that certain of those documents can give us some insight into some general ways in which his psychic life and his work impinge upon one another throughout his career. Among other things, I'd like to describe a peculiar arc to his career that seems to me related to certain aspects of his psychic life.

One of the most remarkable documents in Blotner's one-volume revision and update of his two-volume biography is an astonishing letter that Faulkner wrote to his publisher Hal Smith, probably in the very late spring of 1929, just after he had finished writing *Sanctuary*, asking to borrow $500 with which to get married: "Hal," he wrote:

> I want $500.00. I am going to be married. Both want to and have to. THIS PART IS CONFIDENTIAL, UTTERLY. For my honor

and the sanity—I believe life—of a woman. This is not bunk; neither am I being sucked in. We grew up together and I dont think she could fool me in this way; that is, make me believe that her mental condition, her nerves, are this far gone. And no question of pregnancy: that would hardly move me: no one can face his own bastard with more equanimity than I, having had some practice. neither is it a matter of a promise on my part; we have known one another long enough to pay no attention to our promises. It's a situation which I engendered and permitted to ripen which has become unbearable, and I am tired of running from devilment I bring about. This sounds a little insane, but I'm not in any shape to write letters now.

"I'll give you a note," Faulkner continued,

with ten percent interest or whatever you wish, due the first of next March, with the reversion of all accruing royalty on the two novels of mine you have in case I die, and I will promise in writing to deliver you a third novel before that date; if it fails to please you, the note and interest to be paid on the above date. . . . I need not say this is confidential—the reasons, I mean—and urgent. I believe it will be the last time I'll bother you for money before time, because from now on I'll have to work. And I work well under pressure—and a wife will be pressure enough for me.[8]

I'd bet that Smith did lend him the money, for Faulkner dedicated *As I Lay Dying,* his next novel, to him.

This letter is remarkable in a number of respects: first, for its suggestion that whatever Smith's reason for delaying publication of *Sanctuary* for more than a year and a half after its completion, it probably had little to do with any fear of public outrage or of legal complications, as Faulkner later claimed. Second, for Faulkner's claim of having fathered an illegitimate child—though this, of course, may be more brag than anything else. And third, for the letter's apparent confirmation of suspicions that we have all entertained about Faulkner's marriage. We know from numerous sources that it was a stormy relationship, which caused both Faulkner and Estelle much unhappiness over the years. This letter suggests that it was a marriage which he did not want to make, one he went into with considerable resentment, even desperation.

Faulkner and his fiancée, Estelle Oldham, had been childhood sweethearts. Her parents had disapproved strongly of
Faulkner and had pushed her into a marriage with a more
promising young man, Cornell Franklin. Although Faulkner
urged her to elope with him, Estelle somewhat languidly acquiesced to her parents' decision and married Franklin in 1918. The
Franklins moved to Shanghai and had two children. Faulkner
continued to torch for her throughout the twenties: he wrote
and bound for her a pamphlet of poems, *Vision in Spring,* and
saw her whenever she returned from Shanghai on furlough. He
was also, and very practically, pursuing other women at the
same time, notably Helen Baird. At about the same time he was
writing and binding *Vision in Spring* for Estelle, he was inscribing another little hand-printed book, *Mayday,* to Helen. In the
spring of 1926, when Estelle was actually making arrangements
to divorce Cornell, Faulkner was preparing yet another such
booklet, *Helen: A Courtship,* for Helen, and in September of
that year he finished *Mosquitoes* and dedicated it to Helen; in
late October, however, he made for Estelle a pamphlet of his
New Orleans Sketches which included a new one, a monologue
by one Hong Li, a Chinese gentleman trying to come to terms
with a lost love.

Faulkner's desperate letter to Smith allows us to infer that
during the times that Estelle and her children came home on
furlough from Shanghai, she and Faulkner took up more or
less where they had left off, doubtless Faulkner more or less
sincerely—probably less—promising how wonderful their lives
could be if only she weren't married; obviously when she
began making plans in 1926 to get that divorce, Faulkner was
somewhat shaken, and as the papers were filed and the divorce
proceedings actually instituted, the full reality of what he had
gotten himself into became more and more evident. We may
get some sense of his deepest feelings about his upcoming
marriage and about his upcoming wife when we read, in *Sanctuary,* that Temple Drake wears an expensive Chinese robe while
she lives in Miss Reba's whorehouse, and when we note that he

specifies June 20, *his wedding day,* as the day on which Lee Goodwin's trial begins—the trial during which Temple lies to protect her original ravisher and thereby causes an innocent man's death. I wonder whether at some psychological level Faulkner ever forgave Estelle for having cuckolded him—indeed, *pre*cuckolded him—before they were married.

Sometime between 1925 and 1928, at about the time Estelle told Faulkner she was getting a divorce, Faulkner began but did not finish a patently autobiographical piece entitled "And Now What's To Do?" The narrator of this fragment outlines a background similar to Faulkner's family life and adolescent preoccupations in Oxford, then notes how his happy childhood had been upset by the onset of desire, "his changing body"; he began watching the girls, "watching their forming legs, imagining their blossoming thighs, with a feeling of defiant inferiority"—an interesting and significant phrase, I think, for a man so physically small and delicate as Faulkner: "There was a giant in him, but the giant was muscle-bound." He sees the girls "with their ripening thighs and their mouths that keep you awake at night with unnameable things—shame of lost integrity, manhood's pride, desire like a drug. The body is tarnished, soiled in its pride, now. But what is it for, anyway?" He continues, somewhat ambiguously, "A girl got in trouble," but he does not clarify whether he himself got the girl in trouble; he then describes his escape on the train, and continues with a revealing mediation on the nature of women and of men, and on what was apparently his first sexual experience:

> Nothing to girls. Dividing legs dividing receptive. He had known all about it before, but the reality was like reading a story and then seeing it in the movies, with music and all. Soft things. Secretive, but like traps. Like going after something you wanted, and getting into a nest of spider webs. You got the thing, then you had to pick the webs off, and every time you touched one, it stuck to you. Even after you didn't want the thing anymore, the webs clung to you. Until after a while you remembered the way the webs itched and you wanted the thing again, just thinking of how the webs itched. No. Quicksand. That was it. Wade through once, then go on. But a

man wont. He wants to go all the way through, somehow; break out
on the other side. Everything incomplete somehow. Having to back
off, with webs clinging to you. "Christ, you have to tell them so
much. You cant think of it fast enough. And they never forget when
you do and when you dont. What do they want, anyway?"[9]

"And Now What's To Do?" then, provides an early autobiographical background for the sorts of problems that plague so
many of his male characters: the fear and loathing of women,
the shame and filth associated with sexuality, the immutability
of desire, and the absolute inextricability of the desire and
the shame.

Over and over again, as nearly all critics have noted, male
characters in Faulkner have problems that are traceable to sour
relationships with and attitudes toward and expectations of
women; even women characters have problems traceable to
sour relationships with other women, and it is undeniable that
much of Faulkner's work is marked by gynophobia if not always
by outright misogyny. Women in his fiction are nearly always
associated not just with sex and shame but also with filth,
excrement, pain, and death. And in the years following Estelle's
announcement that she was getting a divorce and so would be
available to fulfill all of Faulkner's dreams, we may locate the
beginnings of several themes in his work which equate women
with whores and shame and betrayal and prison and other
assorted traps. In the years immediately following Faulkner's
marriage, these concerns become extremely intense in the
fiction.

In *As I Lay Dying*, Faulkner's first novel after his marriage—
and the novel he offered Hal Smith as security for the loan—
Cash Bundren says of Jewel, when he thinks Jewel is having at
it with a married woman, "A fellow kind of hates to see [a young
boy] wallowing in somebody else's mire."[10] Very soon after his
marriage Faulkner wrote a series of short stories centered
around very curious ménages à trois in which fully impotent or
at least weak husbands allow, encourage, permit, their wives to
be sexually serviced by other men. Of the twenty-five stories

we know he sent out between January 23, 1930, and March 16, 1931, at least a dozen explore this kind of relationship,[11] and it recurs over and over again as a central motif in, for example, the relationship between Popeye and Red in *Sanctuary;* between Byron Bunch and Lucas Burch and between Gail Hightower and his wife's lovers in *Light in August;* between Roger Schuman and Jack Holmes in *Pylon;* between Rat Rittenmeyer and Harry Wilbourne and between the tall convict and the father of his lady's baby in *If I Forget Thee, Jerusalem;* and between Flem Snopes and Manfred de Spain in *The Town.*

Mink Snopes, in *The Hamlet,* makes the homoerotic component of this triangulation very specific; as he makes love with his wife, the former "lord of the harem" in which he found her, he is constantly "surrounded by the loud soundless invisible shades of the nameless and numberless men—that body which . . . was anterior even to the two-dollar marriage which had not sanctified but sanctioned them, which each time he approached it, it was not garments intervening but the cuckolding shades which had become a part of his past too, as if he and not she had been their prone recipient. . . ."[12] In marrying such a woman, Mink feels he has been denied the one thing that every man holds sacred, the right to his own virgin. He approaches sex with his wife in terms that sound very like those of Faulkner's protagonist in "And Now What's To Do?": "he would contemplate [her used body] even from the cold starless night-periphery beyond both hatred and desire and tell himself: It's like drink. It's like dope to me" (*Hamlet* 938). Mink's feelings, as here articulated, with their complex combination of hetero- and homo-eroticism, may well be those of numerous men in Faulkner.

The extent to which these husbands reflect Faulkner's own state of mind during this time is, of course, highly problematical. But the external evidence of his life suggests plenty for him to be angry, nervous, and frustrated about. If he clearly was not enthusiastic about his marriage, doubtless neither was Estelle completely happy. She spent a good deal of their honeymoon drinking heavily and either tried at one point actually to commit suicide or made a dramatic gesture in that direction. After all, she had left a relatively affluent and glamorous life in Shanghai to marry a poor and unsuccessful novelist whose future could not have inspired much confidence. Doubtless she also sensed her new husband's lack of enthusiasm, and so felt no less trapped and desperate than he. Estelle's daughter Cho-Cho told Joseph Blotner years later that she thought that Estelle regretted marrying Faulkner and that she "believed that somehow Cornell would come back to her."[13] Estelle must have felt considerable tension between herself and her new mother-in-law, who apparently disapproved of her because she drank too much and thereby encouraged Billy to do the same. Faulkner must have felt caught in the tension between his problematic new wife and a domineering mother who had, according to Phil Stone, tied her sons to her in such a way as to cause them to resent her; she was in part responsible, Stone thought, "for an animosity toward women" in Faulkner (Blotner, 1984, 246). The birth and premature death of his and Estelle's baby daughter, Alabama, in January 1931, must have seemed to the tragedian some sort of cosmic symbol of the destructive nature of his marriage.

In the works of this period, these elements and many related others from the external world of Faulkner's life in Oxford appear in an astonishing variety of combinations and permutations. Whether Faulkner's use of this material from his own life was conscious or unconscious is, of course, the question to which I'd suggest a simple, even simplistic, answer: if it was not conscious use at first, over the course of the several novels and the dozen stories, he became very conscious indeed of how he had worked his own life, this quintessentially private person, into his fiction. This increasing awareness in its turn created its own problems that he, as usual, began to deal with in the fiction.

One important story he wrote in the first quarter of 1931 illustrates. He wrote "Artist at Home" before March 16, 1931. It is about Roger Howes, whose name puns on "house." He is a writer who assists in, indeed arranges, the violation of the home of the story's title. Roger gets married and moves, like Sherwood Anderson, to rural Virginia on the proceeds from the sales of his first novel; there he writes another, less successful novel, and becomes more and more lethargic about his career, until he finally stops writing altogether. He and his wife are fairly cut off from other people except for a stream of New York bohemian/ artist types who come, with or without invitations, to sponge off them. His wife Anne resents their coming very much, but she becomes infatuated with a particularly obnoxious and fey young poet named John Blair, who is remarkably similar to a fey young poet named Faulkner in *Mosquitoes*. Anne's and Blair's first embrace comes in the garden; they are both surprised when Roger suddenly emerges from behind a bush where he has been watching. But Roger is not at all upset, and we learn that he has both anticipated and even hoped for something of this sort to happen; he has, indeed, invited Blair to Virginia. During the next few days he finds ways to throw them together, encouraging their relationship.

As the affair develops, Roger begins to write again, starts to work on his long-delayed third novel. The lovers' trysts are punctuated by the sound of Roger's typewriter, a sound the narrator connects more than once with a "bull market" in typewriting. "And what was it he [was] writing?" the narrator asks: "Him, and Anne, and the poet. Word for word, between the waiting spells to find out what to write down next, with a few changes here and there, of course, because live people do not make good copy, the most interesting copy being gossip, since it mostly is not true" (CS 644). The nub of the story, then, is Roger's deliberate exploitation of his wife's infidelity and of his own part in the triangle. We do not know what Roger writes and we do not know what, if anything, he *feels* about Anne and John, whether he feels anything at all about his cuckolding, or whether it is very difficult to control those feelings in order to channel them into his fiction. But clearly his creative juices respond directly to the erotic tension of his voyeurism, which is itself not always direct but triangulated through his writing. During this time, John Blair writes a poem, published in a non-paying small magazine, which Roger, but not Anne, likes. Roger sells his novel and with his royalties buys Anne a fur coat, which she rejects, refusing to accept financial benefit from her part in the triangle. She gives it to a neighbor woman, who has accidentally seen John swimming naked, and been properly horrified at her accidental vision of the spectacle.

Sedgwick, Tanner, Girard, and others who have written on this and related subjects, have a good deal of interest to say on the subject of cuckoldry. But these critics deal almost exclusively with writers before the twentieth century, and so do not explore the particular twist on the figure of the cuckold in the modern world that allies him with the waste land figure of J. Alfred Prufrock. For centuries, the cuckold was the clown, the object of ridicule, and a culturally acceptable figure of fun because, as Tanner argues, cuckolding a clown—cuckoldry in general, no matter how rife—didn't threaten the institution of marriage. In the nineteenth century, fiction's interest in marriage takes a decided turn, and we may generally say that in large measure nineteenth century fiction's towering and defining figures are its adulterous heroines: Anna Karenina, Emma Bovary, Hester Prynne, and Edna Pontellier. In the twentieth century, however, the defining figures of modernist fiction—at least in our current but rapidly changing sense of literary history—tend to be the man for whom all things sexual and personal are universally problematic: Prufrock's "overwhelming question." In the twentieth century the cuckold is neither a comic nor a tragic figure, but a pathetic one, whose sexual sensibilities define his sense of self and his world view, a world view that he imposes on others as a "universal" view. This is true of both characters and authors: in nothing do William Faulkner and James Joyce resemble each other more particularly than in their relationships with their wives, and in the significance of the figure of the cuckold and the adulterous wife in their fiction.

At first glance, for example, the title, "Artist at Home," merely describes the creator in his domestic surroundings; a closer look invokes the Victorian sense of "at home" as meaning "ready to receive." An even closer look may suggest an active creator *of* home, One Who Arranges Things or Creates Situations at Home in Pleasurable or Profitable Patterns. Whichever meaning Faulkner intended, perhaps all three, the title and what we know of the external circumstances of Faulkner's life invite us to believe that at least at one level the story springs from a conscious recognition of the ways in which he had been exploiting his own psychic life. If we may legitimately make such inferences from the story, we may make ourselves privy to a confession of sorts that Faulkner, at least in the early years of his marriage, felt himself, as artist, to be at best a voyeur, perhaps at worst a pimp. It is very easy, perhaps *too* easy, to invoke *Sanctuary*'s Popeye, and to remember the several ways in which Faulkner, both more and less humorously, identified himself with this most vicious and impotent and voyeuristic of all his characters.

No doubt Estelle was as miserable and insecure, for many of these same reasons, as Faulkner was. *Requiem for a Nun* in 1951 may provide some evidence of Faulkner's growing understanding of the situation his own sensibilities about women had largely created. Up to *Requiem*, Faulkner's concern had been almost exclusively with the cuckold's attempts to deal with a wife who had "betrayed" him with another man—"betrayed" would be the man's term for her past, and not her own. In *Requiem*, Faulkner seems finally to recognize the inherent unfairness in any man's holding any woman responsible for her sexual life before marrying him. In *Requiem*, Faulkner returns once again to Miss Reba's, the Memphis whorehouse of Temple Drake's undoing in *Sanctuary*, and a site which becomes a sort of touchstone, as we now can see, for themes running throughout his career that equate women with filth and sex with shame.

Requiem for a Nun runs in two directions. First, *Requiem* is precisely about Temple's attempt to rescue herself from her

husband Gowan, who, under the guise of forgiving her for her
past in the whorehouse, manages to keep her every day reminded of and so ashamed of that past. And he, who was
largely responsible for her problems in *Sanctuary*, expects large
measures of gratitude from her for his generosity in forgiving
her—a forgiveness which in fact he never quite manages. Second, *Requiem* is about the culture's concerted efforts to bring
her to judgment for her sexual history. That culture, personified
in the ruthless figure of Gavin Stevens, insists not just that she
repent for *having had* a sexual life prior to and independent of
her husband; it demands that she accept and recite the culture's
version of her sexual life and that she admit that her sexual
history is directly responsible for the death of her baby. Stevens
is in *Requiem* not just a surrogate for Temple's husband, but for
the culture itself; indeed, he drags her to the Governor's office
for her confession. The patriarchal culture thus inscribes her
sexual history on her and forces her to recite it, to believe
it—"loved it" indeed.[14] No one seriously tries to hold Gowan
responsible for their baby's murder, although he created the
situation which put her into Popeye's, and therefore Pete's,
grasp.

   In *Sanctuary* Gowan Stevens abandons Temple at the Old
Frenchman place, leaving her to her own devices to deal
with Popeye and the Memphis underworld; Popeye, who is
impotent, rapes her with a corncob, then takes her to Miss
Reba's. Temple's *Requiem for a Nun* version of her time at Miss
Reba's is that her tenure there was relatively chaste—it "was
worse than being the wealthy ward of the most indulgent trust
or insurance company: carried to Memphis and shut up in that
Manuel Street sporting house like a ten-year-old bride in a
Spanish convent, with the madam herself more eagle-eyed
than any mama"[15]—until she fell in love with Red, the surrogate
lover Popeye brought in to make love to Temple while he
watched.

   Gowan's version of Temple's past, even though he was not
there, is that she spent time in a Memphis whorehouse and,

being a woman, of course became a whore and "loved it." He assumes that she became one of the girls, even though she engaged in sex with nobody but Red; there is plenty of evidence that she was in love with Red, and plenty more that she had very little choice in the matter. Nevertheless, after Temple's rescue and the trial, Gowan marries her, out of his own sense of guilt over having abandoned her, and out of some sense of honor. Gowan's Uncle Gavin, the prosecutor who forces Temple, unnecessarily, to dredge up that past, analyzes the husband this way:

> And when I say 'past,' I mean that part of it which the husband knows. . . . Because it was not long before she discovered, realised, that she was going to spend a good part of the rest of her days (nights too) being forgiven for it; in being not only constantly reminded . . . but say made—kept—aware of it in order to be forgiven for it so that she might be grateful to the forgiver, but in having to employ more and more of what tact she had . . . to make the gratitude . . . acceptable to meet with, match, the high standards of the forgiver. But she was not too concerned. Her husband . . . had made what he probably considered the supreme sacrifice to expiate his part in her past; she had no doubts of her capacity to continue to supply whatever increasing degree of gratitude the increasing appetite—or capacity—of its addict would demand, in return for the sacrifice which, so she believed, she had accepted for the same reason of gratitude. (*RN* 581–82)

Temple had earlier described their marriage as a plan for redemption gone awry:

> And then maybe there would be the love this time—the peace, the quiet, the no shame. . . . Love, but more than love too: not depending on just love to hold two people together, make them better than either one would have been alone, but tragedy, suffering, having suffered and caused grief; having something to have to live with even when, because, you knew both of you could never forget it. And then I began to believe something even more than that: that there was something even better, stronger, than tragedy to hold two people together: forgiveness. Only, that seemed to be wrong. Only maybe it wasn't the forgiveness that was wrong, but

the gratitude; and maybe the only thing worse than having to give
gratitude constantly all the time, is having to accept it—(*RN* 577)

Precisely, I think.

In *Sanctuary* Temple is a victim of a variety of forces,
including her own youth and inexperience, but she *is* a victim:
by the time of *Requiem* she is an eight-year-married woman
with two children who has spent a long time trying to be
respectable, trying to live down a past which her husband and
her culture have conspired to make her feel responsible for,
guilty for, ashamed of, and in need of forgiveness for. But Gavin
Stevens, patriarchy's advocate and chief prosecutor, is mired in
Temple's sexual past, moves through it deliciously, voyeuristi-
cally concerned with Temple's sexual pathologies. Despite
Requiem's richly historical prologues, it is the burden of the
present, not of the past, that pushes Temple to the desperate
measure of escaping from her marriage, which attempt in turn
precipitates the central crisis of the novel, the murder of one of
her children by their black servant.

Faulkner's sympathy for Temple is unmistakable, and the
novel's ending, with her return to Gowan, is unambiguously
bleak in offering her the rest of her life with a husband who has
not learned anything, who is still mired in self-pity and in
loathing of Temple's sexual past, and who will doubtless add
Temple's more recent sins to the list of things he has to be
honorable about and that she will have to be grateful for being
forgiven for. But Faulkner perhaps had learned something, by
looking at the problem from the woman's point of view, and in
fact his final novel, *The Reivers*, may represent a resolution of
many of his own problems about such matters. In *The Reivers*,
Faulkner returns once again to Miss Reba's whorehouse, looking
at that world through eyeglasses *deliberately* rose-colored, I
think, and seeing through those glasses *Sanctuary*'s unstable
world of whores, of voyeurists, of sexual shame and of impend-
ing violence, but denuded here of the shame and the terror, the
nightmare, that was the essence of *Sanctuary*'s vision. At the

center of *The Reivers* Boon Hogganbeck extracts Everbe Corinthia from her employment at Miss Reba's in order to marry her. He goes to her in the whorehouse, accepts her for what she is, and marries her for what she is going to be: there is no recrimination for her past, there are no troublesome ghosts of that legion of other men. The idea of *forgiveness* for that past is not even remotely an issue between them; the baby they have at the end of the novel is some indication that they will not build their future upon the unsteady counterpoint of forgiveness and gratitude, but rather upon a solid base of love, mutual respect, and mutual acceptance of each other's past, present, and future.

The artist as cuckold, then, is one who exploits his or her own inner and very private life as the material of fiction. The early Faulkner may be the Artist as Cuckold, the artist as civilian, in mufti, sporting his various neuroses and frustrations and fears and resentments of women in public, disguising them as intensely tragic fiction. By the last decade of his life he is more comfortably, more agreeably, the Artist at Home, still exploiting his own inner life, but whose work by then reflected his softening intensity about women, a considerable mellowing of his sense of sexuality as something shameful, an abatement of his sense of women and of domesticity as middle class traps, and a larger, more generous sense of women as complete human beings, as something other than their genitals: as something more than spittoon for men who only want to chew.

Eula Varner Snopes, her daughter Linda, and Maggie Mallison, in *The Town* and *The Mansion,* seem to me fully realized, complex portraits of three completely different, but equally magnificent women. In *The Town,* Eula Varner Snopes lives her life in this most domestic of Faulkner's novels almost completely outside the respectable: she is an adulteress, one who has, like Estelle Oldham, pre-cuckolded her husband and brought into their marriage a child which is not his. She has continued the cuckolding, more or less publicly, through her affair with her husband's employer for eighteen years, a length of time that indicates that the relationship has more than just sex going for it: compared to this infidelity, Temple's liaison with Red at Miss Reba's is little more than a one-night stand. If we believe Chick Mallison, everybody in the town knows of Eula's adultery, and Eula knows that everybody knows and that everybody has even more or less conspired to support the sham in the name of respectability. She, who is so completely out of the range of the ordinary, lives a lie for eighteen years, staying with an impotent husband in an unsatisfying sterile marriage. Yet she commits suicide suddenly when her illicit relation threatens to become in fact public.

In all kinds of ways, the town itself, the community of men and women too, is the cuckold in *The Town*, the desiring subject, and Major de Spain the mediator: in its collective imagination Jefferson invests Eula with its own fantasies to titillate its own respectably repressed libido. She is the wife of a banker and a deacon; at the same time, with the community's voyeuristic cooperation, she violates the most sacred of their mores of respectability. The town *creates* her and then, through its mouthy representative, Gavin Stevens, exploits her, even in her death, by erecting a marble monument over her grave. In idealizing her in her death, the community makes her the mediator in a triangle in which the object of desire is wholeness, respectability. After following her sexual exploits over the years, at her death the town remakes her into a monument to its own virtue, forgiving her, and themselves, for their sexual shame: they have revelled in the titillation she has brought them, but refuse at last to let her be what she was. Stevens and Ratliff conclude that she committed suicide because she was bored. Perhaps they are right. As Dawn Trouard puts it,

> Eula arrives where she has always been heading. By the time of *The Town*, Faulkner's sympathies and understanding of what male-female relationships have done to women allow him to get the image right, and in putting a marble nymph in the Jefferson cemetery, he may be offering us his profoundest and most moving rendering of what it must be like to be a sexual female in such as

Yoknapatawpha. The marble faun of 1924 looks out over a fructive garden whose vital life he cannot participate in; the marble nymph—perhaps a more tragically apt symbol of the twentieth century's wasteland than a marble male faun—looks out over a dead dead world of men, and women too, who cannot either accept what she has to offer, sexual or otherwise, or reconcile themselves to their failure of her, and so must force her to join them in the cemetery.[16]

Eula, like Temple Drake, was in an impossible situation. I rather suspect that Faulkner learned something in writing *The Town* about the bind that he and all masculine others have put all women in. It may have been in some ways liberating for him. Hee Kang has convincingly demonstrated that in *The Mansion* Faulkner constructs a "radically creative and unprecedentedly modern feminine" in the figure of Linda Snopes Kohl, Eula's daughter:

> Refusing to surrender herself as a victim of the patriarchy, Linda, in her deaf voice, defiantly breaks the "vault of silence," conceives her own seductive yet threatening feminine desire by interrogating men's logic, and finally undoes and subverts the patriarchal authority, law, and language. . . . In *The Mansion* Faulkner, through Linda, changes the landscape of woman's space in his fictional world, tracing a trajectory from the space of victimization, betrayal, and death to a newly configured feminine space of desire, autonomy, and freedom.[17]

From this point of view, perhaps it is possible to see *The Reivers*, its rose-colored overview of his misogynist world, as a deliberate reinscription of the scene of the primal crime in his work, in which Faulkner quietly elides from it the sexual shame and the sexual terror, the fear and loathing of women that mar so many of his characters. Thus *The Reivers* may be a kind of implicit message to his grandchildren, to whom the novel is dedicated, and to us, that there are enough things in this world to loathe and be fearful of without seeking them out in the unoffending spaces of our wives', mothers', and sisters' sexual lives and sexual histories.

I do not mean to suggest any of this as a "happy ending" for

Faulkner the artist or Faulkner the citizen. Nor do I want to absolve Faulkner of the peculiar kinds of misery he created in his own home. I doubt very seriously that as a result of writing *The Town* or *The Mansion* or *The Reivers* he altered very many of his social presumptions about male-female relations or positions, though it seems to me demonstrable that at least part of his political engagement during the fifties was a direct response to the racial morality of, say, *Go Down, Moses* and *Intruder in the Dust*. I believe it would be very difficult to write such novels and not learn *something* in the process of confronting the narrative materials of those books. Whether his aging, his mellowing, his renewed fictional understanding of gender problematics would ever have prompted him to a similar social and political engagement is of course impossible to say. But the change in his fictional treatments of gender problems from his earliest books to his latest seems to me undeniable.

In his late career, Faulkner seems to understand that men cannot claim their own histories until women can claim theirs, too, and tell their stories themselves: if they choose and in their own voices, their own language, without yielding to the cultural narrative that binds us all to a singular story too often reducible to sexual pathology. Like Faulkner's, and like Jefferson's, a good deal of the specific energy of our own cultural narratives is based in our voyeuristic fascination with the supreme primal cracked foul oozing unscratchable chaste and utterly insatiable uterus. Faulkner knew this, I think. He knew more about desire than René Girard and Eve Sedgwick, and probably more about adultery than Tony Tanner and Emma Bovary. At any rate, he knew that for male communities to place women on the pedestals of their desire is to be cuckolded by death—whom we, like Quentin, prefer above all else.

NOTES

1. *Absalom, Absalom!*, The Corrected Text (New York: Random House, 1986).
2. See Daniel Ferrer, "Editorial Changes in the Chronology of *Absalom, Absalom!*: A Matter of Life and Death?" *Faulkner Journal* 5 (Fall 1989): 45–48; Noel Polk, "Where

the Comma Goes: Editing William Faulkner," *Representing Modernist Texts: Editing as Interpretation*, ed. George Bornstein (Ann Arbor: University of Michigan Press, 1991), 241–58.

3. E.g., Estella Schoenberg, *Old Tales and Talking: Quentin Compson in William Faulkner's "Absalom, Absalom!"* and Related Works (Jackson: University Press of Mississippi, 1977), 81–82; and Dirk Kuyk, Jr., *Sutpen's Design: Interpreting Faulkner's "Absalom, Absalom!"* (Charlottesville: University Press of Virginia, 1990), 8.

4. John Irwin, *Doubling and Incest/Repetition and Revenge: A Speculative Reading of Faulkner* (Baltimore: Johns Hopkins University Press, 1975), 43 *et passim*.

5. See " 'The Dungeon Was Mother Herself': William Faulkner: 1927–1931," in *New Directions in Faulkner Studies: Faulkner and Yoknapatawpha*, 1983, ed. Doreen Fowler and Ann J. Abadie (Jackson: University Press of Mississippi, 1984), 61–93.

6. René Girard, *Deceit, Desire, and the Novel: Self and Other in Literary Structure*, trans. Yvonne Freccero (Baltimore: Johns Hopkins University Press, 1965); Eve Kosofsky Sedgwick, *Between Men: English Literature and Male Homosocial Desire* (New York: Columbia University Press, 1985); Tony Tanner, *Adultery in the Novel: Contract and Transgression* (Baltimore: Johns Hopkins University Press, 1979).

7. William Faulkner, *Collected Stories* (New York: Random House, 1950), 374.

8. Joseph Blotner, *William Faulkner: A Biography*, One-Volume Edition (New York: Random House, 1984), 240.

9. "And Now What's To Do?" in *A Faulkner Miscellany*, ed. James B. Meriwether (Jackson: University Press of Mississippi, 1975), 146–47.

10. *As I Lay Dying*, in *Novels: 1930–1935*, ed. Joseph Blotner and Noel Polk (New York: Library of America, 1985), 85.

11. See, for example, "Mistral," "The Brooch," "Fox Hunt," "Honor," "Hair," "Divorce in Naples," and "A Justice" in *Collected Stories;* "Idyll in the Desert" and "A Dangerous Man" in *Uncollected Stories*, ed. Joseph Blotner (New York: Random House, 1977).

12. *The Hamlet*, in *Novels: 1936–1940*, ed. Joseph Blotner and Noel Polk (New York: Library of America, 1990), 938.

13. Blotner, 245. There is some evidence that Faulkner liked Estelle's first husband, Cornell, very much. According to Malcolm, he would drive the family, Estelle and Estelle's children, to Columbus for visits with Cornell.

14. See Janet Wondra, " 'Play' within a Play: Gaming with Language in *Requiem for a Nun*," *Faulkner Journal*, 8 (Fall 1992): 43–59.

15. *Requiem for a Nun*, in *Novels: 1942–1954*, ed. Joseph Blotner and Noel Polk (New York: Library of America, 1994), 568.

16. "Eula's Plot: An Irigararian Reading of Faulkner's Snopes Trilogy," *Mississippi Quarterly* 42 (Summer 1989): 294–95.

17. "A New Configuration of Faulkner's Feminine: Linda Snopes Kohl in *The Mansion*," *Faulkner Journal* 8 (Fall 1992): 21–22.

Faulkner's Crying Game:
Male Homosexual Panic

JOHN N. DUVALL

Before/After My Paper

About a week and half before I was to give my paper at the conference, as I sat at my desk looking over what was essentially the completed draft of my essay, I got a phone call. It was from a reporter for the Memphis paper, *The Commercial Appeal*, who was preparing a story on the conference. He had gotten a packet of information that included the titles of the various papers. "Mr. Duvall," he asked, "I couldn't help noticing the title of your paper. What exactly do you mean by homosexual panic?" I must admit I had there and then my own moment of panic. How, I thought, can I describe my work in a way that won't become misrepresented?

Then it came to me—the perfect way to explain the concept. There had been a wire service story in the paper just the day before (July 22, 1994). It was a story of gay bashing, but one so bizarre that if it were the plot for a made-for-tv movie, one would dismiss it as some script writer's pathology. Down in Florida, a group of rugby players (including the local prosecutor) decided to spoof the Ladies' Professional Golf Association, so they dressed in drag and staged their own tournament. Several hours after finishing their golf game and still dressed in drag, they went to a local gay bar where they smashed glasses and mirrors, overturned tables, and insulted patrons with shouts of "homos" and "fags."

As Melville's Ishmael doubtless would say, "Surely all this is not without meaning," but I don't think one needs to be Dr. Freud to figure this one out. The point of this story is that the more furiously men wish to define their masculinity in opposition to the feminine, the more distinctly we see male heterosexuality implicated in what it wishes to deny. In other words, male heterosexuality is always already unstably positioned between women and gays.

After I hung up the phone, it became clear to me the extent to which I had become implicated in the very concept I was using to interpret Faulkner. My conversation with the reporter taught me an important lesson: the problem is identification, not how someone identifies me or my work.

Because William Faulkner wrote at a time of significant change in the way of naming the behavior of women, his fiction, not surprisingly, has proved useful to feminist analysis of both the position of women and the cultural feminine.[1] Relatively less has been written about Faulkner's representations of masculinity.[2] To the extent that masculinity defines itself in relation to femininity, Faulkner's fiction offers an equally complex rendering of masculinity in crisis as it attempts to know itself in a now more fluid and decentered representational field. I'd like, then, to examine the issue of embattled masculinity in Faulkner to suggest that what we see in his fiction is the working through of a larger cultural pathology in male sexual self-identification. (Already, though, there is a problem with the language I have just used to speak of such matters; "sexual identity" with its values of sameness, essence, and stability hardly seems appropriate to the difference and plurality about which I will speak.)

To take up Faulknerian masculinity necessarily leads to a discussion of gender. A distinction in feminist analysis that has proved enormously productive opposes a base line of biological sex (female/male) to culturally constructed gender (feminine/masculine).[3] This distinction, however, has come under increasing scrutiny in the last few years from a variety of perspectives. What Judith Butler asserts theoretically in *Gender Trouble*, Thomas Laqueur demonstrates in *Making Sex* with his historical examination of the shift from the pre-Enlightenment one-sex model to the Enlightenment's two-sex model; namely, that sex is always already gendered.[4] Eve Kosofsky Sedgwick casts matters somewhat differently, although in a way compatible with Butler and Laqueur. Sedgwick asserts that *sexuality* is a missing (and in some sense mediating) term in the feminist sex/ gender opposition; thus, sexuality is "virtually impossible to situate on a map delimited by the feminist-defined sex/gender distinction" because there is a part of sexuality that seems of a piece with chromosomal sex—the given—and another part of sexuality that seems "even more than gender" to occupy the position of "the relational, the social/symbolic, the constructed, the variable, the representational."[5]

Sedgwick introduces the complementary yet distinct opposition between hetero- and homosexuality as a way to produce a more nuanced account of the effects of power on gendered bodies. Sedgwick's analysis is most supple in its account of the homoerotic within homosocial male bonding. Her deployment of the concept "homosexual panic" proves a useful strategy for producing dissident readings of a hegemonic/heterosexual masculinity that sees homosexuality as a totally othered minority.[6] Homosexual panic posits that male heterosexual "identity" is intimately tied to a definitional crisis since "male friendship, mentorship, admiring identification, bureaucratic subordination, and heterosexual rivalry all involve forms of investment that force men into the arbitrarily mapped, self-contradictory, and anathema-riddled quicksands of . . . male homosocial desire."[7] The cultural function of homosexual panic, then, is to police the border between hetero- and homosexuality; in a culture that stigmatizes same sex sexuality, the fear of being labelled homosexual, by others or oneself, haunts heterosexuality. It is through the concept of homosexual panic that I wish to think about several moments in Faulkner's life and fiction.

It would be possible to construct an argument that Faulkner's aesthetic is a gay aesthetic, given Faulkner's pilgrimage during his 1925 tour of Europe to Oscar Wilde's grave or his drawings influenced by Aubrey Beardsley. Moreover, Faulkner's special relationship with his mentor Phil Stone or his friendship with men whom Frederick Karl identifies as homosexual, such as Stark Young, Ben Wasson, and Bill Spratling, could be employed to speculate about Faulkner's sexual orientation.[8] But it is not my purpose here to assert that Faulkner was a latent homosexual because, if we follow Sedgwick and other articulations of queer theory, we may discover there is no such thing simply because the homoerotic is embedded in, not opposed to, masculinity.[9]

A number of the things I will point to in this paper occur at the level of language's connotation.[10] In the everyday, we employ the hierarchized relation of denotation (the primary or literal meaning) over connotation (secondary or figurative meanings). But as Roland Barthes points out at the beginning of S/Z, "denotation is not the first meaning, but pretends to be so; under this illusion, it is ultimately no more than the *last* of the connotations (the one which seems both to establish and to close the reading), the superior myth by which the text pretends to return to the nature of language, to language as nature."[11] In short, all denotation is reified connotation. For D. A. Miller, connotation, "the dominant signifying practice of homophobia," constructs "an insubstantial homosexuality" while "tending to raise this ghost all over the place"; connotation, of course, can always be denied, simply by uttering " 'But isn't it just . . . ?' before retorting the denotation."[12] I am urging here an openness to the countercommunication of connotation.

There is a story we—members of the Faulkner interpretive community—all know. It is about a little man rejected in love who joins the Royal Air Force. A young man who dreams of flying, killing, and mastery in the sky. But he is denied this dream by the ending of the European War. He never even flies an airplane. But no matter. He returns to Oxford and assumes a role—the wounded war pilot. As Judith L. Sensibar suggests, "posing for a series of snapshots of himself as wounded war hero, Faulkner created a firmly masculine image, an acceptable front behind which he could practice his art," which would have been seen as a feminine pursuit.[13] What is interesting about this theatrical enactment of gender is that it is a compromised masculinity, a masculinity that falls short of wholeness—a cane, a limp, a wounded leg. It is as though Faulkner created himself as a kind of Jake Barnes-*cum*-Eliotic Fisher King before the letter. This already compromised masculine image of the war hero seems further and self-consciously undercut by Faulkner's other self-fashioning, his equally theatrical enactment of a role—the decadent dandy/French symbolist poet. If writing poetry was perceived as a feminine occupation, Count No 'Count was perceived by his Oxford contemporaries as downright "queer," as Ben Wasson's reminiscences make vivid.[14] One day in the fall of 1919 Faulkner handed Wasson a copy of Conrad Aiken's *Turns and Movies and Other Tales in Verse*. According to Wasson, Faulkner

> persuaded me to go to the campus with him.
> He selected a place near one of the ubiquitous Confederate monuments. We sat there together on the grass, and he read the book aloud to me as students passed to and fro, glancing questioningly at us. Bill read without stopping, straight through the contents. What Aiken had set down moved me greatly.[15]

Small wonder that Wasson recalls questioning glances: had Wasson been a young woman, the passing students would have incorporated the moment as part of normal heterosexual courtship. Seeing two young men, though, defamiliarizes the moment. Indeed, had the students known of the frank treatment of homosexuality in Aiken's *Turns and Movies*, their glances perhaps would have been outraged.[16] Could it be that Faulkner in a sort of one-man guerilla theater was throwing back to his community its own assumptions about gender and sexual orientation? And what does it mean for Faulkner repeatedly to claim for himself the position of failed poet? These questions seem especially pertinent in light of how Faulkner himself conceived of the poet and the artist.

In Freud's master narrative, the move from the polymorphously perverse infant to the successful heterosexual adult involves loss and repression, but his civilization-and-its-discontents model at least means you don't have to decide each morning what you're going to be that day. But for Faulkner as a young man, such certainty—as his dueling personas indicate—seems elusive. To the extent that Faulkner's texts engage the Freudian presumption of bisexuality, the fact of dressing—both in Faulkner's life and fiction—is always already a cross-dressing, an instance of the body in drag.

Certainly the role of the wounded pilot is one that Faulkner tried to suppress as his increasing fame made it clear that biographers eventually would expose this guise. But the pilot is reluctant to land, just as the poet won't quit the scene; in a sense, both pilot and poet migrate back and forth between life and art. These two figures—the man in a uniform and the artist—comprise a sustained consideration of masculinity in the texts of William Faulkner. Together they create a textual logic that explores male violence, homophobia, and misogyny, while at the same time serving as a starting point for refiguring a masculinity that acknowledges the feminine as a constitutive component. In his consideration of masculinity, Faulkner puts into play moments of homoerotic figuration and possibility. Perhaps what I am trying to say can only be expressed through the apparent double negative of litotes: the fiction of William Faulkner does not disavow male homosexuality. At the time Faulkner was writing, the model of inversion was the standard way of naming deviance; in this model, a homosexual male can only be effeminate. Yet part of the way that Faulkner's texts refuse to disavow homosexuality is by unhinging the presumed conjunction of heterosexuality and masculinity. In other words, one can be a male and a heterosexual and still not be a "man." Faulkner's fiction thus opens out the question of masculinity in multiple ways.

The more we learn about Faulkner's life, the more we see Faulkner's autobiographical appropriations in his characters. In *Soldiers' Pay*, Donald Mahon, the severely wounded pilot who returns to his Georgia home to die, as Frederick Karl notes, "is

a not too disguised version" of Faulkner's persona, a character
"who has lost his sexual function, and thus, his manhood."[17] Yet
Faulkner 's war hero guise seems split between Mahon and the
naive boy in uniform, Cadet Lowe, who—like Faulkner—has
the war end on him too soon, a point I will return to later with
Percy Grimm. Characters, however, for whom the war did not
end soon enough provide additional clues about Faulknerian
masculinity. Just as Faulkner used the Sartoris family to fiction-
alize parts of his family history, so does he use the Sartoris twins
as aspects of his wounded aviator persona. Johnny and Bayard
Sartoris in *Flags in the Dust,* "Ad Astra," and "All the Dead
Pilots" provide Faulkner the means to project himself into
the homosocial world of the war pilots and into the war he
never fought.

The Bayard one sees in *Flags in the Dust* seems to embody a
hypermasculinity: he drinks heavily, is reckless, violent, and
taciturn—but he is also a wounded pilot, scarred psychologically
by the death of his twin. He is also literally wounded from his
repeated efforts to reproduce the danger of the aerial combat
that took his brother's life. He "courts" Narcissa Benbow while
he lies recuperating from injuries sustained in an automobile
accident. One afternoon, Narcissa visits the bedridden Bayard;
this moment, during which Bayard recounts Johnny's death, is
figured, psychologically, as a rape, a rape made possible by the
sexual metaphorics of aerial combat. In short, Bayard "rapes"
Narcissa with a story of manly death:

> She tried to free her wrist, but he held it in his hard fingers, and
> her trembling body betrayed her and she sank into her chair again,
> staring at him with ebbing terror and dread. He consumed the
> cigarette in deep, troubled draughts, and still holding her wrist he
> began talking of his dead brother, without preamble, brutally. . . .
> [A]nd she sitting with her arm taut in his grasp and her other hand
> pressed against her mouth, watching him with terrified fascin-
> ation. . . .
>   He talked on and her hand came away from her mouth and slid
> down her other arm and tugged at his fingers. "Please," she
> whispered. "Please!" He ceased and looked at her and his fingers

shifted, and just as she thought she was free they clamped again, and now both of her wrists were prisoners. She struggled, staring at him dreadfully, but he grinned his white cruel teeth at her and pressed her crossed arms down upon the bed beside him. [18]

The passion of this moment between Bayard and Narcissa, figured as it is in terms of heterosexual violation, depends, however, on the story of the German pilot's shooting down Johnny Sartoris's plane, a story fraught with homoerotic implications. Bayard is forced to watch his brother's plane penetrated by the bullets of another man. Johnny's jump to certain death is the climax of this interaction between two men. Important here is that what the German does to Johnny, Bayard figuratively repeats with Narcissa: the German feminizes Johnny, while Bayard shows that even women must be feminized, if he (Bayard) is to secure his masculinity. Doubly connoted but not directly denoted in both pairs (Johnny-German pilot, Narcissa-Bayard) is that masculinity is the power to feminize the other. If this scene implies a dominating masculinity, it is an implication, I hope to show, that is not left to stand unexamined in related narratives.

In Faulkner's 1931 short story "Ad Astra," the narrator tells us of Bayard's immediate response to his brother's death. Using another plane as bait, the next week Bayard shoots down three Germans in a scenario that allows him each time to "save" his brother. What Bayard fails to realize is that a homoerotic element is part and parcel of the homosocial world he inhabits as a pilot; indeed it is integral to aerial combat. Each time a German dives on the decoy plane, Bayard responds. To do what? To meet the German in a much mythologized but seldom enacted face-to-face dogfight? No. To penetrate him from the rear.

The larger narrative structure of "Ad Astra" supports such homoerotic implications. The story tells of an international group of pilots on Armistice Day in France. One of the central concerns of the story is identity. The narrator begins "I dont know what we were," a sentiment echoed by other characters. [19]

Although this sentence explicitly refers to national identity, it also implies the uncertainty of identity along other axes. The story ostensibly delineates a "safe" all-male space of hegemonic masculinity—acceptable male bonding through drinking and through bragging about fighting and heterosexual exploits— even if it is a wounded, wasteland masculinity. (The Indian soldier comments, "All this generation which fought in the war are dead tonight" [CS 421].) The story distinguishes, however, between Sartoris and Bland. Bland, the lady's man, is not well liked by the other men; although Bland and Sartoris are both Southerners, their attitude toward fighting is opposed. When confronted by the enemy, Bland seems content to fly the other way because, "unlike Sartoris, in the five months he had been out, no one had ever found a bullet hole in his machine" (CS 408). This points to an odd paradox: to be recognized as a man's man in this fraternity means risking penetration, yet to be penetrated is to be a woman. Stated differently, merely being heterosexual in one's object choice, as Bland is, is insufficient to establish manhood.

This dynamic clearly is in play in the relation between the American Monaghan and his prisoner, a German pilot he has downed that morning. Monaghan violates protocol by bringing his prisoner, who has a bad head wound, into the café where his comrades are "celebrating" the end of the war and announces to the group:

> "I'm going to take him home with me."
> "Why?" Bland said. "What do you want with him?"
> "Because he belongs to me," Monaghan said. He set the full glass before the German. "Here; drink." . . .
> "I haf plenty," the German said. "All day I haf plenty."
> "Do you want to go to America with him?" Bland said: [sic]
> "Yes. I would ligk it. Thanks."
> "Sure you'll like it," Monaghan said. "I'll make a man of you. Drink." (CS 412)

But Monaghan is not trying to make a *man* out of the German. Like Billy's reading poetry to Ben, something seems askew here

that, if this were between a man and a woman, the reader, like
the Ole Miss students, would process as part of the natural and
normal. That is, had Monaghan brought in a French woman,
tried to get her drunk, and promised her a trip to America, who
would think twice? The war's over; boys will be boys. But what
happens in the café is a seduction that exceeds the boundaries
of this homosocial world, and it is precisely that the war is over
that leads to the homoerotic subtext of this scene. The war over,
it is no longer acceptable to penetrate the body of another
man's plane, so how does one keep this feeling alive? Bland's
question—What do you want with him?—strikes close to the
heart of the matter. The homoerotic reading casts a different
light on the "French people's shocked and outraged faces" (*CS*
411–12); in one sense the French crowd obviously reacts to the
presence of an enemy soldier, but at a different level, their
disgust registers the unspeakable in this male community.

The tension occasioned by the presence of the German flyer
escalates into a brawl. In the aftermath of the fight, Comyn and
Monaghan leave Sartoris, Bland, and the narrator to go to a
whorehouse, half carrying the wounded German pilot with
them. Bland speaks directly to the homoerotic implications of
the story: " 'What will they do with him? . . . Prop him in the
corner and turn the light off? Or do French brothels have he-
beds too?' " The unnamed narrator's response is " 'Who the
hell's business is that' " (*CS* 426–27). The point here is not that
Comyn and Monaghan are taking the German off to sodomize
him; nevertheless, the German's presence insures that the
sexuality that is to occur will be between men. What Comyn
and Monaghan literally do with the prostitute, they figuratively
do to the German. We see in this moment women devalued in
a sexual economy; the prostitute will serve primarily as an agent
to effect a displaced homoerotic consummation. This paradigm
is not isolated to this story but also is central to Faulkner's major
fiction as, for example, in *Absalom, Absalom!*, where Judith
similarly serves to legitimize Henry's homoerotic desire for Bon.

Acknowledging the homoerotic subtext of "Ad Astra" casts a

useful light on another of Faulkner's wasteland stories, "All the Dead Pilots." In this story, Johnny Sartoris struggles with his superior officer, Captain Spoomer, over a young woman who is not exactly a prostitute, but who has been available to the enlisted men. The conflict is this: when Sartoris arrives, he wins for a period the exclusive affections of the young woman; after some time, Spoomer takes over Johnny's position with the woman. While the enlisted men were content to let the hierarchy stand, giving way when Sartoris takes the woman, Sartoris will not submit to a superior officer stealing his woman because he believes he is the superior pilot/man. Spoomer only has flown as an observer; Sartoris, as a combatant. So Sartoris responds by letting Spoomer's dog loose. If Spoomer has gone to visit the woman, the dog runs to town; if Spoomer has gone elsewhere, the dog goes behind the men's mess to eat garbage. Spoomer is furious if the dog gets in the garbage and hides the dog in a different place every time he leaves the base. This relationship between Sartoris and Spoomer is the central mystery for the narrator: " 'Do you mean that Captain Spoomer objects to the dog eating kitchen refuse?' " (CS 516). The symbolic logic that makes sense of Sartoris's and Spoomer's obsession with this dog is as full of thick evasions as the Freudian dreamwork. The first step is easy. Spoomer's dog is Spoomer. The narrator learns from one of the soldiers that, except for the uniform, "he and the dog looked alike" (CS 518). The second connection is less obvious. From another of the soldiers, the narrator learns that the young woman is known to the soldiers as Kitchener (Kit for short) "because she had such a mob of soldiers" (CS 514).

So why then does Sartoris take pleasure in freeing Spoomer's dog? Precisely so that the dog (who, recall, is a symbolic substitute for Spoomer) will go and root/rut among the kitchen/er refuse. Part of Spoomer's anger is that the dog eats the enlisted men's rather than the officers' garbage. So that at a certain level, Sartoris's act is an insult that reminds Spoomer that he, like his dog, is enjoying sloppy seconds, Kitchener's refuse. Spoomer's rank should entitle him to a better class of woman, so that his taking Kit, a common woman (common property), is as inappropriate as it would be for him to eat with the enlisted men.

The officer's uniform in "All the Dead Pilots" also adds an odd inflection to masculinity, since Johnny seems cathected not to articles of his lover's clothing but rather to the clothing of his lover's lover. When he first learns that Spoomer has usurped his place, Sartoris gets drunk and takes one of Spoomer's uniform tunics. Johnny's theft leads to what one might call a dressing at cross-purposes that points to the story's literal mo-ment of cross-dressing. After taking the tunic, Sartoris wakes a corporal, an ex-professional boxer who is wearing only his underwear, and makes him put on Spoomer's tunic; the two of them "stood there in the dawn, swinging at one another with their naked fists" (*CS* 515). Here, as elsewhere in Faulkner, there emerges a symbolic equivalence between fighting and fornicating. This fight between Sartoris and the corporal is repeated by a fight Sartoris has with a different corporal (the body?). Knowing that Spoomer is again with Kitchener although the town is under attack, Johnny gets drunk and flies his plane to a nearby field, then steals an ambulance (with the drunken driver still in it) to drive to the café. He bursts into the woman's room and hears her scream but sees only a closed closet door and Spoomer's pants and tunic, which he takes. One might note that what is shameful here, what must be closeted, is heterosexuality—the woman and a naked Spoomer. On his way out, Johnny is stopped by a French corporal who wonders what Sartoris is doing there. A fight ensues and, after the corporal pulls a gun and shoots point-blank at Johnny (an attempt at phallic penetration), the tables are reversed and Sartoris femi-nizes the corporal, trampling on the man's hand: "the corporal began to scream like a woman behind his brigand's moustaches. That was what made it funny, Sartoris said: that noise coming out of a pair of moustaches like a Gilbert and Sullivan pirate" (*CS* 525). After knocking out the corporal, Sartoris enacts a true moment of the unconscious. Drunk and having sustained several sharp blows to the head, Sartoris "didn't know then what he intended to do. . . . [H]e didn't realize it even when he had dragged the unconscious driver out of the ambulance and was dressing him in Captain Spoomer's slacks and cap and ribboned tunic" (*CS* 525). Sartoris then writes Spoomer's name and squadron number on a piece of paper, places it in the tunic pocket, and returns to the aerodrome.

When the ambulance driver, dressed as Spoomer, is returned to the aerodrome, Spoomer, of course, is disgraced. But how exactly has he dishonored his uniform? Johnny's sartorical she-nanigans function symbolically to castrate and feminize Spoomer. The next day Spoomer returns to the aerodrome "in a woman's skirt and a knitted shawl" (*CS* 527) and is summarily returned to England because he has been "outed" from his closet as a *hetero*sexual, a situation Sartoris finds humorous: " 'He's got to go back to England, where all the men are gone. All those women, and not a man between fourteen and eighty to help him' " (*CS* 528). The Spoomer who returns to England may be a male heterosexual, but he isn't a man. Again, hetero-sexuality appears neither as a sufficient (or apparently necessary) condition of masculinity because the assertion Sartoris makes about masculinity devalues heterosexual fornicating in favor of homoerotic fighting. Johnny Sartoris may symbolically castrate Spoomer, but it is an act which is simultaneously a self-castra-tion, for he too is punished by being transferred to a squadron with inferior planes, which proves to be the cause of his death. While castration and castration anxiety may be treated humor-ously in "All the Dead Pilots," elsewhere in Faulkner's fiction it takes a more sinister cast.

In *Light in August*, the story of a grim, small boy-man named Percy—the individual who kills and castrates Joe Christmas—serves as another embodiment of Faulkner's war hero persona, one that engages fully the problematic of male homosexual panic.[20] The initial delineation of Percy Grimm, who Faulkner would later claim was a "Nazi Storm Trooper" before the fact,[21] reads eerily like autobiographical reminiscence, particularly the relationship with the father:

> He was too young to have been in the European War, though it was not until 1921 or '22 that he realised that he would never forgive his parents for that fact. His father, a hardware merchant, did not understand this. He thought that the boy was just lazy and in a fair way to become perfectly worthless, when in reality the boy was suffering the terrible tragedy of having been born not alone too late but not late enough to have escaped first hand knowledge of the lost time when he should have been a man instead of a child. [22]

And like Billy, Percy finds a way toward minimal acceptance by donning a uniform. Here the similarities end, for Percy really is a captain in the Mississippi National Guard and not, as Faulkner was, a simulated soldier. Wearing the uniform, however, gives Grimm only "the selfconscious pride of a boy" (*LA* 498). This portrait of Grimm crucially reveals a young man who is insecure about his masculinity and who believes that there is some choice he can make that would create a stable identity. But in so believing, Grimm makes a category mistake, since, as this part of the narrative suggests, there is no stable masculinity to be achieved, certainly none that essentializes a sexual orientation.

Grimm's ostensible reason for wanting to lead a special patrol of veterans is to insure that Christmas will be dealt with by "the law" rather than by a lynch mob. But there is another motive operating here, one that Grimm doesn't acknowledge: he wants to be accepted by the men of Jefferson, to enter their homosocial world, something from which he has felt distanced. Yet what Percy fails to realize is that to be a man is, paradoxically, to be one of the boys. But by insisting on being their leader, Grimm is excluded from the serious play of the men's "holiday," their two-day long poker game and their reenactment of their war experiences. After a while the force of their actions "began to reassure Grimm's men in their own makebelieve" (*LA* 504).

Part of this dynamic is to have contempt for authority; when they perceive a threat to their poker game, they respond with utterances such as "Ware M.P.'s" and "Throw the son of a bitch out" (*LA* 504–5). Their project becomes a multiple paradox. They have gathered in the name of the law to represent the will of the law only to see themselves as restricted by that law, as boys before the law. Power is always elsewhere for "Grimm's men," and to be one of Percy's men is to be a boy; Percy's problem may be that he's not boy enough to be a man.

A clear portrait of male homosexual panic emerges, then, in Grimm's killing and castration of Joe Christmas. It is particularly important that it is Christmas whom Percy Grimm mutilates because in doing so Grimm completes a piece of textual logic focusing on black blood that shows the extent to which, for Faulkner's white Southern male, the otherness of the woman and the "Negro" serve as material figurations of a male crisis in sexual self-definition. Christmas's racial ambiguity and his gynophobic reaction to menstrual blood particularly merge in the figure of "black blood." When Joe learns about menstruation from his first love, Bobbie Allen, he runs from her into a dark woods, as black "as though in a cave"; from this black, invaginated space "In the notseeing," Joe "seemed to see a diminishing row of suavely shaped urns in moonlight, blanched. And not one was perfect. Each one was cracked and from each crack there issued something liquid, deathcolored, and foul" (*LA* 208–9). Overcome by this vision, Joe vomits. In Joe's unconscious, blackness and the female inexorably are linked.

When Grimm emasculates Christmas, the text marks the primary coordinate of identity as racial: " 'Now you'll let white women alone, even in hell' " (*LA* 513), Grimm asserts. Blatantly expressed as it is in this formulation, we hear a white man sending a message to black men about the possession of white women. But a homoerotic subtext also is at play in this moment. When Hightower attempts to intervene with the claim that he and Christmas were together the night Joanna was killed, Grimm responds with immediate fury at the prospect: " 'Jesus Christ!' Grimm cried, his young voice clear and outraged like that of a young priest. 'Has every preacher and old maid in Jefferson taken their pants down to the yellowbellied son of a bitch?' " (*LA* 512). Christmas becomes doubly threatening to Grimm; in addition to violating the taboo against miscegenation, Christmas (as well as Hightower) is perceived as a pervert. Grimm's outrage and his excessively violent response can be read as an instance of homosexual panic.

In *Epistemology of the Closet*, Sedgwick speaks of the "homosexual panic" defense in hate crimes against gay men; the defendant "accused of antigay violence implies that his responsibility for the crime was diminished by a pathological psychological condition, perhaps brought on by an unwanted sexual advance from the man whom he then attacked"; for Sedgwick,

> the homosexual panic defense performs a double act of minoritizing taxonomy: that is, it asserts, one distinct minority of gay people, and a second minority, equally distinguishable from the population at large, of "latent homosexuals" whose "insecurity about their own masculinity" is so analogous as to permit a plea based on diminution of normal moral responsibility. . . . The reliance of the homosexual panic plea on the fact that this male definitional crisis is systemic and endemic is enabled only, and precisely, by its denial of the same fact.[23]

Percy's rage and his excessive use of force result from his confrontation with the unspeakable in a community that values male bonds but demonizes male same-sex desire; to be thus confronted is a grim moment for Percy indeed, one that must be experienced with the force of a homosexual proposition. Significantly, it is Grimm's immediate interpretation of Hightower's claim, a logical leap turning a vague implication into the denoted truth, that shows how close to the surface of Percy's psychic life the homoerotic lies; if it is a proposition, it is a self-proposition.

What can we then make of Percy's response? It is the homophobia of homosexual panic that is figured through homoerotic images. While chasing Joe, Grimm calls Christmas a "good man" (*LA* 510) based on Joe's skill at avoiding capture. When Grimm hears Hightower's alibi, Christmas ceases to be a good man and, in fact, becomes an embodiment of manhood that must be erased. Grimm doesn't just shoot Christmas; rather, he "emptied the automatic's magazine into" Joe's body (*LA* 512). Yet Grimm's passion is not yet spent. His castration of Joe completes a certain symbolic logic. The "black blood" that flows from Christmas's hips and loins is metaphorically and metonymically menstrual blood; Joe bleeds where women (and only women) bleed.[24] At the sight of Joe's "menstrual" flow, "one of the men gave a choked cry and . . . began to vomit," a confirmation that the thought or sight of this shameful flow is not simply Joe's (or Faulkner's) personal pathology but a collective one of Yoknapatawpha masculinity; the man's vomiting repeats Joe's vomiting upon learning of menstruation from Bobbie Allen. Thus Christmas, in addition to being forced to the communal definition of himself as "nigger murderer" also must be seen in death occupying the gendered role of woman. The matrix of otherness that has been recognized in Faulkner's fiction—the mirrored relation between the subject positions of African Americans and women—must be broadened to include the otherness of homosexuality as a feared and fantasized space of blackness.[25] I spoke earlier of Grimm's belief that he could make a choice and that the choice he makes, like the Sartoris brothers', is an identification of masculinity with the ability to castrate. But because the father is always already a son, no amount of castration or castration anxiety ever can create a stable site of masculinity.[26] Grimm may castrate Christmas, but that doesn't make Grimm a man, and in fact completes his exclusion from the other men of Jefferson.

By December of 1933 William Faulkner had received his pilot's license and owned an airplane, facts that show his long-time passion for flying hadn't faded and that served to legitimize his postwar persona as a wounded pilot. In February of 1934, Faulkner attended the dedication of Shushan Airport in New Orleans, which serves as the backdrop for his lightly regarded novel *Pylon*. As I have argued elsewhere, *Pylon* deserves more careful consideration.[27] Faulkner examines the social otherness of the barnstormers who travel from air show to air show.

Particularly the ménage à trois of Roger and Laverne Shumann and Jack Holmes proves a bisexual space that challenges the patriarchal assumptions in conventional marriage. The multiple ambiguities of this group make them perhaps Faulkner's most radical experiment in thinking gender. Laverne, "a woman not tall and not thin, looking almost like a man in the greasy coverall, . . . a tanned heavyjawed face in which the eyes looked like pieces of china," is another of Faulkner's epicene women, so troubling to an earlier generation of Faulkner's readers.[28] And Jack Holmes is delineated with equally ambiguous features: "He wore a narrow mustache above a mouth much more delicate and even feminine than that of the woman" (P 31). Roger Shumann, as a figuration of the masculine, is perhaps the most interesting of the three, especially in his relation to the child of this group, Jack Shumann, whose paternity is undecidable. Roger works and ultimately dies working to support a son who might not be his and a child not yet born who he believes is not his. Shumann's willingness to give his patronymic to a child he cannot be certain is his represents an antipatriarchal urge.[29] Shumann, then, in accepting the son he cannot know is his is the antithesis of Thomas Sutpen, the father who denies a son he knows to be his own. *Pylon*, as a novel literally framed by the writing of *Absalom, Absalom!*, can be read against the more famous novel in ways that remind me of the contrapuntal relation between "The Wild Palms" and "Old Man." Certainly the veiled homoeroticism of the Henry-Judith-Bon triangle can be apprehended more fully if juxtaposed against the more openly bisexual space of Jack, Laverne, and Roger. I am only half-facetious when I suggest that the corrected text of *Absalom, Absalom!* should have had *Pylon* embedded in it.

Whatever possibilities that existed for a sustained refiguration of masculinity through fictional flyers end, however, a few months after the publication of *Pylon*, when on November 10, 1935, William's youngest brother was killed in the crash of the plane Faulkner had purchased the year before. After Dean's death, the pilot figure and flight as metaphors for sexual ambiguity seem unavailable for Faulkner. But although the pilot had been grounded, the other side of the faultline of Faulkner's masculine subject, the artist, remains a site to consider.

A useful starting point for a consideration of the artist is in Faulkner's second novel, *Mosquitoes*, which focuses on the New Orleans literati and questions of aesthetics and poetics. The novel is also rife with questions of gender and sexuality. In a promising move, Frann Michel, in her reading of *Mosquitoes*, attempts a synthesis of the Freudian model of the male child's relation to the father and Nancy Chodorow's emphasis on the pre-oedipal primary identification with the mother; masculine identity thus emerges as a "normal" pathology, at least as much as Freud's account of woman's assumption of adult feminine sexuality. To the extent that masculinity defines itself in opposition to the feminine, masculinity is doubly fragile: "to escape feminization of identification with and engulfment by the mother, the male child turns to a relation with the father. But the escape offered by the relation with the father entails the threat of castration by the father."[30] The threat of feminization almost seems to be a constitutive part of masculine identity. Michel argues that Faulkner's delineation of Eva Wiseman, a poet, constitutes a moment of lesbian identification.[31] Wiseman is linked, as John Irwin first pointed out, to the funny little black man, a writer named Faulkner, whom one of the characters in *Mosquitoes* recalls meeting one time.[32] In addition to this fictional Faulkner, Eva Wiseman also is related to the historical Faulkner. Her poem expressing desire for an epicene woman with boy's hands and a woman's breast Faulkner will later publish in his 1933 collection, *The Green Bough*. Dawson Fairchild, the Sherwood Anderson figure of *Mosquitoes*, reads Eva Wiseman's poetry as "emotional bisexuality" to which his companion responds: " 'A book is the writer's secret life, the dark twin of a man: you can't reconcile them.' "[33]

The other representation of the artist I wish to take up points precisely to the writer's secret life and dark twin; this figuration occurs in "Afternoon of a Cow." On June 25, 1937, Faulkner read a typescript of this story, written he claimed by Ernest V. Trueblood, to several male friends—notably Maurice Coindreau, who was then translating *The Sound and the Fury*, and Ben Wasson—as the prelude to a poker game. As in *Mosquitoes*, Faulkner again appears as a character, only this time he is central.

In this story, Mr. Faulkner and Trueblood's afternoon of drinking is interrupted by a black servant's news that Faulkner's son, Malcolm, with two other boys, had set the pasture on fire. The men then hurry to the pasture to save a cow, Beulah. Faulkner and the cow fall into a ravine. After the fire has passed, the three men attempt to help the cow out. The cow, however, falls back on Faulkner and, as Trueblood puts it, Mr. Faulkner "received the full discharge of the poor creature's afternoon of anguish and despair."[34] Mr. Faulkner then leads the cow the long way home by taking it to where the ravine levels out. He cleans himself and resumes drinking with Trueblood.

Michael Grimwood is correct in asserting that this story "rehearsed an insecurity about his literary identity" and that the farmer becomes an important persona for Faulkner later in life.[35] What I would add is that by 1937, Faulkner felt a need for a different, safe masculine cover for his feminine vocation as a writer now that the pilot had become too painful to use. In a sense, then, the farmer replaces the pilot, but something more than literary identity is at stake here. "Afternoon of a Cow" asserts that identity itself is always already a fiction or a theatrical production.[36] Early in the story, Trueblood reveals that "I have been writing Mr. Faulkner's novels and short stories for years" (*US* 425). Trueblood is more than a secretary, but less than a writer. Mr. Faulkner, the fiction asserts, tells Trueblood what subjects to write about each afternoon; Trueblood then does the actual writing. The point here is that Mr. Faulkner is not William Faulkner without Ernest V. Trueblood. And whatever is produced under that name William Faulkner is always an unstable collaboration, and whatever can be said about masculinity in this story occurs in the negotiations between these two figures. A taciturn, heavy drinking man of action who reads nothing deeper than detective fiction, Mr. Faulkner is a type of the hypermasculine associated with Faulkner's war pilots. Ernest V. Trueblood is a fussy prude, whose euphemistic style refuses to name bodily functions and deletes all of Faulkner's expletives. What really is Ernest V. Trueblood but Count No 'Count grown up, that "queer" Faulkner who wanted to be a poet? In "Afternoon," then, Mr. Faulkner plays the "straight" man to Trueblood's comically effeminate verbal mincing. But is Trueblood's style merely comic affectation? Describing the cow just prior to its shitting on Mr. Faulkner, Trueblood says

> I seem to have received, as though by telepathy, from the poor creature (a female mind; the lone female among three men) not only her terror but the subject of it: that she knew by woman's sacred instinct that the future held for her that which is to a female far worse than any fear of bodily injury or suffering: one of those invasions of female privacy where, helpless victim of her own physical body, she seems to see herself as object of some malignant power for irony and outrage; and this none the less bitter for the fact that those who are to witness it, gentlemen though they be, will never be able to forget it but will walk the earth with the remembrance of it so long as she lives. . . . (US 430)

This is self-parody in more than one way. Although Mr. Faulkner authorizes Trueblood to tell this story in Trueblood's own style, the style is clearly "Faulknerian," with its embeddings, delays, and rhetorical excess—on the whole, something one might expect in the Faux Faulkner contest.[37] The above passage is also an embarrassment inasmuch as it serves as a reversed reminder of Faulkner's figuration of certain female characters, such as Lena Grove, Dewey Dell, and Eula Varner, as bovine; here the cow is figured as a woman. Doubtless it would be easy to read this as another instance of Faulkner's bad faith representation of women or his conventional treatment of homosexual males as effeminate. And yet in this moment, an interesting transformation occurs in this Mr. Faulkner. He quietly accepts this engulfment by the female, and in that acceptance the shit-besmeared Mr. Faulkner has a brief moment of critical distance on his particular enactment of masculinity. Mr. Faulkner is born again as Trueblood, or at least becomes true to his blood, as the masculinity Mr. Faulkner has projected falls away temporarily. When the men near the barn they encounter the three boys, with singed hair and charred clothes, who expect punishment from the father: "They stood looking at us in complete immobility until Mr. Faulkner said, again with that chastened gentleness and quietude which . . . has been Mr. Faulkner's true and hidden character all these years: 'Go to the house' " (*US* 433). This Mr. Faulkner, who had been linked with the war-pilot hypermasculine, at a critical moment avoids the anger and violence of Sartoris masculinity. "Afternoon of a Cow," then, does not simply reproduce hegemonic stereotypes or reactionary images of women and effeminate men; the story also recognizes that masculinity is always inescapably an enactment, whether it is inflected in terms of the hegemonic norm (Farmer Faulkner) or of queer alternatives (Ernest V. Trueblood).

At the outset I said I was not here to imply that William Faulkner was a homosexual, but I know that the connotations of this paper are beyond my control. Yet what is it that we think we know when someone names (or we name for someone) their sexual orientation? The question is analogous to what we think we know if we fix someone's paternity or racial identity. We believe we have determined stable coordinates of the subject. What I hope to have suggested is that in unhinging masculinity from a particular sexual practice, Faulkner's texts at certain moments disavow the notion of "sexual identity." As part of this move, what Faulkner in his life and work does not disavow is the male homosexual.[38]

NOTES

1. The work of Minrose Gwin, Deborah Clarke, Susan V. Donaldson, Doreen Fowler, Judith Wittenberg, Judith L. Sensibar, Philip Weinstein, and others has helped

dislodge the older Agrarian model of Faulkner's women and the feminine. Recently Diane Roberts in *Faulkner and Southern Womanhood* (Athens: University of Georgia Press, 1994) has shown just how the extensive shifts from Old South models of womanhood to those of the 1920s and 1930s created tensions in the South between women's "growing social freedom" at a time of "hardening traditional values" (13). See particularly chap. 1.

2. Anne Goodwyn Jones uses Klaus Theweleit's work on the fantasies of the German Freikorps to note parallels between fascist male figurations of women and Faulkner's; see " 'The Kotex Age': Women, Popular Culture, and *The Wild Palms*," in *Faulkner and Popular Culture*, ed. Doreen Fowler and Ann J. Abadie (Jackson: University Press of Mississippi, 1990), 142–62. In "The 'Masculinity' of Faulkner's Thought" (*Faulkner Journal* 4.1 & 2 [Fall 1988/Spring 1989]: 67–81) Gail L. Mortimer, using the work of Nancy Chodorow and Carol Gilligan, argues from certain male characters that Faulkner's language is masculine because of its emphasis on "issues of loss and control" (80); despite the useful emphasis on a masculine-feminine continuum, the essay tends both to essentialize masculinity and femininity and to presume heterosexuality.

3. This distinction is first fully articulated in Gayle Rubin's anthropological essay The Traffic in Women: Notes on the 'Political Economy' of Sex," in *Toward an Anthropology of Women*, ed. Rayna R. Reiter (New York: Monthly Review Press, 1975).

4. Judith Butler, *Gender Trouble: Feminism and the Subversion of Identity* (New York: Routledge, 1990). Thomas Laqueur, *Making Sex: Body and Gender from the Greeks to Freud* (Cambridge: Harvard University Press, 1990). As Laqueur puts it: "almost everything one wants to *say* about sex—however sex is understood—already has in it a claim about gender. Sex . . . is situational; it is explicable only within the context of battles over gender and power" (11).

5. *Epistemology of the Closet* (University of California Press, 1990), 29. More problematic still from Sedgwick's perspective is what she identifies as "a damaging bias toward heterosocial or heterosexist assumptions . . . in the very concept of gender. . . . [T]he ultimate definitional appeal in any gender-based analysis must necessarily be to the diacritical frontier between different genders. This gives heterosocial and heterosexual relations a conceptual privilege of incalculable consequence" (31).

6. My use of the term "dissident reading" is borrowed from Jonathan Dollimore's *Sexual Dissidence: Augustine to Wilde, Freud to Foucault* (Oxford: Oxford University Press, 1991) and Alan Sinfield's *Faultlines: Cultural Materialism and the Politics of Dissident Reading* (Berkeley: University of California Press, 1992).

7. Sedgwick, *Epistemology*, 186.

8. In *William Faulkner: American Writer* (New York: Weidenfeld and Nicolson, 1989), Karl identifies as homosexual individuals who made at least some effort to closet their sexuality. See for example his discussion of Wasson, 502n. Also, as Robert Dale Parker pointed out to me, Spratling's autobiography is less clear about his sexual identity than Karl indicates.

9. Susan Faludi's portrayal of Shannon Faulkner's attempt to join the Corps of Cadets at The Citadel serves as an interesting metonymy for my discussion of William Faulkner and the issue of masculinity ("The Naked Citadel," *The New Yorker*, 5 Sept. 1994: 62–81). For Faludi, the particular enactment of masculinity at The Citadel turns upon open misogyny, gynophobia, feminization of freshman "knobs," and of course a Southern gentleman's respect for ladies. Most telling is Faludi's visit to a gay bar in Charleston and her conversation with the drag queens there, who discussed the relationships they had with Citadel cadets. Faludi cleverly parallels the drag queens' enactment of femininity (as they help one another prepare themselves for a show) with the cadets' obsessive concern about their uniform. In particular, the cadets' enactment of uniformed masculinity requires the proper shirt tuck: a cadet must have another man take the former's shirt and tuck it deeply into his unbuckled pants.

A point of Faludi's article—as with the anecdote prefacing my essay—is that the set of "latent homosexuals" may be so large that to say male heterosexual or latent homosexual would be to name the same set; in other words, latency is so endemic to heterosexuality that to call someone "latent" fails to identify anything at all.

10. Here I am following D. A. Miller in his use of Barthes. See "Anal *Rope,*" *Representations* 32 (Fall 1990): 114–33.

11. *S/Z,* trans. Richard Miller (New York: Hill and Wang, 1974), 9.

12. "Anal *Rope,*" 118–19.

13. "Faulkner's Fictional Photographs: Playing with Difference," in *Out of Bounds: Male Writers and Gender(ed) Criticism,* ed. Laura Claridge and Elizabeth Langland (Amherst: University of Massachusetts Press, 1990), 300.

14. Although "queer" did not explicitly carry the connotation in the 1910s that it does for us now, the term clearly tended in that direction by signifying deviance from a presumed norm. See Sedgwick's meditation on the meanings of "queer" in *Tendencies* (Durham: Duke University Press, 1993), 5–9.

15. *Count No 'Count: Flashbacks to Faulkner* (Jackson: University Press of Mississippi, 1983), 32–33.

16. See particularly "II. The Apollo Trio," "V. Gabriel de Ford," and "XII. Aerial Dodds" in *Turns and Movies and Other Tales in Verse* (Boston: Houghton Mifflin, 1916).

17. Karl, 209.

18. *Flags in the Dust,* ed. Douglas Day (New York: Vintage, 1974), 280–81.

19. "Ad Astra," in *Collected Stories of William Faulkner* (New York: Vintage, 1977), 407. All subsequent references to "Ad Astra" and "All the Dead Pilots" are to this edition; hereafter cited as *CS*.

20. Robert Penn Warren first notes a link between Faulkner and Percy Grimm. See "Introduction: Faulkner: Past and Present," in *Faulkner: A Collection of Critical Essays,* ed. Robert Penn Warren (Englewood Cliffs, N.J.: Prentice-Hall, 1966), 3.

21. *Faulkner in the University,* ed. Frederick L. Gwynn and Joseph L. Blotner (New York: Vintage, 1965), 41.

22. *Light in August,* The Corrected Text (New York: Vintage, 1987), 496–97; hereafter cited as *LA*.

23. *Epistemology of the Closet,* 19–20.

24. Here I follow Joseph R. Urgo's position in "Menstrual Blood and 'Nigger' Blood: Joe Christmas and the Ideology of Sex and Race," *Mississippi Quarterly* 42, No. 3 (Summer 1989): 391–401; see particularly 401.

25. Doreen Fowler correctly reads Christmas's death as a confirmation of the mirrored figuration of women and African Americans in the novel. See "Joe Christmas and 'Womanshenegro' " in *Faulkner and Women,* ed. Doreen Fowler and Ann J. Abadie (Jackson: University Press of Mississippi, 1986), 144–61.

26. John T. Irwin first makes the point in relation to Faulkner's texts about fathers as always already sons. See *Doubling and Incest/Repetition and Revenge* (Baltimore: Johns Hopkins University Press, 1975), 104.

27. See my *Faulkner's Marginal Couple: Invisible, Outlaw, and Unspeakable Communities* (Austin: University of Texas Press, 1990), 81–97. For recent readings of *Pylon* that complement my sense of the novel's radical portrayal of gender, see John T. Matthews, "The Autograph of Violence in Faulkner's *Pylon*" in *Southern Literature and Literary Theory,* ed. Jefferson Humphries (Athens: University of Georgia Press, 1990), 247–69 and Vivian Wagner, "Gender, Technology, and Utopia in Faulkner's Airplane Tales," *Arizona Quarterly* 49 (Winter 1993): 79–97.

28. *Pylon,* The Corrected Text (New York: Vintage, 1987), 21; hereafter cited as *P*.

29. In this regard, Shumann seems to embody the sentiment of the German pilot in "Ad Astra": " 'the word *father* iss that barbarism which will be first swept away; it iss the symbol of that hierarchy which hass stained the history of man with injustice of arbitrary instead of moral; force instead of love' " (*CS* 417).

30. "William Faulkner as a Lesbian Author," *Faulkner Journal* 4.1 & 2 (Fall 1988/Spring 1989), 9. Michel sees in *Mosquitoes* Faulkner's use of lesbian identification as a "focus for the multiple feminizations of the male author and a defense against male homoeroticism" (16–17).

31. For Michel, this is ultimately a bad faith gesture on Faulkner's part, a way of appropriating feminine subjectivity and the possibilities of writing for men (17).

32. *Doubling and Incest,* 167.

33. *Mosquitoes* (New York: Boni and Liveright, 1927), 208.

34. "Afternoon of a Cow," in *Uncollected Stories of William Faulkner,* ed. Joseph Blotner (New York: Random House, 1979), 430; hereafter cited as *US*.

35. " 'Mr. Faulkner' and 'Ernest V. Trueblood,' " *Southern Review* NS 21 (1985): 371.

36. I would disagree with Grimwood when he claims the story "not only dramatizes the pastoral symbiosis between 'farmer' and 'writer,' but projects that relationship out of one man's identity" (368). My point is that there is no unitary identity prior to the split and that the two characters—the farmer and the aesthete/writer—are a negotiation of masculinity.

37. See Grimwood on this point (364).

38. I wish to thank Patrick Murphy, Paul Naylor, Robert Dale Parker, and Susan Scheckel for their questions and comments on drafts of this paper. This work was supported by a grant from The University of Memphis Faculty Research Grant Fund. This support (I am required to add) does not imply endorsement by the university of research conclusions.

Sex and Gender, Feminine and Masculine: Faulkner and the Polymorphous Exchange of Cultural Binaries

ROBERT DALE PARKER

Three models of sex and gender identity inform this discussion. In the first model, still active culturally but here treated as obsolete, people are born with a sex, male or female, which determines and equals their gender. In this model, as Freud puts it, anatomy is destiny.[1] By the 1970s and mid-80s, feminist theory settled into a new orthodoxy that offered a second model, in which sex refers to the biological, including the female and male, while gender refers to the more variable arenas of the cultural and discursive, including the feminine and masculine. In this model, females and males are born, whereas (to paraphrase Simone de Beauvoir and the U.S. Marine Corps) women and men are made. This second model has proved extraordinarily useful because it no longer essentializes gender into a stable certainty. Nevertheless, it continues to essentialize sex by reading the categories of female and male as if they were underlying biological essences independent of culture. For many observers that kernel of essentialism is part of the second model's appeal. But others, among whom Judith Butler may be the best known, have argued for a third model that sees both sex and gender as constructed, reading biology as part of culture rather than antecedent to culture.[2] In this model, as Thomas Laqueur puts it, destiny is anatomy.[3]

Here I work from this third model on the logic that we cannot conceptualize anything—not even anatomy—as female or male

73

independently of our cultural concepts of feminine and masculine. Feminine and masculine can always trump female and male, because the supposedly pure biology is always already seen through lenses colored by cultural and linguistic expectation and expression.

Two brief clarifications. One, in this context, the word "sex" refers to a supposedly anatomical identity, such as the male sex or the female sex, not to an activity. And two, even though I work from the third model, which reads gender as producing or helping to produce sex, so that the two are finally indistinguishable, I will sometimes differentiate sex from gender when I address the continuing assumptions of model two, the dominating cultural illusion that sex precedes and differs from gender.

My focus is a polymorphous and typically Faulknerian dizziness before a linked pair of binaries: the binary between sex and gender and the binary between masculine and feminine genders. Faulkner oscillates between needs to see sex as determining gender, as different from gender, or as determined by gender, and he oscillates between seeing the binary of feminine and masculine genders as stable and seeing it as unstable. I will look at these oscillations in a sampling of much studied and little studied works, with no pretense to producing a complete list of any particular kind of example. Then I will discuss how these sometimes commonplace preoccupations take on specifically Faulknerian shapes. My overall argument is that Faulkner feels queasier about the burdens on masculinity than about the more concretely threatening burdens on women. For women, he imagines or at least tries to imagine the dialectic between sex and gender in terms of individual women, whereas for men, he imagines sex and gender through a more frankly puzzled uneasiness about the broader possibilities for masculinity.

Faulkner's biological fascinations have been remarked before. Ilse Dusoir Lind proposes that Faulkner was the first to "put the biological facts of female life into fiction" and "the only major American fiction writer of the twenties and thirties who incorporates into his depiction of women the functioning of the organs of reproduction."[4] Lind cites Faulkner's references to menstruation, menopause, and the uterus, although she does not mention Temple Drake's or Addie Bundren's striking descriptions of their own genitalia.

Those who read sex as a biological essence rather than a cultural process might see Addie's body as an example of anatomical femaleness determined independently of femininity. In many ways, the problem of *As I Lay Dying* is the problem of what to do with Addie's body, and she herself imagines her body in thoughts that Faulkner renders with a stunning mixture of explicitness and indirection. She thinks about her husband Anse's "name until after a while I could see the word as a shape, a vessel . . . : a significant shape profoundly without life like an empty door frame; and then I would find that I had forgotten the name of the jar. I would think: The shape of my body where I used to be a virgin is in the shape of a   and I couldn't think *Anse,* couldn't remember *Anse.*"[5]

This remarkable passage poses several questions for the exchanges between sex and gender, masculine and feminine. Addie conceives her sexual biology in terms that almost deincarnate the biological by deriving it so extravagantly from figures—*shape, vessel,* and *jar*—that mold her ideas of her own anatomy. Indeed, the derived status of her sexual identity is overdetermined, for it comes also from Anse's sexual biology, so that even her autoerotic sensation of her own femaleness is channeled through heterosexual and patriarchal imperatives into a citation of Anse's maleness. Yet Anse's biology is itself rendered in overdeterminedly discursive form, as a continuous deferral in a chain of rhetorical figures like a hall of mirrors, with no underlying signified or biological endpoint. The figures blend into each other rather than precipitating out as distinct entities, but the rough outline envisions Anse's sexuality as (1) a blank space graphed in (2) the palimpsest of (3) Addie's forgotten name for (4) the sensation of (5) his empty shape, as if shape were opposed to a substance it can never reach, to a signified *Anse* free of corrupting signifiers.

Addie's medley of unnameables (shape, blank space, couldn't think, couldn't remember) is therefore not simply the blank space that some critics have called it. It is neither a fault in language nor a castratingly feminized absence or lack. Addie's blank space, her writeable anatomy, is full with gendered discourse. It is language, and it bespeaks its own alphabet in an eloquence at once alongside and outside the received system of alphabetic inscription. Addie's alphabet scripts her anatomy both in relation to and in resistance to Anse's, both derivatively and independently. She at once erases Anse by her inability to think or remember his name, and italicizes the name that she cannot think or remember, and together these reactions and assertions write the feminine-masculine space that Anse's world and its received alphabets would erase.[6]

Thus Addie's concept that there is a place *"where"* she "used to be a virgin" reads back onto physiology a gendered cultural category. It underlines how we cannot conceptualize physiology independently of culture, and how the biology of sex, the supposed antecedent to gender, is always already gendered. Addie is not born with the biological shape she now feels, so much as she and Anse and their cultural matrix produce that shape. Through the material, tactile discourse of sexual contact, they produce her sensation of interior vaginal contour.

Addie's thoughts recall the passage in *Sanctuary* where Temple remembers yearning to switch sexes because a sex change would oblige a behavior change in the men who threaten to rape her. They could still rape her—or him—if she exchanged her female genitalia for male genitalia, but nothing in Temple or the novel remotely countenances such an idea. The confident boundaries of Temple's fantasy thus tell us much, especially when we recognize them so readily as to take for granted that a sudden sex change—fantastic though it is—would produce the safety she yearns for. And that readers have taken her expectations for granted is testified to by the paucity of comment that her fantasy has evoked in a body of criticism that otherwise has much to say about Temple.[7]

In some ways, then, Temple, despite her "boy's name,"[8] takes the boundaries between sexes much more for granted than Addie does. Even when she imagines switching sexes, she conceives the switch as immediate and complete: "It made a kind of plopping sound, like blowing a little rubber tube wrong-side outward. It felt cold, like the inside of your mouth when you hold it open" (S 220). Temple sees sex in such anatomical terms that in her fantasy the inner surface of tissue, the shape that so puzzles and fascinates Addie, reverses and becomes the outer surface with an abruptness—figured in the "plopping sound"—that bisects sex into two opposite poles, male and female, suppressing any continuum between them or any place outside the continuum. It is as if she lingers so memorably over the physical sensation of tissue in part to insist on its concreteness as the corporeal signified of sex, of a maleness and femaleness made suddenly more intensely perceptible by the unprecedented shift from one to the other.

But as with Addie, the difference between female and male is not so concrete as Temple, in her desperate wish to escape the violence that men inflict on women, yearns to imagine. If a woman turned inside out becomes a man, then we could as well note the likeness as the difference between men and women. Such likeness was exactly the emphasis in Western medicine before the eighteenth century, Laqueur argues. He quotes Galen: "Turn outward the woman's, turn inward, so to speak, and fold double the man's [genital organs], and you will find the same in both in every respect."[9] The site of difference is so fluid that, as Temple puts it, "I'd wonder if I could tell when it happened." Then she adds quickly "I mean, before I looked" (S 217), as if trying to reassert the disturbingly deferred physiological. But for Temple the physiological always derives from the psychological. The sex change she imagines comes not from a biological impulse but from her own thoughts: "I was thinking about if I just was a boy and then I tried to make myself into one by thinking. . . . Then I thought about being a man, and as soon as I thought it, it happened" (S 216, 220). Here body is so contingent on mind and sex is so contingent on gender that, as with Addie, the distinctions between them appear like relics of a defunct social narrative, active only as yearned-for simplifications rather than as determining facts.

As Temple recalls wishing for a change, Rosa Coldfield of *Absalom, Absalom!* claims that once, for the length of an adolescent summer, she did change—and then apparently changed back: *"That was the miscast summer of my barren youth which . . . I lived out not as a woman, a girl, but rather as the man which I perhaps should have been."*[10] That summer, she insists, her gender differed from her sex, and the intense recollection evokes her continued investment in the long-ago transformation. She thinks that she *"should have"* been *"weaponed and panoplied as a man instead of hollow woman"* (AA 117). Elsewhere I have written about the social and psychological forces that pressure Rosa to define her feminine position in oppressively narrow ways, leading her to fear women's roles and to suppose that she has failed as a woman.[11] She turns to fantasies of masculinity and androgyny, I argued, to escape the burdens imposed on women. Hence the nervous evasions that weave through her account of her erotic fascination for Thomas Sutpen. And hence, when she celebrates her adolescent crush on Charles Bon by dubbing herself *"all polymath love's androgynous advocate"* (AA 117), she mixes a grandiloquent celebration of heterosexual sexuality with an evasive denial of the sexual difference it depends on.

While that reading continues to seem part of the story to me, and in Rosa's case perhaps the largest part of the story, it also sidesteps Rosa's sex and gender ambiguity by reading it only as a defense against something else. It misses how Rosa's shifting among assertions of the feminine, masculine, and androgynous shows her not only suffering from but also challenging the rigid binaries between sex and gender, feminine and masculine, and female and male. Rosa's assertions not only defend against the burdens imposed on the feminine side of those binaries. They

also craft fluidly androgynous spaces that the binaries themselves defend against by denying.

If characters like Temple and Rosa, classified as women,
sometimes imagine themselves vaulting to the other side of the
binary, for Faulkner characters classified as men the switch
more often occurs in other characters' minds than in the minds
of characters who are thought to switch. In Faulkner's world, it
is much safer for women to imagine themselves as men than for
men to imagine themselves as women. The worried sense that
men live under more threat than women evokes the fragility of
masculine identity in a world where we could argue that men
actually offer women much more material danger than women
offer men, and it defensively reacts against women's increasing
assertiveness.

Let us look at three sets of examples: (1) Carl and George,
the bisexual but predominantly gay couple in Faulkner's rarely
discussed story "Divorce in Naples" (their sexuality has probably
frightened off critical discussion[12]); (2) the Harvard students'
description of Shreve MacKenzie as Quentin Compson's "husband" in *The Sound and the Fury;* and (3) the townspeople's
descriptions of several heterosexual male acquaintances as homosexual in *Light in August,* namely, Joe Brown/Lucas Burch's
relation to Joe Christmas and Gail Hightower's relations both to
his black male cook (whose name and sexual preference go
unmentioned) and to Christmas.

"Divorce in Naples" keeps trying to deny homosexuality in
ways that reassert it. The homosexual-heterosexual binary is too
deeply intertwined with the binaries between masculine and
feminine genders and between sex and gender for Faulkner to
let go of it. Early in the story, five seamen from an American
ship, including the narrator, sit chatting with three Italian
prostitutes, the "women in Italian, the men in English, as if
language might be the sex difference, the functioning of the
vocal cords the inner binding until the dark pairing."[13] This
description assumes that the binary between men and women
is a precondition of sexual attraction, an odd assumption for this

story, where it turns out that two of the seamen are a gay couple (though it remains unclear how far their sexual contact goes) and where the narrator's sexual preference remains curiously ambiguous and unspoken. On the other hand, the odd description fits the story perfectly, because the heterosexual seamen and the narrator feel compelled to attribute feminine gender to Carl, one member of the gay couple. When they joke that Carl is George's "wife" or "girl" (CS 877, 878, 889) but never apply feminine terms to George, they try to describe the homosexual couple as if it were heterosexual.

Their need to feminize Carl draws on the inversion model of homosexual or queer desire, in which gay men are gendered as women and lesbians are gendered as men.[14] But as long as it stays within the assumptions of compulsory heterosexuality, the inversion model has a limited reach. For when heterosexual assumptions steer the inversion model to discover opposite genders in same sex couples, it can only "invert" the gender of one side of a couple. It therefore ends up reasserting the very homosexuality it is called on to resist, because the two people who desire someone of a different gender still desire someone of the same sex, in contrast to the pairing of feminized men and masculinized women like Horace Benbow and Belle Mitchell's sister Joan Heppleton in *Flags in the Dust*. Hence "Divorce in Naples" keeps trying to deny homosexuality in ways that insist on its presence. The tone of teasing jocularity eases the story's emerging recognitions. When the characters chuckle at homosexuality and describe it in heterosexual terms, they both derogate it and help themselves learn to accept it.

The subtlest limit to that acceptance appears in the unspoken position of the narrator, the only one of the five shipmates never to pair up with a man or a woman, implying that the story marks the narrator's wish to cipher out his own sexuality. His ambiguity suggests something like what Eve Kosofsky Sedgwick calls homosexual panic, by which she refers not to homosexuals but rather to heterosexuals' anxiety that they might be homosexual.[15] Thus the urge to attribute feminine gender to one but only one man in the gay couple expresses both disdain and comfort. By making Carl into George's wife and George into Carl's husband it asserts their unfamiliarity and softens it into the familiar. But it also changes the familiar, for even while it others queerness, it queers sameness. Men do not look the same to the narrator of "Divorce in Naples" after he sees George and Carl.

The Sound and the Fury repeats the pattern of "Divorce in Naples" when other Harvard students tease Quentin about his relation to Shreve. "Calling Shreve my husband. Ah let him alone, Shreve said, if he's got better sense than to chase after the little dirty sluts, whose business. In the South you are ashamed of being a virgin. Boys. Men."[16] If the feminizing of Quentin amuses others and so puts him in Carl's position, his self-doubts echo the "Divorce in Naples" narrator's implicit uncertainties. Shreve continues the joke, and spoofs it, by saying that when they part he "will never love another,"[17] but no one questions Shreve's gender. They only question Quentin's just as they only question Carl's, thus at once both undermining the gender binary and reasserting it.

In *Light in August,* a similar pattern assumes a different shape under the additional pressure of hateful race relations. Brown blames his roommate Christmas for murdering the white Joanna Burden. When the sheriff sounds doubtful and Brown realizes that he himself looks suspect, he suddenly blurts out that Christmas is black, as if that were his trump card. Immediately then, on the basis of a shaky attribution from the prime suspect, the investigation completely changes direction to point at Christmas and make him the despised object of a manhunt, while Brown becomes merely a witness. "Like he had knowed," as Byron Bunch tells Hightower, "that if it come to a pinch, this would save him, even if it was almost worse for a white man to admit what he would have to admit than to be accused of the murder itself."[18] As long as Brown and his roommate are white, the town (and by "the town" I refer to that fraction of social structure that Faulkner represents by falsely totalizing phrases like "everybody" [101], as if everyone in town were white, straight, and agreed with everyone else) takes them as curious outsiders but otherwise as ordinary—which to them means heterosexual—scum. But as soon as one of them, despite the most suspiciously self-interested motives, says that the other is black, then the town takes it for granted that their relation is homosexual, because they see homosexual desire as the only thing that could make a white man live with a black man.[19] And to the town, only scum like Brown would admit to being homosexual, since they take homosexuality as worse than murder (or "almost worse," in Byron's feeble disclaimer). Byron cannot even name it: he calls it "what [Brown] would have to admit," trusting Hightower to recognize "the love that dare not speak its name."

In this scene, then, Brown's "admission" leaves him hated, and hated automatically, as if that were predictable for any white who makes such an admission. Yet later, instead of hating Brown, the other characters laugh at him as feminine. "I aint interested," the sheriff says, "in the wives he left in Alabama, or anywere else. What I am interested in is the husband he seems to have had since he come to Jefferson," and in response, "The deputy guffaws" (*LIA* 321–22). For the town, therefore, racial difference can mark a gender difference, since they see one man in the couple as husband and—implicitly—the other as wife, and the gender difference they impose on racial difference so threatens them that it fragments their response, or Faulkner's, leading one time to horror and another time to laughter.

Christmas and Brown are like Hightower and his cook, and like Hightower and Christmas, in that none of them is actually a couple; people only think or pretend to think they are a couple. Apparently a real homosexual, mixed-race couple seems too much or too far afield for Faulkner to take on. He comes close enough in "Divorce in Naples," however, to suggest that the idea attracts him, with the Greek George, whom the narrator introduces as "black," and the blond Scandinavian American

Carl, who dance with George's "black head shoulders above Carl's sleek pale one" (CS 877, 892). In *Light in August*, the town eagerly blames Christmas for murdering Joanna Burden, but they do not blame him—as they blame his supposed "wife" Brown—for betraying his sex and becoming feminine. (A number of critics have seen Christmas as feminine, but not in his relation to Brown.) If the town must see a two-man couple as a masculine male and a feminine male, then when they see a black-white male couple they automatically see the white male as feminine.

The town makes racial difference represent Christmas and Brown as a gay couple, but when Hightower hires his male cook, the town has more than racial difference to provoke its reading, since it already has a history of reading Hightower as sexually different. Because Hightower's wife arrives in town seeming anything but insatiably nymphomaniac and yet turns "bad on him" by slipping "off to Memphis now and then" for "a good time," they assume "he couldn't or wouldn't satisfy her himself" (*LIA* 59). After she dies in Memphis, Hightower

> still kept the cook, a negro woman. . . . [T]he people seemed to realise all at once that the negro was a woman, that he had that negro woman in the house alone with him all day. . . . [T]he whispering began. About how he had made his wife go bad and commit suicide because he was not a natural husband, a natural man, and that the negro woman was the reason. And that's all it took. . . . One day the cook quit. They heard how one night a party of carelessly masked men went to the minister's house and ordered him to fire her. Then they heard how the next day the woman told that she quit herself because her employer asked her to do something which she said was against God and nature. . . . So he did his own cooking for a while, until they heard one day that he had a negro man to cook for him. And that finished him, sure enough. Because that evening some men, not masked either, took the negro man out and whipped him. (*LIA* 71–72)

When Hightower still won't leave town, they tie him to a tree and beat him unconscious.

Byron and Faulkner, at least, have no patience for this brutal nonsense. On the one hand, the idea is that Hightower "couldn't or wouldn't satisfy" his wife because he is not a "natural" man or husband, implying that he is impotent or gay. But then he supposedly goes "against nature" with his female cook, implying that he is neither impotent nor gay and that the alternative "unnaturalness" of mixed-race desire somehow returns him to his "natural" heterosexual potency, or else that he is impotent á la Popeye, and that mixed-race desire works like Popeye's corncob and voyeurism, "unnaturally" releasing a sexuality that he otherwise cannot express. The tone suggests that hardly anyone believes the first cook's coerced accusation. Rather, the most phobic white men make her, like the male cook and then Hightower, their brutalized medium for homophobic and racist hysteria, so that the implicitly unified opinion of "the town" increasingly fragments, which is why it takes hooded violence to prop it up. When the violent men then forgo their masks to beat the male cook, they seem to argue that if the town cannot quite agree on the propriety of beating up black women, it better not even entertain the possibility of not agreeing on the propriety of beating up gay men.

Here we might recall Leslie Fiedler's famous argument that American culture and classic American literature are preoccupied with mixed-race, male homosocial couples—Natty Bumppo and Chingachgook, Ishmael and Queequeg, Huck and Jim, and so on—because the forbidden combinations turn safely permissible when the taboo against same-sex couples and the taboo against mixed-race couples combine, in effect, to cancel each other out. The couple can achieve a comfortably intimate friendship without fearing the homosexual side of their homosocial desire, because people of different races supposedly don't do that, and without fearing the prohibition against mixed-race couples, because people of the same sex supposedly don't do that either.[20] In Hightower's case, however, Fiedler's model turns upside down. Because racial difference provides such a good alibi to make sexual likeness safe, it only looks the more suspect. Anybody with that carefully set up an alibi must be guilty.

In response, Hightower colludes in his own feminization. Jealous of Byron's newfound heterosexual masculinity, Hightower warns him: "[W]hat woman, good or bad, has ever suffered from any brute as men have suffered from good women?" (*LIA* 316). Here he self-servingly denies the actual relations between genders, feminizing himself by inverting which gender most abuses which. To assuage his resentment, Hightower sits down to read. He could read, well, Byron, for example, but instead Faulkner has him read Tennyson and closes the chapter with a loving swipe at Tennyson and Hightower that mixes homosexual panic with acid insight. Reading Tennyson, Faulkner says, "the gutless swooning full of sapless trees and dehydrated lusts . . . is like listening in a cathedral to a eunuch chanting in a language which he does *not* even need to *not* understand" (*LIA* 318, emphasis added). For Faulkner here, an effeminate man is not a woman so much as a castrato whose lack reproduces itself in a cascade of negatives. In one sense this bolsters the distinction between sex and gender, because it sees a feminine man as a man, even if a castrated one, rather than as a woman, but in another sense it more ambiguously reaches for the eunuch, the man who lacks male equipment, to figure the feminine man who has it, turning gender back into anatomy all over again.

Eventually, after delivering Lena's baby, Hightower reasserts his masculinity. "Life comes to the old man yet," he thinks. He decides not to wash the dishes or take a rest, thinking, "That's what a woman would do." "He moves like a man with a purpose now, who for twentyfive years has been doing nothing at all. . . . Neither is the book which he now chooses the Tennyson: this time also he chooses food for a man. It is Henry IV" (*LIA* 404–5). If Hightower resorts to such silly tactics to shore up his masculinity, then his tower is bound to tumble soon. For once he is suspect, every act to confirm his masculinity also unveils his need to have it confirmed.

Finally, he tries to cash in that double bind in a desperate effort to give Christmas an alibi, falsely claiming—again without naming the love that dare not speak its name—that Christmas was with him the night of Joanna Burden's death.[21] Hightower and Joanna are pariahs, unrepresentative of the rest of the town, but Percy Grimm's response to Hightower's lie insists that their difference is so precarious that it can only be sustained by social policing and vigilantism: "Jesus Christ," he yells, reassuring his needy masculinity with the masculine lingo of a curse, yet a curse that invokes the effeminate male icon of a therefore self-deconstructing masculine propriety. "Has every preacher and old maid in Jefferson taken their pants down to the yellowbellied son of a bitch?" (*LIA* 464). Then Grimm fires his phallic gun into Christmas, the modern incarnation of the Jesus Christ he hopelessly appeals to, and then castrates the threateningly masculine Christmas into Grimm's notion of femininity. Thus the feminine men, the supposedly gay men, the men caught up in homosexual panic like Grimm, and the racially ambiguous men, though all border crossers or pariahs, yet lie somehow at the center of the community and its imagination of itself,[22] with gender collapsing into sex, sex collapsing into gender, and both continually rerefracting through varyingly imagined structures of race.[23]

Not all Faulkner's stories worry so tensely over borders. For contrast, let us look at a barely known story, a cartoon Faulkner drew for Meta Carpenter that shows how they pass the day on a California weekend.[24] Here borders, from social borders to the lines that join and separate the rows of cartoon frames, are everywhere broken and everywhere asserted and nowhere worried over. Unlike Faulkner's prose fictions, this story has no forthright conflict. It begins in happy rendezvous and ends in happily relaxed erotic union. It is prolific with differences of gender and sex, behaviorally and corporeally, with the figures readily distinguished as men or women by their bodies, clothing, or coiffures, except perhaps on the beach in panel 7, where the swimsuits look almost the same, as they do again in the last panel where they appear next to more conspicuously gender-specific clothing. In panel 1, you might say that Bill takes the

initiative, casting himself as subject to Meta's object, but the
eagerness of his early start meets its match in the casual eroticism of her pose as she slides on her stockings, as if pleasurably
contemplating her own body or its relation to the eager man
who knocks at her door. The door thus enforces a boundary and
figures its own permeability. Bill too, in drawing this gentle
caricature of his profile, contemplates his own body, studying
his hawklike face as Meta studies her long legs. Each contemplates the other, and each contemplates her or himself, including her or himself contemplating the other. Meta contemplates
her body again in panel 8, inspecting her reflection in a compact
like Temple Drake, but sunnily rather than sullenly; and Bill
contemplates the contemplating Meta, drawing this cartoon so
that she can contemplate Bill contemplating Meta contemplating herself, and so on in a series with no particular endpoint,
but instead with a continuous exchange of object position and
subject position, quite unlike the gendered object and subject
positions in the Hollywood cinema that Bill and Meta help
produce on weekdays.[25]

Meanwhile, Meta exhausts Bill with her superior forehand at
Ping-Pong and then outruns him to the beach. We might read
her athletic superiority and the mock prostration of his defeat in
a variety of ways, as self-effeminizing, as a courtly patronizing
that finds her superiority amusing, or simply as a modest and
accurate portrayal of the day's activities. (Her memoir claims
that she was indeed a better Ping-Pong player.) Not much
hinges on the options, at least for this story. It might matter
whether he is patronizing, effeminate, modest, or accurate if
that had much bearing on the ending, for example, but it
doesn't. The ending is satisfied and comfortable. First Meta and
Bill veer off in pairs of women and men to drink beer with
another couple (Sally Richards and John Crown) at the Hofbrau
(panels 10 and 11), rearranging themselves at the table in boy-
girl, boy-girl sequence, if we count around the circumference,
or in like-gender pairs if we count by who faces whom, thus
offering complementary assertions of gender difference and

likeness. Then in the last panel, they merge symmetry and difference, as two differently sexed bodies deposit their differently gendered clothing—except for those bathing suits—on the symmetrically placed chairs. It is indeed a "good night," a night as undisturbed as the sign requests. Thus the rendezvous of the opening panel begins a path from early morning separation to late evening union.

Or does it? The morning's separation also suggests a transience in the evening's union, for this couple does not ordinarily spend the night together, and this very cartoon seems designed to memorialize the week's exception rather than its rule. This is the day when they eat breakfast together in a restaurant and don't go to work. Bill may jokingly dub them "Mr & Mrs" in panel 2,[26] but she is not Mrs. Faulkner, and someone else is. In the last panel, the "DO NOT DISTURB" sign faces the wrong way, as if their evening bliss is so fragile that they need to tell each other not to disturb it, need to remind each other not to remember how soon it will end.

By contrast, in the powerful but little discussed story "Honor," a character that strays from marriage returns happily and abruptly, but the permutations of gender distribute across a much more polymorphous exchange. As a story of barnstormers and a sexual triangle, "Honor" anticipates *Pylon*, and the novel has perhaps distracted attention from the story.[27] Buck Monaghan signs on as a wing walker for the pilot Howard Rogers who, with his wife Mildred, befriends Monaghan. The friendship grows strangely close; Mildred and Monaghan sleep together; and then she announces her decision to divorce Rogers for Monaghan. As they arrange the divorce, Monaghan focuses more on Rogers than on Mildred. The next day, in narrative charged with suspense and sexual double entendre, Monaghan and Rogers do their act in the air. In an elaborate sexual pantomime that the title tries to contain as merely a duel of honor, Monaghan invites Rogers to tumble him off the wing. After Monaghan slips or is made to slip, Rogers does an out-of-cockpit walk of his own to save Monaghan. In response, Mildred goes back to Rogers.

On the one hand, we can read this as the sort of triangle Sedgwick describes in *Between Men*, where, building on the classic discussions of Claude Lévi-Strauss, Gayle Rubin, and Luce Irigaray, she describes how men negotiate their homosocial relation to each other through the exchange of women, in this case Mildred. On the other hand, the relation between Monaghan and Rogers seems homosexual as well as homosocial.[28] Moreover, with their relation to Mildred as well as to each other, they are bisexual, a structure that Mildred eagerly if unconsciously exploits so that she can have her fling with Monaghan and also set up a fling between Monaghan and Rogers, thus flinging Rogers back to a new appreciation of her and her back to a new appreciation of Rogers. The relation "between men" may surprise some readers, but Mildred herself sets it up. She has Rogers invite Monaghan to dinner and, clad in her apron, apologizes that they can't afford to go out: "I told him you'd just have to take us as we are." Soon, Monaghan says, "she had bought one for me to wear, and the three of us would all go back to the kitchen and cook dinner. . . . 'It's because we are so poor. We're just an aviator.'" She feminizes the men into her aproned domesticity and condenses herself and her husband into one entity, so that for Monaghan to feel drawn to either of them is also to feel drawn to the other, a bisexuality that Monaghan confirms and encourages in his response: "Well," he says, "Howard can fly well enough for two people" (*CS* 554).

The double entendres intensify as Mildred announces her plans for divorce while in Monaghan's mind the referent of the word "her" glides back and forth between Mildred and the airplane: Rogers "was looking at me," recalls Monaghan, "and she running her hands over my face and making a little moaning sound against my neck. . . . I wasn't thinking about her at all. I was thinking that he and I were upstairs and me out on top and I had just found that he had thrown the stick away and was flying her on the rudder alone and that he knew that I knew the stick was gone and so it was all right now." By telling Monaghan about the divorce in front of Rogers, Mildred tries to structure their relation to her through their relation to each other and their relation to each other through their relation to her. But Monaghan plays his part almost too well for her pleasure. He deserts the heterosexual side of his bisexuality, ignoring her to focus on Rogers. "Don't you love me anymore," she asks. "God damn it," he thinks, "if you'll just keep out of this for a little while! We're both trying our best to take care of you" (CS 557–58). Even as he wants her to keep out of it so that he can concentrate on Rogers, he envisions his homosexual relation to Rogers both through the heterosexual language of flying "her" and—in the vision of Rogers throwing the stick away—through the strain of language that structures homosexuality as a castrating gender inversion.[29]

Monaghan figures that Rogers sets up their air show the next day, "laid for me, sucked me in. . . . 'You've got me now, haven't you?' " he asks, more hoping than complaining, because he wants Rogers to have him or suck him in. "Take the stick yourself," Rogers responds. "I'll do your trick. . . . I can, as long as you fly her properly" (CS 559). In the air, the double entendres between pilot and wing walker continue to proliferate, and the specifically heterosexual innuendoes give way to homosexual if still less conscious innuendoes—presumably less conscious for the author as well as for the character-narrator: "I was falling. I made a half somersault . . . when something banged me in the back. . . . I knew that if I tried to sit up against the slip stream, I would go off backward. I could see by the tail and the horizon that we were upside now . . . , and I could see Rogers standing up in his cockpit, unfastening his belt, and I could . . . see that when I went off I would miss the fuselage. . . . After a while I saw his legs slide into the front cockpit and then I felt his hands on me" (CS 561–62). Immediately after that scene, Mildred returns to Rogers, as if his homosexual relation to Monaghan in the air re-establishes the ground for his heterosexual relations.

The agency thus seems widely dispersed. Mildred sets up the triangle and Monaghan willingly joins it, and then Rogers sets up the air show and Monaghan willingly joins that too. Hence Mildred may be an object of exchange between men in the familiar pattern of men's exchange of women, but in this case the woman is at least as much the negotiator and the exchanger of men, until the relation between object and subject status and between the systems of sex and gender, masculine and feminine, and heterosexual and homosexual all spiral round too quickly to settle into any stable binary.

Which can take us to the question of what about any of this is particularly Faulknerian. Part of the answer is: not much. Faulkner was of his times and places. He was not the only one to feel threatened and comforted by the resources of sex and gender, masculinity and femininity. But of course, Faulkner also had his own takes on cultural structure and exchange. Moreover, to an extent, he had to find his own takes, because the changing attitudes that all of us live among, and contribute to, help keep any one position inside or outside the binaries from stabilizing.

Through the run of examples we have looked at, Faulkner sets things up—whether convincingly or not—to make the female characters' uncertainties seem relatively personal: as if Addie just happens to marry a hopeless bore, as if Temple just happens to get stranded among criminals, as if Rosa's adolescent passion and lonely eloquence were sui generis. Eula Varner might make a prominent exception to that pattern, but only so long as Faulkner portrays her, like Lena Grove, as a mythological figure or, at her most human, a freak of nature. As she ages and turns sexually active, he increasingly particularizes her plight. By contrast, Faulkner sets up the male characters' uncertainties not only as personal but also as the anguished consequence of their not knowing how to articulate the personal to some larger group, such as homosexuals, women, or white racists. The point is not that such articulations are any harder for men or easier for women, but rather that Faulkner paints them that way. In a world where women's agency is growing but men still hold hegemony, Faulkner worries much more about masculine weakness than about feminine weakness. That is one reason that feminist critics can find so much emergent agency in Faulkner's women characters, even amidst all his misogyny.[30]

Thus if, as Lind suggests, Faulkner is remarkable for his frank attention to and respect for women's "organs of reproduction," he is much more concerned with men's organs. And almost always when he pays attention to male sexual anatomy, he turns to figures of castration, whether the literal castration of some of his most famous characters, like Benjy Compson and Joe Christmas; or the countless figurative castrations of men who are physically deformed or impotent, psychically weak, self-castratingly suicidal, or effeminized, such as Donald Mahon, Ernest Talliaferro, Horace Benbow, young John and Bayard Sartoris, Quentin, Anse and Darl Bundren, Popeye, Hightower, the reporter in *Pylon*, Charles Bon, Flem Snopes, Labove, Ike McCaslin, and many more, including the many men who shoot guns that won't go off, or who cannot or will not shoot guns that could go off—such as Quentin, Bayard Sartoris in *The Unvanquished*, Mink Snopes, Lucas Beauchamp, Boon Hogganbeck, or Ike McCaslin, or who break or injure their limbs—such as Cash Bundren, Thomas Sutpen, Ab Snopes, Hoake McCarron, and Henry Armstid. Faulkner worries much more about whether males are real men than about whether females are real women. Indeed, female characters whom Faulkner sees as masculine or boyish, like Joan Heppleton, Laverne in *Pylon*, Drusilla Hawk, or Charlotte Rittenmeyer, often seem to excite him. None of this is only Faulknerian. Much of it appears, to take a prominent example, in Hemingway. But if it is not only Faulknerian, it is still obsessively Faulknerian.

Again and again, Faulkner returns to the border regions of gender performance. The fear that gender differs from sex provokes a need to see gender and sex as the same, so that females are real women and—more important to Faulkner—

males are real men. But so confining a regimen provokes a reinvigorated alertness to the differences between sex and gender, differences that attract Faulkner by allowing for many different ways to be feminine or masculine. Those differences threaten the social regimen, which reasserts itself in the need to make sex and gender into one and the same thing all over again. Hence any effort to merge sex and gender can provoke an effort to differentiate them, and any effort to differentiate them can provoke an effort to merge them. For Faulkner, then, gender performance is an ongoing narrative with a narrative structure like his novels. There is always another way to tell the story, always another version, even as the fascination of endless discourse depends on its contrast to the stubborn illusion that under the clothing of all that tale telling lies one true story.

NOTES

1. "The Dissolution of the Oedipus Complex," in *The Standard Edition of the Complete Psychological Works of Sigmund Freud*, ed. and trans. James Strachey, 24 vols. (London: Hogarth Press, 1961), 19:178.

2. Judith Butler, *Gender Trouble: Feminism and the Subversion of Identity* (New York: Routledge, 1990); and *Bodies That Matter: On the Discursive Limits of "Sex"* (New York: Routledge, 1993). My paraphrase oversimplifies the sometimes labored nuances of Butler's arguments. For an astute, well-informed, wide-ranging survey, see Donna J. Haraway, " 'Gender' for a Marxist Dictionary," in her *Simians, Cyborgs, and Women: The Reinvention of Nature* (New York: Routledge, 1991), 127–48. For a history, see Thomas Laqueur, *Making Sex: Body and Gender from the Greeks to Freud* (Berkeley: University of California Press, 1990).

3. Laqueur, chap. 2.

4. Ilse Dusoir Lind, "Faulkner's Women," in *The Maker and the Myth: Faulkner and Yoknapatawpha*, ed. Evans Harrington and Ann J. Abadie (Jackson: University Press of Mississippi, 1978), 92–94.

5. William Faulkner, *As I Lay Dying*, The Corrected Text (New York: Vintage International, 1990 [1930]), 173.

6. Paul R. Lilly, Jr., "Caddy and Addie: Speakers of Faulkner's Impeccable Language," *Journal of Narrative Technique* 3 (1973): 179–80, discusses the blank space as expressive language, an idea repeated with variations by John T. Matthews, *The Play of Faulkner's Language* (Ithaca: Cornell University Press, 1982), 40–42; André Bleikasten, *The Ink of Melancholy: Faulkner's Novels from "The Sound and the Fury" to "Light in August"* (Bloomington: Indiana University Press, 1990), 159; Minrose C. Gwin, *The Feminine and Faulkner: Reading (Beyond) Sexual Difference* (Knoxville: University of Tennessee Press, 1990), 154; and Diane Roberts, *Faulkner and Southern Womanhood* (Athens: University of Georgia Press, 1994), 200. Constance Pierce, "Being, Knowing, and Saying in the 'Addie' Section of Faulkner's *As I Lay Dying*," *Twentieth Century Literature* 26 (1980): 294–305, in an excellent article that has many implications for this

passage, notes how Addie's "incantation" both intensifies and evacuates Anse and "his shape in her vaginal space" (300). On the blank space as a Lacanian absence or lack, see James A. Snead, *Figures of Division: William Faulkner's Major Novels* (New York: Methuen, 1986), 69.

7. In the huge quantity of commentary about Temple, the fullest and most interesting discussion I know of on this moment comes in Homer B. Pettey, "Reading and Raping in *Sanctuary*," *Faulkner Journal* 3:1 (1987): 80. In general, my view of Temple and of rape differs very much from Pettey's, as he does not join the rereading of Temple called for by many critics such as Joseph R. Urgo, "Temple Drake's Truthful Perjury: Rethinking Faulkner's *Sanctuary*," *American Literature* 55 (1983): 435–44; Robert Dale Parker, *Faulkner and the Novelistic Imagination* (Urbana: University of Illinois Press, 1985), 62–65; Elisabeth Muhlenfeld, "Bewildered Witness: Temple Drake in *Sanctuary*," *Faulkner Journal* 1:2 (1986): 43–55; Dianne Luce Cox, "A Measure of Innocence: *Sanctuary*'s Temple Drake," *Mississippi Quarterly* 39 (1986): 301–24; and John N. Duvall, *Faulkner's Marginal Couple: Invisible, Outlaw, and Unspeakable Communities* (Austin: University of Texas Press, 1990), 61, 74–75. These and other recent discussions argue against the tendency of earlier critics to blame the victim.

8. William Faulkner, *Sanctuary*, The Corrected Text (New York: Vintage International, 1993 [1931]), 147. Subsequent references to this edition appear in the text parenthetically, indicated by the abbreviation *S*.

9. Laqueur, 25.

10. William Faulkner, *Absalom, Absalom!*, The Corrected Text (New York: Vintage International, 1990 [1936]), 116. Subsequent references to this edition appear in the text parenthetically, indicated by the abbreviation *AA*.

11. Robert Dale Parker, *"Absalom, Absalom!": The Questioning of Fictions* (Boston: Twayne, 1991), 73–81.

12. The only substantive discussion of "Divorce in Naples" that I have found is the very good article by Edmond L. Volpe, "A Tale of Ambivalences: Faulkner's 'Divorce in Naples,' " *Studies in Short Fiction* 28 (1991): 41–45, which focuses on the heterosexual side of the characters that I describe as bisexual but predominantly homosexual. For examples of other discussions of homosexuality in Faulkner's fiction, see Don Merrick Liles, "William Faulkner's *Absalom, Absalom!*: An Exegesis of the Homoerotic Configurations in the Novel," *Journal of Homosexuality* 8:3/4 (1983): 99–111; and Frann Michel, "William Faulkner as a Lesbian Author," *Faulkner Journal* 4: 1–2 (1988/89): 5–20.

13. *Collected Stories of William Faulkner* (New York: Random House, 1950), 877. Subsequent references to this edition appear in the text parenthetically, indicated by the abbreviation *CS*.

14. See Eve Kosofsky Sedgwick, *Epistemology of the Closet* (Berkeley: University of California Press, 1990), 86–90.

15. Sedgwick, *Epistemology*, 19–21, 182–212; and Sedgwick, *Between Men: English Literature and Male Homosocial Desire* (New York: Columbia University Press, 1985), 83–96.

16. William Faulkner, *The Sound and the Fury*, The Corrected Text (New York: Vintage International, 1990 [1929]), 78, also 171.

17. Faulkner, *The Sound and the Fury*, 106.

18. William Faulkner, *Light in August*, The Corrected Text (New York: Vintage International, 1990 [1929]), 97. Subsequent references to this edition appear in the text parenthetically, indicated by the abbreviation *LIA*.

19. We might note Brown/Burch's curious racial status as a "dark complected" (*LIA* 51, 55) man who is assumed to be white (Snead, *Figures of Division* 92), who chooses the alias Brown, and who calls his coworkers "*slaving* bastards" (emphasis added), until they press him to say "I was just talking to myself," which they then call "God's truth" (*LIA* 45–46). "Like to like" (*LIA* 43), a coworker says to describe Brown's relation to Christmas.

20. Leslie Fiedler, *Love and Death in the American Novel* (New York: Stein and Day, 1960).

21. For excellent discussions of Hightower's lie that he was with Christmas, see Donald M. Kartiganer, *The Fragile Thread: The Meaning of Form in Faulkner's Novels* (Amherst: University of Massachusetts Press, 1979), 53; and Duvall, *Faulkner's Marginal Couple*, 34–35. On that and the larger pattern of male pairings in *Light in August*, see Philip M. Weinstein, *Faulkner's Subject: A Cosmos No One Owns* (Cambridge: Cambridge University Press, 1992), 20. On Christmas as homosexual, see especially Roberts, *Faulkner and Southern Womanhood*, 173–78.

22. On pariahs in *Light in August*, see Cleanth Brooks, *William Faulkner: The Yoknapatawpha Country* (New Haven: Yale University Press, 1963); and Duvall, *Faulkner's Marginal Couple*.

23. Cf. Gail L. Mortimer, *Faulkner's Rhetoric of Loss: A Study in Perception and Meaning* (Austin: University of Texas Press, 1983), 81: "In Faulkner . . . the blurring of any boundary both produces anxiety and is, paradoxically, quite appealing. Consequently, a number of his stories are concerned in very particular ways with such themes as miscegenation, necrophilia, incest, androgyny, cannibalism, and homosexuality."

24. Reprinted from Sally Davis, "The Secret Hollywood Romance of William Faulkner," *Los Angeles Magazine* 21:11 (Nov. 1976): 131–34, 206–7. Meta Carpenter Wilde and Orin Borsten, in *A Loving Gentleman: The Love Story of William Faulkner and Meta Carpenter* (New York: Simon and Schuster, 1976) 64, 68, 78–82, describe the drawings and their context, although not all their details match the actual drawings' rendition.

25. I am thinking especially of the classic study by Laura Mulvey, "Visual Pleasure and Narrative Cinema" (1975), reprinted in her *Visual and Other Pleasures* (Bloomington: Indiana University Press, 1988), 14–26, and the wide array of responses it has provoked.

26. Wilde describes "Mr. & Mrs. Bowen" as Faulkner's running joke, a homespun analogue to John Thomas and Lady Jane in *Lady Chatterley's Lover* and the name that Meta and Bill registered under at the hotel depicted in the cartoon (62–63, 78, 81).

27. The best discussion of "Honor" comes in an excellent article by Vivian Wagner: "Gender, Technology, and Utopia in Faulkner's Airplane Tales," *Arizona Quarterly* 49:4 (Winter 1993): 79–97.

28. Wagner, 96. James Ferguson, *Faulkner's Short Fiction* (Knoxville: University of Tennessee Press, 1991), also notes the homosexual side of "Divorce in Naples" and "Honor," although he makes a point of saying that they are not very good stories and that such ideas, including the triangle in "Honor," are "peculiar" (66, 72–73, 172). By contrast, Sedgwick's *Between Men* shows that something very like that triangle is actually routine.

29. In the discussion following this paper at the conference, Elizabeth Dobbs helpfully noted the title's pun, "on her," and that prompted Jay Watson to remind us of the relevant limerick: "She offered her honor. / He honored her offer. / And all night long / It was honor and offer." I would also like to thank John N. Duvall for his comments on a draft of this paper.

30. Thus to find "strong female characters" is not necessarily or only to find the "respect for women" that so-called images of women criticism often seeks. That approach, though now much maligned, is still much practiced, especially in the classroom. In themselves, images of women are often not reducible to strength or weakness, respect or disrespect. For such images, even as they mediate and change the larger system around them, are also always mediated by it, by a system that sometimes uses such images to bolster misogyny. If a misogynist system—in this case a self-pitying masculinity—can sometimes launder its images of women to convert them into its own capital, then those images and their relation to the larger system need a more patiently nuanced critical scrutiny.

Maternalizing the Epicene: Faulkner's Paradox of Form and Gender

DAVID ROGERS

What is henceforth necessary for any human subject who desires to describe the modern world will be to walk through the mirror, dismantle the frame held together by the Big Dichotomies and operate a transposition of the boundaries and spaces now tangled in a figurative confusion.[1]

ALICE JARDINE

I found out that not only each book had to have a design, but the whole output or sum of an artist's work had to have a design.[2]

WILLIAM FAULKNER

Concepts of the epicene character in Faulkner have always had an air of fancy about them. There may have been relatively widespread agreement that, in the novels at least, epicene in its most literal instances refers clearly to representations· of androgynous women, young women such as Cecily Saunders from *Soldiers' Pay* and Temple Drake from *Sanctuary*, or the parachutist Laverne from *Pylon*, whose somatic ambiguity and dubious moral actions appear to signify, as Michel Gresset suggests, the essence of an equally ambiguous postwar period.[3] But there has been far less consensus about what else or to whom, in a wider and much more general sense, the word might refer. Indeed, if any common ground has emerged with regard to the more suggestive and abstract references of epicene, it has probably come in the recognition that the variety of contexts in which the sign appears is so eccentric and so

97

diverse—the ambiguity of epicene so much an exaggerated example of the consequences of Faulkner's modernist aesthetic—that any attempts to affix to it an ultimate or consistent set of stable references must finally prove impossible. Sergei Chakovsky, in fact, appears to speak to this view when he argues that, in "acquir[ing] [its] broad range of specific and general artistic-philosophical applications," epicene eventually "dissociate[s] itself from its original carriers—the particular kind of woman."[4] As a result, the most appropriate definition of epicene, we might say, could be the one that Margaret Powers—herself described in *Soldiers' Pay* as a Beardsleyan figure and hence somatically epicene—gives to Joe Gilligan and Januarius J. Jones in Faulkner's first published novel: "Epicene," she says, "is something that you want and can't get, Joe."[5]

It is easy to appreciate why such perceptions of epicene as perpetually elusive persist: to accept the arbitrariness of signs in general is one thing; to have to encounter an example is another. Yet clearly a different approach to the problem is necessary if the fate of epicene is not to continue to act as something of a drag on our understanding of the sign's significance and the possible inference from Chakovsky's comment—that a word must remain denotative if it is to maintain its associations and hence to signify meaningfully—continue to stand. If, however, we change interpretative tact and, in effect, accept rather than resist the actions of the sign; if we take its shifts, not as moves that distort or mystify its meaning, but as that which represents what, finally, *epicene* may actually signify, then not only does the confusion over its signification almost immediately recede, but the larger ramifications of the function of the sign also become apparent—both for the individual novels themselves and for the entire range of Faulkner's corpus, the "sum" of Faulkner's text. Read for what it is, in other words, a sign continually in a state of creative and increasingly immaterial becoming, *epicene,* we begin to realize, does not so much sever its association with particular "carriers" as compound it—move it, extend it, and accumulate it; spread it out, so to speak, in a way that seems reminiscent of the movement implicit in the pragmatist William James's famous image of the grease spot: "Novelty soaks in," writes James, "it stains the ancient mass; but it is also tinged by what absorbs it."[6]

Considered in this fashion, epicene becomes, then, something of a comprehensively compositional and textualizing figure, an emerging "vector" for what amounts to a wholesale undoing of Western images and tropes throughout the novels.[7] As much that which is signified as that which does the signifying, it starts to suggest a space somewhere between, but not precisely in the middle of, the two concepts. Neither one nor the other, but both simultaneously, it connotes a sexual uncertainty that "engenders" and "surrounds" (as Faulkner writes to describe Lena Grove and the narrative that contains her in *Light in August*) the larger cultural uncertainty that is contingent in Faulkner with late capitalism and the still more comprehensive and paradoxical material uncertainty which distinguishes Faulkner's apocalyptic world. This latter world is, on the one hand, beyond meaningful articulation, as André Bleikasten has argued,[8] and, on the other, meaningfully articulate, "shot through with relations," as Katherine Wheeler writes in describing the material reality of James.[9]

In keeping with the pervasively paradoxical quality of Faulkner's novels in general, the development of the compositional nature of epicene involves something of a paradox itself—at least in the light of so much contemporary literary theory and gender studies. In both areas, the formal and figural dimensions of literary texts—what Henry Louis Gates, Jr., in his theory for the tradition of "signifyin(g)" in African American writing calls a novel's "literariness"—have been practically allegorized, and for many sound reasons, as patriarchal, repressive, and, with regard to modernism specifically, reactionary and defensive.[10] As a consequence, considerations of such literary qualities as historically specific conventions in their own right, potentially variable in their implications and appropriateness, and capable of providing some of the most intriguing and radical qualities of period texts, have been largely overshadowed by political concerns drawn from what amounts to a construction of formal aesthetics that risks becoming itself ahistorical and problematically universalized. As Gates has shown, however, to politicize such literariness too dogmatically or dismissively is not only possibly to distort the understanding of a particular historical period but also to overlook a key textual dynamic. For when understood intertextually and within its historical context, the "literary" may—as it does with Faulkner and the African American texts Gates examines—manifest a decidedly deconstructive potential all its own.

It is partly because the Faulknerian epicene amounts essentially to a formal figure, its quality implicit in (rather than obscured by) a range of disparate and at first glance seemingly unlikely carriers who are distinguished by specific figural details and particular formal acts, that such a reformist potential emerges across the novels. The example of one of the least considered (and most fully dissociated) carriers of epicenity in Faulkner—the mosquitoes of the novel that bears their name—illustrates the point. Somatically epicene, the mosquito appears to duplicate the activity of the sign for which it proves both metonym and synecdoche. As Cleanth Brooks first noted, neither the signifier *mosquito* nor its plural appears anywhere in the novel, save as its title.[11] The reader knows of these "little darts of fire," as Faulkner calls them occasionally, not by their visible presence, but by the signs of their absence: a spot of blood on the skin, the sound of a slap on the wrist or the leg, the changed directions of their victims. Like the more comprehensive epicene, these apparently immaterial carriers seem to mock "without relevance inherent themselves . . . the significance they [ought to] affirm," to paraphrase from Quentin Compson in *The Sound and the Fury*.[12]

Quentin makes his remark in reference to the "shadowy" and "paradoxical" "visible forms" that "all stable things" seem to take in the "gray half-light." In calling such forms "antic and perverse," he not only exposes the concept that for Gresset

defines what is "evil" in Faulkner, but he also calls attention to
the specific term that seems to explain more accurately than any
other the deconstructive activity that Faulkner (and Gates's
African American narratives) display.[13] For as Jonathan Dollimore observes when writing about sexual dissidence, the perverse represents the "most extreme threat" in Western culture.
It does so not because it jeopardizes the so-called true form of
something through the shape of its "absolute opposite or its
direct negation," but, by contrast, because its form is "inextricably rooted in the true and authentic" itself. This paradox—the
perverse as alien yet not other—generates what Dollimore
calls the "perverse dynamic," that movement which—like that
conditioned by the sign *epicene*—directs the potential of the
paradox to destabilize, to undo. Characterized by the paradoxical and initiated by its accompanying dynamic, the perverse is,
according to Dollimore, therefore "doubly insurgent." Its threat
coming "from outside in, and from inside out," it exposes, as
Dollimore argues, "the potential inherent in all social orders as a
consequence of their own structure and developmental logic."[14]

For Faulkner and the South, the most compelling figure of
such potential insurgence is arguably the mulatto, that alien
figure grounded in the supposedly authentic form of whiteness.
A figure neither white nor black but somewhere indefinably and
unlocatably between the two, the mulatto appeared to threaten
the social system of the South by breaking down the strictly
dichotomous distinction of color upon which slavery and its
continuation were based. In attempting to ward off the threat of
the mulatto and prevent the emergence of what Stanley Elkins
refers to as a "free mulatto class," the slaveholding South shifted
the determinate for the identity of the slave child from father to
mother.[15] As it did, however, the white South succeeded only
in creating a new and an even more subversive figure in the
shape of the unwed mother. The accompanying elevation in the
legal status of this figure not only ironically implied the breakdown of the hegemony of patriarchal law, but, given the symbolic value of woman in Western tradition, it also ironically

connoted the wholesale emasculation of patriarchal authority in
general while denying any ideal of rational law or an absolute,
patriarch God.

As a consequence, the South's unwed mother of the slave
comes to occupy a place amidst such nineteenth-century literary
figures as Hawthorne's Hester Prynne, Gaskell's Ruth, and
Hardy's "spouseless mother" Tess. Like these unmarried figures, she posits a world that is Darwinian in its "brimfulness,"
to quote Hardy, and its indeterminacy, a world wherein all
children, in a sense, may be said to be mulattoes, no longer
seen to be made in the exact image of their f/Father; a perverse,
naturalistic world where, as James observed in 1906, "She" [by
which James means nature] it is who dominates, who "stands
firm," the increase in the size of the material universe and
the diminution of "man's importance" brought about by the
"discoveries of science" having left "Man . . . no longer the
lawgiver to nature," the one who must now "accommodate
himself."[16]

Not surprisingly then, the perversity of this ironic twist
emerges in Faulkner with an otherwise unlikely epicene figure:
the mule, one of Faulkner's favorite creatures and connected
etymologically to the figure of the mulatto. "Ugly, untiring and
perverse," as Faulkner writes in the infamously purple passage
in *Flags in the Dust,* because "he can be moved neither by
reason, flattery, nor promise of reward," the mule, an "object
of general execrations; unwept, unhonored, and unsung," is
something of a Derridean undecideable, a figure known more
by what it is not than by what it is.[17]

For all the mule's attraction for Faulkner, however, it is the
mosquito that most crucially enacts the significance of the
epicene. Physically embodying the perverse as "turned the
wrong way around," as the OED defines the term, the "demon,"
as Faulkner once wrote, "whispering" to him at night equates
perversity with the natural world. Moreover, "armed and potent" and representative of "even more than a mere natural
principle: a divine one," as Gavin Stevens says in *The Town*

about the malaria bearing female that is "turned upside down
and backward," the mosquito helps to distinguish those characters whose formal actions make them configurations of the
epicene and participants in the paradoxical dynamic of the
sign.[18]

The earliest indication of the infectiously perverse effect of
mosquitoes comes in Faulkner's second novel when the insects
divert Patricia Robyn and David West—actually turn them the
wrong way around—once the would-be lovers have left the
yacht *Nausikaa* and attempt to make their way to Mandeville,
site of the type of formal marriages that traditionally connote
the "sane and sound polarity between the sexes" that Gresset
considers the "guarantee of an ethical order in Faulkner's
work."[19] As Dollimore reminds us, to pervert means to deviate
or cause a deviation from the "straight and narrow," this last
phrase being one of the "trite commonplaces" of Western
thought and language that exposes its ideal of stasis and such
accompanying concepts as law, order, and coherence in general
and therefore bears "the trace of Western metaphysics."[20] Yet
Robyn and West, the latter's surname casting him as a representative Western man, are forced from such a linear path. They
become not only victims of the "divine principle" of the perverse, but, in becoming "wanderers" or "wayward" travelers
once they have been driven from the road to Mandeville,
marked out by the "patriarchal pines" that line it, they also
acquire the mantle of perversity themselves.

Pat Robyn's change from a merely somatic epicene to one
figuratively indicative of a wider material perversity further
illustrates the transformation of epicene from denotative sign to
connotative activity, from a sign seemingly linked "naturally" to
its carrier to one holding together both sign and signified. The
im/materiality of the world conveyed by the composite sign of
epicene and, in this instance, Robyn typifies the world inferra-
ble from Faulkner's texts. (Old Ben and the rattlesnake embody
the same im/materiality in the collection of short stories/novel
Go Down, Moses, where the similarly depicted appearance and

disappearance of these figures, apparently as antithetical for Faulkner as the mule and the mosquito, imply that they both physically manifest the same spiritual element of the woods— the same divine principle. Indeed, they suggest that the two, the material and the divine, should not be taken to distinguish different things.) Within this context, the waywardness enacted by Robyn and West connotes the deviance they themselves personify once they have been victimized by the mosquitoes. They become characters who now reveal, through their wandering, their own wayward, inverted actions, the sign of their own perversity; they emerge as newly formulated epicene figures.

As a result of this shift, the young couple exposes an initial, broad category of figural "carriers" of epicenity. Epicene, it now becomes apparent, refers to all those in Faulkner who wander, who are wanderers; all those characters who either by choice or fate seem to be travelling without a precise idea of their destination or whose route to that destination is circuitous or haphazard or constantly altered. Gendered as male, such epicenity often manifests itself as a condition of rootlessness or orphanage. Gendered as female, however, it appears generally in the shape of a greater threat: the figure of the wayward or "loose" woman, for lack of a better term, the supposedly questionable morals of whom associate her simultaneously with the original, somatically ambiguous epicenes and those nineteenth-century figures like the unwed slave mothers of the Old South.

The effect is again twofold and seemingly paradoxical. First of all, Faulkner's rendering of these newly realized epicene women, as if in concert with the accumulative quality of the sign *epicene*, seems to trope the period's androgyne figures. At the same time, however, it represents an almost logical extension of the implications of their compositional quality. Though first acted out with Patricia Robyn, the accumulation begins earlier with Margaret Powers. Like Robyn, Powers is, physically, one of the original epicene carriers. Nevertheless, from the opening of the novel she is unmistakably epicene with a difference. Married and widowed, she is never, as is Robyn or

Cecily Saunders, aligned remotely with the virginal. What they can still lose, she has already lost. Moreover, with her second marriage to Donald Mahon, his surname pronounced as if it were spelled M.A.N., she becomes "Mrs. Mahon," as Faulkner repeatedly refers to her, and the nominal sign for a figure who, in progressively acquiring the "powers" of "man" (Margaret Powers Mahon), consequently aligns Faulknerian perversity, as does the mosquito, with the inverted, naturalistic world of James.

With her change, however, Margaret Mahon also emerges as the first of the newly composite figures of Faulknerian epicenes we might call *maternalized* epicenes.[21] As such, as Mrs. Mahon, she initiates the convergence of the original figure with a set of Faulknerian figures of women who might appear as much its opposite as the men with whom the somatic epicene is implicitly joined. I am referring here to the supposed earth mother types in the novels, those "young, married or marriageable women," as Karl Zink once wrote, who are "usually already pregnant, wed or unwed" and who are, "despite their individuating features," virtually the "same woman" since "they share so many generalized traits." For Zink, this repeated figure of woman depicts the "channels" for what he calls "the more obvious natural processes."[22] Yet in the guise of the maternalized epicene, this generalized figure, like its counterparts, the unwed mothers of the nineteenth century, only casts such processes as both "obvious" and "natural," if we consider *natural* and *perverse*, not as antonyms in the novels, but synonyms. (To speak of the material world of the novels is, as with the figures that represent it—Old Ben, the rattlesnake, the maternalized epicenes—to speak of the naturally perverse or perversely natural, the two words existing, not in irresolvable tension, but in amoral oscillation).

To consider the two in this fashion is to exchange for good the notion that Faulkner's "habit of mind" was oxymoronic for one of its being epicenic. Although evidence for this switch is pervasive, nowhere is it more telling, especially as it affects our thinking about Faulkner and gender and our understanding of

Faulkner's personal accommodation of the perverse and all it implies, than in the rhetoric of color that distinguishes the novels. As Gresset, for one, has remarked, an understanding of that rhetoric provides a crucial perspective on Faulkner's fiction; and, as suited to the dynamic implicit in the actions of the epicene, Faulkner's rhetoric gradually and progressively shifts the color associated with the maternalized epicene from black—the absolute opposite of white, the color conventionally assigned to the so-called pure or true form of woman—to faded blue.

The appropriateness of the change lies in the uncertainty, the indefinable nature, of the latter color. As denim wearers appreciate, faded blue is a color constantly in a state of change. Like epicene, it exists in an unspecific space from which it is impossible to construct an unending series of syntheses and antitheses; somewhere between blue and gray, those two colors in Faulkner's rhetoric which typically connote, on the one hand, idealism, as we can see in the phrases "constant blue" or "ultimate blue" or "horizon blue" at various times associated with Faulknerian idealists, and, on the other, death, as with the doctor in *The Wild Palms* and the cloth cap and trousers Flem wears throughout the Snopes trilogy (not to mention the opposing sides in the Civil War). Faded blue is a color that defies definition and defers location on any color band.

The further importance of this exchange, however, comes with the quality of its development. Part of what the movement of epicene makes apparent is how an understanding of any figure or formal act in Faulkner depends upon an inter/intratextual relationship with figures or acts of a similar kind in other novels, and the first instance of black's connection with epicene occurs with Margaret Powers. There it is largely a manner of speaking and almost wholly metonymic: described as "dark" and "black-headed" and "black-eyed," Powers is, though "white," nevertheless for Cecily Saunders "that black ugly woman."[23] As black shifts to Dilsey, the spouseless mother in *The Sound and the Fury*, it appears to duplicate the action of the Jamesian inkspot, spreading out and absorbing Dilsey as it becomes more comprehensively physical and synecdochic. Dilsey, in other words, is, as an African American, a more completely black figure of woman. Yet at the opening of the fourth section of *The Sound and the Fury* when she appears for the second time in the doorway of her cabin, a similarly metonymic detail appears with her as well. Having first been dressed flamboyantly, "a black straw hat perched upon her turban" and a "mangy and anonymous fur" bordering the "maroon velvet cape" she wears over "a dress of purple silk," Dilsey, who is almost always read as if she were simply a nurturing figure of the earth mother in the guise of what is also usually considered to be the unproblematic figure of the South's black mammy, stands clothed in an outfit— "a man's felt hat and an army overcoat"—that casts her paradoxically as somatically epicene (and hence "epicenizes" the maternal). Only now, just visible "beneath the frayed skirts" of that coat, hang the "uneven balloonings" of a "blue gingham dress."[24]

With this glimpse of gingham, Dilsey stands as a second transitional figure. She not only marks and undoes the traditional dichotomy of color central to Western thought and to the South, but, at the same time, she articulates the progression of maternalized epicenes with a third—and at first equally suspect—figure of natural perversity, Lena Grove of *Light in August*. Almost routinely read as bucolic and benignly passive, Grove is generally distinguished as the one positive exception among Faulkner's disturbing figures of female fecundity; but, as Faulkner describes her at the beginning of that novel, she not only appears from the start as problematically perverse, but, perhaps the paradigm of Faulknerian wanderers, she represents the first comprehensive figure of the maternalized epicene as a figure of faded blue:

> From beneath a sunbonnet of faded blue, weathered now by other than formal soap and water, [Lena, sitting in Armstid's wagon as she moves haphazardly—*wanders*—toward Jefferson] looks up . . . quietly and pleasantly. . . . Beneath the faded garment of that same weathered blue her body is *shapeless* and immobile. The fan and the bundle lie on her lap. . . . In the halted wagon Armstid sits,

humped, bleacheyed. He sees that the rim of the fan is bound
neatly in the same faded blue as the sunbonnet and the dress
(my emphasis). [25]

As suggestive as this gradual shift in the color of the epicene
may be figuratively, its articulation transforming the shapless-
ness of the androgyne into that of the pregnant Grove, its full
impact only emerges when we read the figural along formal
lines. In novel after novel—for most of which readers have
argued for a basic bipolar structure "beneath" the opacity of
Faulkner's individual formal experiments—versions of the
newly maternalized epicene appear to stand problematically
opposite another set of typical Faulknerian figures: those figures, usually, but not always, of men, who either reject or
disavow both the natural perversity of the world and of themselves. Like Quentin Compson, these figures are, in general,
Faulknerian idealists. As often as not they are depicted as fliers
and tainted by unadulterated colors of blue, and they eventually
refuse to adjust to the diminution or effacement which they
typically connote through a physical injury, either through a
scar, say, like Donald Mahon does, or a head injury, as does
Bayard Sartoris. In the end, they succumb to a vainglorious
pursuit, as so many critics have observed, and perish, following
the imperative of their idealism to an inevitable loss of consciousness after they realize they cannot transcend their condition or find a satisfactory escape.

Just as inevitably, however, after the death or symbolic loss
of consciousness of these figures, an epicene-like transference
occurs: the formal places and roles of the idealists within the
novels pass to members of a second group of men. These second
figures, who seem initially tangential to the original figures of
antithesis in the novel and whom we might therefore consider
"marginal," are always cast, as the nameless lance corporal is
literally, as anonymous and diminished in the Jamesian sense.
Usually they bear an explicit sign of their own epicenity, as we
see in Cash Bundren and later in the parachutist Jack Holmes
in *Pylon*, in the form of an actual or metaphorical lameness that

Dollimore again reminds us is generally yet another Western sign of perversity. (The "acting" corporal represents the epitome of such perversity in a novel where his apparent resurrection from the dead is just one detail in what amounts to Faulkner's deconstruction of the central narrative of New Testament Christianity.)[26]

As it does for the idealists from whom they take over, the maternalized epicene initially appears to represent, in Faulkner's idiom, the "outrage" of the world for these figures. They therefore seem to perpetuate the bipolar quality of their novels. Yet these figuratively small and anonymous men, unlike the figures whom they replace, eventually expose the illusion of this bipolarity by accepting a new relationship with the maternalized epicene. Faulkner encodes this acceptance implicitly with at least three specific and interrelated formal acts. In each, these men formally converge with their respective figures of the maternalized epicene, both in the individual novels and, as it were, collectively. As the individual figures appear to pass the figural baton among themselves inter/intratextually, their successive acts of convergence serve to suspend the closure of each separate novel and effectively convert the novels into something like chapters within a larger, more comprehensive—and singly designed—text. Their collective articulation of a single convergence across the entire range of Faulkner's corpus, especially, creates, as we will see, a still more inclusively compositional epicene that appears both to anticipate Jardine's gambit and provide a new way of understanding the quote of Faulkner's with which I started.

The first of these formal acts I call the act of "companionate marriage." The term comes from a Judge Lindsay of Denver who spoke in the twenties of premarital cohabitation as a "trial" or "companionate" marriage.[27] Margaret Mahon suggests its appropriateness for Faulkner when she counters Gilligan's offer of marriage with the proposal that the two of them live together outside of marital convention; that they should cohabitate, as "fellows." Gilligan refuses. He chooses instead to return to the humanist refuge of his adopted father, Reverend Mahon. He later rejects a second chance to enter the space of the naturally perverse by turning his back on the "winding road" at the end of the novel on which the two men have just passed the tellingly "pregnant" orchard and heard the "crooning *submerged* passion" (my italics) of black female voices that represent simultaneously, as we can see now that epicene eventually does, "everything" and "nothing," as Faulkner writes.[28]

Here again, a single act in the novels typifies the deconstruction involved in the initial shift in the reference of epicene and the dynamic it signifies for the novels. For both figures of marriage—the one Gilligan proposes and the one Margaret counters with—seem to convey the necessary formal condition for a compositional epicenity. Both imply a convergence of sorts. Yet like the union of two genders into a simply somatic androgyne, the formal act of conventional marriage only amounts to an illusory union. With traditional figure and formal act alike, the mastery of the male remains: in the former by way of the deference to the physical shape of the man, and in the latter by virtue of the retention of the masculine hegemony sanctioned by the church and state. By contrast, Faulkner's companionate marriage breaks the phallocentric bond between the gendered antithesis and, in first drawing attention to the traditional symbol and then undermining it, tropes it and the epicene from problematic to solution. Margaret Mahon expresses the sense of newfound freedom concomitant with this switch as she waits for Gilligan to buy her ticket for the train to New York. "Freedom," thinks Mahon to herself,

> comes with the decision: it does not wait for the act. . . . It is best just to be free, not to let it into the conscious mind. To be consciously anything argues a comparison, a bond with antithesis. Live your dream, do not attain it—else comes satiety. Or sorrow.[29]

The second formal act of convergence, which I have referred to elsewhere as the act of "getting on the wagon," complements and extends the act of companionate marriage by providing a recurring dramatic situation in which the subsequent marginal men indicate the progressively greater degree to which they are prepared to accept implicit offers to live as "fellows" and, by resisting the desire to think themselves consciously free, forfeit the attainment of their idealistic dreams. Epicene, since its connotation relies upon its signifying on two figural dimensions at the same time, this act has its association with the perverse dynamic of the novels exposed explicitly with the almost constant identification of Lena Grove with the wagon as a means of transportation. Almost paradoxically, then, given the reference to the self-enforced sobriety connoted by the slang phrase its physical site conjures up, it casts the perverse condition of indefinite wandering and precarious identity as a state of virtual drunkenness. Those on the wagon seem generally to feel, as Joe Christmas does after he hitches the ride that he assumes will take him to Jefferson but which, instead, carries him to his death in Mottstown, as if they were "somewhere between and among them, suspended . . . without thought, without feeling," having "lost account of time and distance."[30]

Getting on the wagon, however, not only defines Christmas's problem, but it also signals his adaptation to the indeterminacy he himself represents as a mulatto. Yet its connotation of the appropriately "sober" attitude for coming to terms with such a perversely epicene state of suspension does not refer to the kind of self-enforced abstinence suggested by the idiomatic phrase for which the physical detail is a sign. Instead, the attitude of acquiescent accommodation occasioned by the second act of convergence comes to represent, as if to avoid the bond Mrs. Mahon's imperative warns against, the sense of immeasurable moderation which that most integral of Faulknerian figures, the hunter, gains by drinking just the right, but unquantifiable, amount of whiskey. Neither strictly sober nor drunk, the experienced hunter may then manifest the correct blend of courage and humility when he comes face to face with the embodiments of the divine principle of the woods.

Part, then, of a series of related scenes of more literal drink-

ing, the formal act serves, as a result, to restate the expression of
Margaret Mahon's wisdom. The terms of this figural translation
emerge first in *Flags in the Dust*. Bayard Sartoris, his ribs
broken after the first of his two automobile accidents, finds
himself in the back of a mule-drawn wagon driven by a black
man and his son. He discovers there that he must, if he is to
ease the pain in his side, "remember to breathe shallowly."[31]
Bayard does not heed his own advice for long. But the expression of moderate aspiration implicit in the pun that informs his
dictum comes to signify that peculiarly Faulknerian attitude of
sobriety acquired by those subsequent figures of marginal men
who converge with their respective figures of the naturally
perverse, either by assuming their place aboard a wagon or
some variation of it or by taking the conscious decision to join
them there.

The third formal act of convergence I will call the act of
narcissus/a or narcissa/us (the slash and reversals are meant to
imply the amoral oscillation I referred to earlier). Especially as
it is enacted by the idealists in the novels, Faulkner's frequent
use of the conventional myth has been well attended by critics.
Of all of them, John Irwin comes closest to exposing the
connotations of the epicene that Faulkner exploits with his
observation that Faulknerian figures of narcissus, like all narcissi
in general, look into a "medium whose very constitution, in
relation to the ego, seems, paradoxically, to be dissolution."[32]

Again, however, as with the sign *epicene* in general, such
formal acts of looking in Faulkner signify more figuratively than
even Irwin suggests. In addition to the more immediately
apparent surfaces represented by images of water and mirrors,
the surfaces that provide the opportunity for the individual to
examine an image of the self in Faulkner include the still more
figural ones implicated within the mythic narrative because they
"frame" the individual as if she or he were looking in a mirror.
The most frequent of these figural images of reflection involves
an individual who looks through a window or an open door.
There the "surface" s/he faces is illusory rather than material;
the image s/he sees is not that of the self but the form of

an Other, a narcissa/us figure in the shapeless shape of the maternalized epicene—a perverse figure, if for no other reason than the strikingly simple fact that all reflections are inversions, an image of the self turned, like the female mosquito, around and backwards. (I earlier referred to the epicene as a composite figure, and Faulkner uses the word "composite" for such a figural image in *As I Lay Dying* when Cash Bundren sees his mother Addie through the window of their house while he saws the boards for her coffin. Perhaps one of the most revealing examples, however, occurs when Ike McCaslin in *Go Down, Moses* views the unwed mulatto mother of Roth Edmonds's child through the flap door of his tent; dressed "in a man's hat and a man's slicker," she, like Old Ben and the rattlesnake, appears and disappears as if of some divine principle.)[33]

Nowhere is this figural dimension more evident, however, than in the opening of the fourth section of *The Sound and the Fury* I have already alluded to. There Dilsey first steps into the frame of her cabin to face the "bleak and chill" dawn. Arguably a figure of the sort Zink has in mind when he speaks of the "channels" of "obvious natural processes," Dilsey nevertheless appears during the course of this short scene to embody the formal and figural signs of all three categories of characters I have mentioned. Initially, she seems formally and figurally to take over a position within the progression of those beleaguered narcissists from the first three sections of the novel: Benjy, Quentin, and Jason Compson. Described now as no longer nearly the size she once was and wearing an "anonymous" fur coat, however, Dilsey seems less like an idealist and more like his replacement figure, a variation on the marginal man. Accordingly, the weather she faces—her "outrage"—is epicene and perverse: it combines motion with stasis and the mechanical with the organic, its "minute and venomous particles" even mimicking the actions of the mosquito, "needling laterally" as they do into Dilsey's flesh. Framed by the open door, however, Dilsey is herself perverse. She reflects the dissolving atmosphere outside. With her "dropsical" skin and "collapsing" face

she is not only a figure of the body; the apparent inversion of
skin and bones that leaves her looking as if her bones were on
the outside of her body also transforms her from a figure of the
body into a figure of the naturally perverse, this final accumulative gesture providing the most comprehensive category of
epicene yet: everybody, it seems, is always already epicene.[34]

As if to continue the formal continuity with the novel's
idealists, however, Dilsey first retreats into her cabin as though
emulating their desire for a traditional sanctuary. Yet she soon
reemerges from the inside and again stands framed within her
doorway. Only now, having exchanged her original costume for
the dress of the somatic epicene, Dilsey is further transformed,
this time into a second sort of composite figure, in whom all
previous figures of men and women have converged and the
process of maternalization has been apparently completed in
reverse. The figure of the maternal now acquires the trappings
of the figure of the somatically uncertain, as if Dilsey were
meant to dramatize the continual oscillation of the epicene.

Unlike Joe Gilligan and Bayard Sartoris, however, Dilsey
chooses to engage the threatening perversity that she, as a
corporeal figure, embodies and symbolizes. She steps out of her
cabin, crosses the yard, and enters the door of the Compsons'
kitchen, where she prepares to face another day. By figuratively
"walk[ing] through the mirror," as Jardine writes in the first of
the two quotes with which I started, Dilsey serves to illustrate
the figural and formal action that the marginal men of Faulkner
must enact if they too are to "dismantle the frame held together
by the Big Dichotomies"; if they are to accommodate themselves
to the natural perversity of the material world (which, as they
come to recognize, they themselves embody) and climb on the
wagon; if they are to accept, as each more and more self-
consciously does in novel after novel, the limits of their aspira-
tions and "submit," as James writes, to "a materialistic universe,
in which only the tough-minded find themselves cogenially
at home."[35]

Although Dilsey undoubtedly fits James's description, the

radically pragmatic role its sentiment cuts for Faulkner's epicenes remains reserved for the last figure in the progression of
marginal men, the later—and even more paradoxical composite—figure of V. K. Ratliff. The claim for Ratliff's marginality is
hardly in question. The figure into whose "active hand" Gavin
Stevens "pass[es] the torch" in the fight against Snopesism,
Faulkner's figure for the perversity of late capitalism, Ratliff
himself admits to being, as he says at various times, indistin-
guished: an "anonymous underhanded son-of-a-gun," an "anonymous meddler," a "low-minded anonymous scoundrel." The
reasons for his epicenity, however, are equally as clear. Panthea
Reid Broughton, for one, even specifically refers to Ratliff as
"epicene." For Broughton, however, the reference is not positive. "[N]either effeminate nor homosexual [but] . . . simply
sexless," Ratliff, she argues, is therefore "irrevocably cut . . .
off" from any "passion and profoundly emotional human
involvement."[36]

Such passivity is not only immediately reminiscent of maternalized epicenes like Lena Grove, who helps Byron Bunch to
join her formally on a figural wagon when she lifts him through
the back door of the truck the furniture dealer drives, but also
Eula Varner, whose sharing of the wagon with Flem Snopes
seems figuratively to spread the signification of epicene indeterminacy to the economic system that Snopesism represents. It
is, therefore, in one sense as negative as Broughton assumes it
must be. Yet Ratliff, as closely identified as any figure in
Faulkner with being on a wagon, though the wagon he drives
on his sales route in *The Hamlet* soon gets transformed—
modernized—into the figure of the pickup truck he has made
from a plain Model T Ford, also tropes the problematic into an
attitude of sober accommodation. He is as much at ease as Lena
Grove with the suspensive, wayward, and drunken motion the
formal figure of the wagon connotes. Just as much the contented
traveller, he is, moreover, ambiguously gendered, equally as
comfortable with the ladies over tea as he is with the men on
Varner's porch, as good a listener as he is a talker. More

crucially, Ratliff is—given the workshirts he makes, washes, mends, and always wears—as complete a figure of faded blue as we get.[37]

Ratliff is, in other words, epicene, but not as Broughton defines it; not because he is emotionally distant, but because his formal and figural role within the Snopes trilogy makes him inter/intratextually so. And in relation to previous figures, Ratliff, as bachelor, functions paradoxically as the figure who, more than any other single figure, formally "weds" the previous converging figures into one configuration as "fellows." In this sense, he crucially degenders the figure of the maternalized epicene, not only positing the final convergence of the progression of maternalized epicenes with that of the marginal men, but joining the waywardness of the likes of the orphan Joe Christmas, whose institution clothes its inhabitants in standard faded blue uniforms, to its female version. Not surprisingly then, Ratliff also shows himself able to appreciate the need to enact the doubly insurgent nature of Dollimore's perverse that he himself represents. Having been tricked by Flem and taught the figural equivalent of breathing shallowly as a consequence of the "gall" bladder problem that leaves him "luxuriating in that supremely gutful lassitude of convalescence" in which he finds "time, hurry, doing, did not exist," and "the accumulating seconds and minutes and hours to which in its well state the body is slave both waking and sleeping now *reversed*" (my emphasis), Ratliff takes to heart the wisdom passed onto him by Mrs. Wallstreet Snopes, wife of Ratliff's business partner.[38] He accepts the fact that the only way to "beat Snopesism" as an outsider is to counter it "from the inside."[39]

The perverse wandering of epicene's own dynamic does not cease with Ratliff and the Snopes trilogy, however. Although Faulkner's "unheroic hero" seems to signal the figural end of the formal convergence that characterizes that dynamic, the final maternalized epicene turns out to be a figure—a pervert—of a somewhat different and less predictable sort.[40] For with the simple two words "Grandfather said" with which Faulkner's last novel, *The Reivers,* opens, the creator of Yoknapatawpha County establishes conditions for his own perverse indeterminacy. The reader may presume to know the identity and the gender of the speaker of these first two words; s/he may take it for granted that they are spoken by the grandson of Lucius Priest. But all s/he knows for sure is that the narrator is a grand*child* of Lucius. Nothing more. The formal space allotted to that child who mimics the story of its grandfather remains forever anonymous and epicene. In this way, the novel's narrative voice manifests "the splendor" of that voice which the French critic Deleuze associates with the anonymous pronoun "One." It represents that "neuter singularity" of modernity that is, for Deleuze, "best apprehended through the philosophy of paradox."[41]

With the deceptively simple creation of such an ungendered and unidentifiable voice, Faulkner, or perhaps I should say, following André Bleikasten's lead, "Faulkner," succeeds in formally dissolving the conventional distinctions between author and text. "He" dismantles the final dichotomy of agency implicit in the paradox of form and gender the novels articulate. As a consequence, the opening of *The Reivers* not only mocks that which it ought to affirm, but, by dissociating the last means by which we might link author and meaning, it serves theoretically to diminish the status of the writer as well—to make "him" anonymous. Dead, but by "his" own hand, the author who once said that it was his "ambition to be as private individual abolished from history, leaving it markless, no refuge save the printed books," appears to have anticipated and outwitted the poststructuralists, achieving, at the same time, a "transposition" of his own amidst the "figurative confusion" Jardine identifies. Formally and figurally erasing the signature from "his" books, "Faulkner," like epicene, moves into a space of "pure becoming," a space "beyond the fixed sexual identities of intersubjectivity."[42]

NOTES

1. Alice Jardine, *Gynesis: Configurations of Women and Modernity* (Ithaca: Cornell University Press, 1985), 88.

2. Quoted in Joseph Blotner, *Faulkner: A Biography* (New York: Random House, 1974), 637.

3. Michel Gresset, *Fascination: Faulkner's Fiction, 1919–1936*, adapted from the French by Thomas West (Durham: Duke University Press, 1989), 82–83.

4. Sergei Chakovsky, "Women in Faulkner's Novels," in *Faulkner and Women*, ed. Doreen Fowler and Ann J. Abadie (Jackson: University Press of Mississippi, 1986), 58–80.

5. William Faulkner, *Soldiers' Pay* (London: Chatto & Windus, 1974), 290.

6. William James, *Pragmatism and Four Essays from "The Meaning of Truth"* (New York: New American Library, 1907), 10.

7. I am grateful to Judson D. Watson III for his recognition of the appropriateness of the term "vector" to the motion of epicene.

8. André Bleikasten, *The Ink of Melancholy: Faulkner's Novels from "The Sound and the Fury" to "Light in August"* (Bloomington: Indiana University Press, 1991), 352–59.

9. Katherine Wheeler, *Romanticism, Pragmatism, and Deconstruction* (Oxford: Blackwell, 1993), 90.

10. Henry Louis Gates, Jr., *Figures in Black: Words, Signs, and the "Racial" Self* (New York: Oxford University Press, 1987), 49.

11. Cleanth Brooks, "Faulkner's *Mosquitoes*," *Georgia Review* 31 (Spring, 1977): 213–34.

12. William Faulkner, *The Sound and the Fury*, ed. David Minter (New York: W.W. Norton & Co., 1987), 103.

13. Gresset, 102: "Evil, for Faulkner," writes Gresset, "first of all signals a *perverted* relation between two beings (or, worse, between an individual and his own consciousness)." My debt to Gresset and my differences concerning both perversion and epicenity in Faulkner will be apparent to anyone who has read his excellent book.

14. Jonathan Dollimore, *Sexual Dissidence: Augustine to Wilde, Freud to Foucault* (Oxford: Clarendon Press, 1991), 125, 121.

15. Stanley Elkins, *Slavery: A Problem in American Institutional and Intellectual Life*, 2nd ed. (Chicago: The University of Chicago Press, 1968), 55. For a more extensive analysis of this point see my essay "The Irony of Idealism: The South's Construction of the Mulatto," in *Discourses of Slavery: Aphra Behn to Toni Morrison*, ed. Carl Plasa and Betty J. Ring (London: Routledge, 1994), 166–90. In many ways, that essay represents an initial consideration of some of the dynamics of epicene and the formal and figural qualities of the novel in which those dynamics manifest themselves.

16. William James, 24.

17. William Faulkner, *Flags in the Dust* (New York: Random House, 1973), 268.

18. William Faulkner, *The Town* (London: Chatto & Windus, 1938), 121.

19. Gresset, 82.

20. Dollimore, 116.

21. Rogers, 172.

22. Karl E. Zink, "Faulkner's Garden: Woman and the Immemorial Earth," *Modern Fiction Studies* 2 (Autumn 1956): 143.

23. William Faulkner, *Soldiers' Pay*, 139.

24. William Faulkner, *The Sound and the Fury*, 158–59.

25. William Faulkner, *Light in August* (New York: Harrison, Smith & Robert Hass, Inc., 1934), 9.

26. Dollimore, 121.

27. Frederick Lewis Allen, *Only Yesterday: An Informal History of the Nineteen-Twenties* (New York: Harper and Brothers, 1931), 118.

28. Faulkner, *Soldiers' Pay*, 319.

29. Ibid, 301.

30. Faulkner, *Light in August*, 321.

31. Faulkner, *Flags in the Dust*, 203.

32. John T. Irwin, *Doubling and Incest/Repetition and Revenge A Speculative Reading of Faulkner* (Baltimore: Johns Hopkins University Press, 1975), 33.

33. William Faulkner, *Go Down, Moses and Other Stories* (New York: Random House, 1942), 252–53.

34. Faulkner, *The Sound and the Fury*, 158.

35. James, 24.

36. Panthea Reid Broughton, "Masculinity and Menfolk," *Mississippi Quarterly* 22 (Spring 1969): 181–89.

37. For a more complete anthology of Ratliff's epicene traits and a more comprehensive treatment of the three formal acts that encode epicenity in Faulkner and comprise the novels' "skeletal structure," see David Rogers, "Articulating the Flesh: The Paradox of Form and Gender in the Novels of William Faulkner," Diss., Rutgers, The State University of New Jersey, 1991.

38. William Faulkner, *The Hamlet* (London: Chatto & Windus, 1965), 68.

39. Faulkner, *The Town*, 132.

40. I want to thank Minrose Gwin for reminding me of Faulkner's association of the artist and perversion in *Mosquitoes*. For further explanation, see her essay in this collection. The phrase "unheroic hero" that I use for Ratliff I borrow from Gresset.

41. Gilles Deleuze, *Logique du sens* (Paris: Editions de Minuit, 1969), 67. Quoted in Alice Jardine, *Gynesis: Configurations of Women and Modernity*, 113.

42. Ibid.

Did Ernest Like Gordon?:
Faulkner's *Mosquitoes* and the Bite of
"Gender Trouble"

MINROSE C. GWIN

In her 1929 feminist manifesto *A Room of One's Own*, Virginia
Woolf tells of finding an imaginary book called *Life's Adventure*
by an imaginary author named Mary Carmichael. Woolf writes
that, as she began to scan the book, it soon became obvious that
something was amiss: "Something tore, something scratched; a
single word here and there flashed its torch in my eyes."
Suddenly, she says, the three words "Chloe liked Olivia" leapt
up off the page. "Do not start. Do not blush," Woolf cautions
her listeners/readers. "Let us admit in the privacy of our own
society that these things sometimes happen. Sometimes women
do like women." "Mary," as Woolf calls her imaginary author,
not only "broke the sentence; now she has broken the sequence."[1] And although Woolf goes on, in a joking way, to
elaborate that Chloe and Olivia were friends and shared a
laboratory, the sentence "Chloe liked Olivia"—with its obvious
homoerotic valence—slashes, within the textual space of a simple sentence, the binarism of heterosexuality. In doing so, it
opens the door to a different story.[2]

I begin with "Chloe liked Olivia" because it is a succinct and
memorable example of "gender trouble," a term recently coined
by contemporary feminist philosopher Judith Butler to discuss
the performative aspects of gender and the imitative structure
of gender identity. In her 1990 book *Gender Trouble*, Butler
argues that gender identity is culturally constructed by "the

regulatory fiction of heterosexuality," and that "gender trouble" may occur when the performative nature of gender is revealed, sometimes through parody, as in the case of drag and cross-dressing, or through any act that disrupts "the regulatory fiction" (as in my example, the simple sentence "Chloe liked Olivia").[3] In her more recent work, Butler goes on to argue that even the materiality of the body is subject to the cultural enforcement of heterosexuality. This cultural production of acceptable genders and bodies requires "the simultaneous production of a domain of abject beings" who represent "uninhabitable" zones of social life—the queer outside that makes the inside normative. In literary texts those socially unsanctioned spaces of abjection and their revealing performances of "queerness" may have disruptive effects that the author may or may not intend.[4]

With Butler's observations in mind, I want to venture into certain spaces in Faulkner's second novel, *Mosquitoes*, that I believe contain disruptive performances of the "queer" abject and thereby reveal the constructedness of both gender and sexuality. Eve Sedgwick has pointed out that the word "queer" has its origin in the Indo-European term that means *across*.[5] In the spirit of this derivation and of the recent body of critical inquiry known as "queer theory," I would like to approach several textual spaces in *Mosquitoes* which I see as crossings; that is, spaces in which the dynamics of gender production are revealed through the display, and perhaps parody, of culturally constructed genders and bodies. In one of the fullest early discussions of the novel, Michael Millgate rightly points out that, in structuring the novel around a group of New Orleans writers, artists, hangers-on, talkers, and young people going on a yachting expedition on Lake Pontchartrain, Faulkner found a "means of exploring a wide variety of sexual relationships, bringing into constantly shifting juxtaposition his group of men and women of different ages and from widely divergent backgrounds." Thus, Millgate illustrates, "We see Jenny and Pete together, Jenny and the young nephew, Jenny and Mr. Tallia-

ferro, Pete and Miss Jameson, Miss Jameson and Mark Frost,
Miss Jameson and Gordon, Gordon and Patricia, Patricia and
David, and so on."[6] I am interested in the "and so on"—not just
in the "and so on" of "queer" people or "queer" stories, but
also in what I see as "queer" spaces that sometimes open up
unexpectedly and create a sense of disruption or uneasiness,
which itself unseats the notion of heterosexuality as natural.[7]
These are spaces in which the performativity of "gender" and
"body" are revealed, and "gender trouble," which is about as
plentiful as talk and insects in *Mosquitoes*, is set to brewing. At
the same time, however, I want to think about the results of
gender trouble: how the denaturalization of sexuality creates
severe anxiety in this text, especially around the ambiguous
presence of male homoeroticism.

Finally, I want to consider how this second novel, one which
is generally considered a somewhat misshapen stepping stone
to Faulkner's "real" oeuvre and one he himself later disavowed,[8]
may reflect, both in its treatment of male homoeroticism and
lesbianism and in its textual history, the enforcement of what
Adrienne Rich has called "compulsory heterosexuality"—that
is, the rigid identification of species survival with emotional/
erotic relationships and the construction of heterosexuality as "a
man-made institution" rather than a natural preference.[9] My
feeling is that *Mosquitoes* was an apprenticeship novel for
Faulkner in more ways than one: in the process of writing and
publishing the book, he very likely discovered not only what he
might be capable of writing but also what he would not be able
to write about openly. Obviously, throughout his career his
works evince an interest in sex and sexuality, gender and
gendered behavior. I believe, though, that, in all probability,
he learned from his experience with *Mosquitoes* that, to be
published in a mass market, he would need, at least in part, to
muffle and veil explicit same-sex eroticism, i.e., "gender trouble" in the flesh.[10]

I need to pause here to differentiate "gender trouble" from
other terms (such as gender disruption or confusion) that have

been used to describe the gender and sexual dynamics of the novel and its publication history.[11] Recent and very provocative commentaries on the novel have variously suggested that the novel is the site of "gender confusion with a vengeance," in which male and female roles become "confused and conflated" (Karen Johnson);[12] Faulkner's preoccupation with male feminization and his positioning of himself as a "lesbian author" by writing as a woman a text coded as feminine (Frann Michel),[13] or his "attraction to and anxiety about the concept of a double-sexed imagination" (Lisa Rado);[14] an exploration of perversion and the theorizing of art as epicenian (Michel Gresset).[15] In what is for me a compelling argument, Judith Bryant Wittenberg shows how *Mosquitoes* " 'plays' with and problematizes the very notion of difference, oscillating between codified 'norms' and radical alternatives in a genderized dialectic." Thus, Wittenberg believes that "the hegemonic codification of sexual difference is itself interrogated" in the novel and "the psychosocial binary structure 'masculine/feminine' " is called into question.[16] "Gender confusion," as Johnson would call it, then ensues. My contribution to this conversation is to suggest that "gender trouble" and the "queer" spaces I want to describe in *Mosquitoes* are disruptive in another way: they call into question not just the binary structure of sexual difference, but also, as I have said, they challenge and subvert the "regulatory fiction" of heterosexuality, which shores up, both Butler and Rich believe, the institution of patriarchal dominance. I want to contemplate what this text and its "queer" spaces—those there and not there, published and expunged—disclose not only about their creator but about the relations of his writing, and narrative in general, to the dynamic and incessant cultural production of sexuality.

It is no surprise, perhaps, that *Mosquitoes* is sexually charged, containing both heterosexual and homosexual material. The novel was written in 1925–26, first in a shortened attempt entitled "Mosquito," then completed in typescript by September of 1926, and published by Boni & Liveright in April 1927.

Virtually the entire year of 1925 Faulkner spent either in New
Orleans—certainly an important American site of flamboyant
sexual masquerade and activity of all sorts—or in Europe,
mainly in Paris. Living and traveling with his homosexual friend
Bill Spratling off and on for two years during this period,
Faulkner mixed with male homosexuals and lesbians at various
bars and houses in the Vieux Carré in New Orleans.[17] Other
homosexual friends included Ben Wasson and Stark Young. In
Paris he found a city of expatriate writers, Natalie Barney,
Gertrude Stein, Renée Vivien, and other homosexual artists,
writers, and patrons of the arts. Since the early part of the
twentieth century, the city also had been the site of cross-
gendered performance and parody, despite middle-class moral
outrage. The "mannish lesbian" was in vogue, and male homosexuality was, as Shari Benstock puts it, "overt, even flamboyant, and was grounded in the aesthetic of the dandy that
dominated the literary and artistic culture of the period."[18]
During his time in Paris, Faulkner stayed at a small hotel only
a short walk across the Luxembourg Gardens, where he strolled
daily, from the well appointed quarters of Stein and her companion Alice Toklas. In the opposite direction, he was only a block
or so from Rue de l'Odéon, site of the National Theatre and the
French and English bookshops of Adrienne Monnier and Sylvia
Beach, publisher of *Ulysses*. In a letter postmarked September
22, 1925, he wrote his mother that he had visited the tomb of
Oscar Wilde and had gone to the Moulin Rouge, where he saw
a naked ballet dancer "with not a rag on except a coat of gold
paint . . . a man stained brown like a faun and a lady who had
on at least 20 beads."[19] Although Faulkner stayed to himself,
working on "Mosquito" and his unfinished manuscript "Elmer"
(which contains, to a lesser degree, some homoerotic material)
and watching children play in the Gardens, he was also surely
aware of the presence of the energetic group of artists, writers,
and patrons, which included Stein and Barney, as well as Joyce,
Picasso, and Hemingway. Moreover, Sherwood Anderson, who
had visited Stein in Paris, seems to have discussed her prose

writing with Faulkner before the younger writer's European trip.[20]

Certainly *Mosquitoes*, especially in its uncut version, exhibits, as David Minter puts it, "a considerable variety of sexual inclination and activity, masturbatory, incestuous, heterosexual, and lesbian."[21] I want to linger over the fact that Minter omits male homoeroticism from this list, as do other critics of the novel who cite the men's homosocial activity but find no evidence of male homoeroticism.[22] (It's often noted, for example, that the men of the novel delight in going below deck to drink, causing their overbearing hostess, Mrs. Maurier, great distress by resisting her pleading that they eat grapefruit at each meal, play bridge, and dance with the women.) Frann Michel believes, in fact, that the lesbian erotic scenes between Pat Robyn, the androgynous niece of the officious Mrs. Maurier, and Jenny Steinbauer, a provocative shopgirl, and those between Jenny and Eva Eiseman, a lesbian and a poet (as well as Faulkner's alignment with Eva Wiseman as an artist), can be read as part of Faulkner's unwillingness to contemplate male homoeroticism.[23] Instead, I find "gender trouble" at work in a variety of "queer" spaces in *Mosquitoes*, including the space of male homoeroticism, which, as I hope to show, is carefully encoded through character, imagery, and dialogue,[24] as well as in the action and conversation related to lesbianism and "perversion," much of which seems to have been deleted in production of the book, with the knowledge of its publisher Horace Liveright, and to Faulkner's initial consternation.

To begin at the beginning, I open *Mosquitoes* to the first page in which the widower Ernest Talliaferro, who we later learn is a commercial buyer of women's dresses and who wears a red bathing suit with a matching red bathing cap on board the *Nausikaa*, is visiting his acquaintance Mr. Gordon the sculptor, a manly man of few words, called only "Gordon" by other characters. The first words of the prologue to the novel are Ernest's to Gordon: " 'The sex instinct' " he says, " 'is quite strong in me. Frankness, without which there can be no friend-

ship, without which two people cannot really ever "get" each
other, as you artists say; frankness, as I was saying, I
believe—' "[25] Obviously Ernest Talliaferro is standing very close
to Gordon while he is saying all this because at this point
Gordon, who is chiseling away, interrupts to ask him gruffly to
move over. Ernest does so, "examining with concern a faint
even powdering of dust upon his neat small patent leather
shoes" (9). At various points during their ensuing conversation,
in which Ernest is trying unsuccessfully to persuade Gordon to
come along on Mrs. Maurier's yachting expedition, Ernest
observes Gordon's body in action: "the rhythmic power of the
other's back and arm," his "muscularity in an undershirt," which
Ernest compares to "his own symmetrical sleeve." After his
unobliging host thrusts "a hard hip into him" again to get him
out of his way, Ernest sits on a block, "watching the other's hard
body in stained trousers and undershirt, watching the curling
vigor of his hair" (9–10). When Gordon finishes his labor he
straightens up, "flexing his arm and shoulder muscles." At that
moment, the light in the studio fades "quietly and abruptly,"
and the room becomes "like a bathtub after the drain has been
opened" (12).

Ernest, who will spend the rest of the novel attempting to
seduce the nubile Jenny Steinbauer and wondering about his
abysmal lack of success with women, seems to have mixed
feelings about Gordon's muscular body. He watches the other's
upper arm muscles bulge the thin cloth of his shirt "with
envious distaste," but when he insists on taking Gordon's empty
unwashed milk bottle to the grocery for milk, he first "watch[es]
the other's shape" receding before beginning his errand. As he
leaves Gordon's flat, he passes "two people indistinguishably
kissing" before hastening out the street door (12–13). And as he
walks down the street, we are told that he thrusts the bottle
beneath his coat, and "[i]t bulged distressingly under his exploring hand." He first wants to "wrap the thing," then throw it
away and "pleasure[d] in its anticipated crash." He feels "like a
criminal" (14–15).

Clearly Gordon doesn't like Ernest. But . . . does Ernest like Gordon? Interestingly, the question hasn't seemed to come up. In her 1979 treatment of Faulkner's life and work, Wittenberg comments, rightly, that the descriptions of Gordon are "sexual and striking" and that the scene with the phallic milk bottle "betrays Talliaferro's distaste for the earthier aspects of that sexuality which he verbally professes to desire."[26] (Ernest talks constantly about seducing women, but seems completely incapable of doing so.) In a convincing argument that *Mosquitoes* carries strong echoes of *Ulysses*, Michael Zeitlin observes that Talliaferro handles the bottle "perhaps more than is strictly necessary" but connects this narrative emphasis to Leopold Bloom's propensity for pocketing items like pork kidneys and lemon soap. Zeitlin regards Ernest's attachment to and revulsion against the bottle as "a kind of 'oral regression' " tied to a fear of castration.[27] Gary Harrington, in a similar vein, believes that Talliaferro's "stilted attempts at communication and . . . inept striving for sexual fulfillment" may be "last-ditch efforts to establish contact with a world of experience denied to him through accidents of temperament, environment and, indeed, physical appearance."[28] In a recent article on the female and textual politics of *Mosquitoes* which I quoted earlier, Wittenberg finds that the novel is replete with "suggestive interrogatory moments [which] are followed by strong reassertions of 'civilized strictures.' "[29] She aligns these oscillations with a dialectic between the opening and resolidification of gender boundaries and, not incidentally for the latter, the repression of female subjectivity. I find this same kind of oscillation occurring in the realm of sexuality and this opening encounter between Ernest and Gordon a "queer" textual space in which gender trouble delivers its first bite.

As Ernest Talliaferro moves through the novel, he carries gender trouble with him, becoming the "queer abject" who hovers between gendered identities and spaces, illuminating their synthetic nature. Now thirty-eight and a widower for eight years after the death of his invalid wife, he had been forced as a child "to do all the things to which his natural impulses objected, and to forgo all the things he could possibly have had any fun doing" (32). "His marriage had driven him into work as drouth drives the fish down stream into the larger waters," and he rose "with comfortable ease" to the position of wholesale buyer of women's clothes through which he attained expert knowledge of "the frail intimate things [women] preferred" (32–33). Though we are told that celibacy, after eight years of widowhood, had begun to oppress him and that he liked to examine women's bodies on the street, he spends "his dinners alone or in company with an available literary friend" (most likely male) and "t[akes] pleasure in his snug bachelor quarters in the proper neighborhood" (33). On board the yacht, he spends much of his time in liminal gender spaces, either with the women and engaged in their activities or running back and forth between the men who are drinking below and Mrs. Maurier's female domain on the upper deck. As fellow voyager and writer Dawson Fairchild says to Eva Wiseman's brother Julius, " 'Mr. Talliaferro,' " as he is called, is more comfortable with women than with men, perhaps because " 'the world does seem a kind of crude place to a man that spends eight hours a day surrounded by lace trimmed crepe de chine' " (71). David Minter has observed that Talliaferro talks constantly of sex (heterosexual sex, that is), but does nothing about it. Besides talking, "he spends much of his time watching, yearning, hoping."[30] Often, Talliaferro's exploits with the opposite sex, such as his comic pursuits of the alluring Jenny on board and off, are exaggerated and laughable.

Butler has pointed out that to lose "social recognition as an effective heterosexual is to lose one possible social identity and perhaps to gain one that is radically less sanctioned"—to inhabit "unthinkable" terrain fully excluded from dominant culture.[31] This terrain seems to be what Talliaferro is most afraid of occupying. At the end of the book we find him walking the streets of New Orleans, with all of its opportunities for sexual expression, "looking forward to marriage with a thin but definite relief as a solution to his problem." He wants to be married (though it appears he may end up with the unappealing Mrs. Maurier) because he knows that "*chastity is expected of married men. Or, at least they don't lose caste by it. . . .*" (ellipsis Faulkner's) (346). A rather odd reason for marriage, one might say. What Talliaferro seems to be thinking is that, in a world of compulsory heterosexuality, marriage will get him off the hook. All he wants is to be like other men; he finds it "unbearable to believe that he had never had the power to stir women, that he had been always a firearm unloaded and unaware of it" (346).

As Butler stresses, the denaturalization and mobilization of gender categories within sexual cultures (both gay and straight) may be enacted by the repetition of heterosexual constructs, especially through parody. This is not, Butler cautions, a parody of an original but a parody of "the very notion of an original." In place of heterosexual coherence, sex and gender are denaturalized through a performance (for example, drag) which dramatizes their separateness and constructedness.[32] Throughout the novel, but particularly at the end, "Mr. Talliaferro" both performs and becomes a parody of gender relations based upon the traditional heterosexual romance motif with its dynamics of the desiring male subject in pursuit of the desirable female object. He is determined to fit himself, though he obviously does not fit, into that heterosexual paradigm. As he soaks his feet in the warm water, he decides to be a "real man" and use force on women, thinking: "*[t]he trick, the only trick, is to bully them, to dominate them from the start—never employ wiles. . . . The oldest technique in the world: a club. By God, that's it*" (348). The parodic effect of such a statement is obvious. It is made by a small middle-aged man with thinning hair (not exactly the he-man type) who, in the opening pages of the book, was admiring a man's body with very keen interest and who is presently sucking a flavored digestive lozenge as he soaks his feet in a basin of warm water. Having arrived at this revelation, the first thing he wants to do (we might have guessed) is to call another man, this time Fairchild, to share his newly discovered caveman approach to heterosexual relations. And, if we have not gotten

the parodic impact fully enough, the female telephone opera-
tor's sarcastic remark—the final words of the book—drives it
home: " 'You tell 'em, big boy; treat 'em rough' " (349).[33]

Faulkner thus begins the novel with a scene drenched in
male homoerotic suggestiveness featuring Ernest Talliaferro
and then ends with a parodic scene featuring, again, Ernest
Talliaferro, who has decided to be " 'cruel and hard, brutal, if
necessary, until she begs for my love' " (349). The result is a
subtle but highly parodic display of the vicissitudes of compulsory heterosexuality. The performance of male homoeroticism,
upon which the display is contingent, is more subtle than the
frequently noticed explicit lesbian material of the novel, perhaps
because of Faulkner's comparative uneasiness at embarking on
any expeditions into the terrain of the male "queer abject" and
its trail leading to the devalued feminine.[34] However, as Butler
observes, the effects of such performatives "cannot be controlled
by the one who utters or writes" and may indeed "continue to
signify in spite of their authors', and sometimes against their
authors' most precious intentions."[35]

This observation leads me to the second part of this essay:
those instances of gender trouble *not* in *Mosquitoes:* the four
deletions which by all accounts seem to have been excised
during the publishing process and are available now only in the
typescript preserved at the University of Virginia Alderman
Library and published in facsimile in the Garland Faulkner
manuscript series. Although this typescript almost certainly
precedes the typescript sent to the printer—a fact which could
problematize the issue of who deleted the material—all available
evidence indicates that four major chunks were cut by Boni &
Liveright in the editorial process, and not by Faulkner himself.
Each of these four deletions contains the presence or suggestion
of some form of same sex erotics. These are the absent spaces,
the zones of gender trouble which were successfully deactivated
before publication, the performatives which *were* controlled,
though most likely not by their author. (Had Faulkner himself
chosen to delete the passages, it could also be argued, I think,

that compulsory heterosexuality was at work in that decision, though it is not my purpose here to argue that point since the preponderance of evidence points to an editorial decision to cut the passages that was made without prior consultation with the author.)

The textual history of *Mosquitoes* is, at least in part, familiar ground for Faulkner scholars.[36] After spending 1925 in New Orleans and Europe, Faulkner settled in with friends in Pascagoula, Mississippi, during the summer of 1926 to finish the book and transcribe it, chapter by chapter, into typescript. He edited the typescript thoroughly, making deletions and additions. Back in Oxford in September, he gave the typed and edited manuscript to Phil Stone and Sallie Simpson for what Joseph Blotner calls "typing assistance."[37] Lillian Hellman, then a young reader for Boni & Liveright, which had published Faulkner's first novel, *Soldiers' Pay*, recommended publication and the publishing firm accepted the book and sent an advance.[38] Apparently, when Faulkner received galley proofs sometimes between mid-January and mid-February of 1927, he found that four substantial passages had been cut.[39] Whether the deletions were initially Horace Liveright's idea is uncertain, perhaps even doubtful, but certainly he agreed to certain excisions from the manuscript and explained the rationale for them in a letter to Faulkner. This is interesting in itself. Liveright had a reputation for liking books that made a splash. With a trade list including Pound, O'Neill, Eliot, Freud, Hemingway, and Dreiser,[40] Boni & Liveright could hardly be said to be a conservative publisher. Faulkner was clearly distressed that material had been deleted from his book. Although we do not have what was apparently his first letter to Liveright on the subject, one which followed, dated February 18, includes an apology concerning the earlier letter: "I'm sorry my letter about 'Mosquitoes' sounded querulous: I was not trying to complain at all. I understood why the deletions were made, and I was merely pointing out one result of it that, after all, is not very important." After a discussion of punctuation problems, which he attributes to a faulty typewriter, Faulkner adds, "Thank you for the enclosed memoranda showing why, etc."[41] (I want to return to the implications of Faulkner's letter.) In short, certain deletions—presumably the four major ones—do not seem to have been Faulkner's idea; he protested but then acquiesced in the matter when faced with the reality of his situation as a fledgling author. When the book was published in April 1927, it was without the offending material.

The available typescript, which seems to be the one Faulkner completed in Pascagoula, was published in 1987 by Garland as part of its Faulkner manuscript series.[42] Though they have been partly quoted and summarized by Blotner, Millgate, and Edwin T. Arnold, and discussed briefly and sometimes inaccurately by others, the four sizable deletions remain buried in a 464-page typescript, which gets progressively more and more difficult to decipher as Faulkner's typing ribbon gets worse and worse. Interesting, also, is the fact that in the Garland facsimile of the typescript, a page containing part of the final deletion is missing—apparently an editorial mistake; thus we have an inadvertent omission within a deliberately censored passage, an absent space within a textual space that is already absent from the published book—a double remove.[43]

I rehearse the textual history of *Mosquitoes* in such detail because I think the nature of the deletions, the reasons they may have been removed, and Faulkner's response to their removal need to be more closely examined. It has been noted that the expurgations contain sexual material which was likely to be shocking, passages dealing with sex or the idea of art as "perversion."[44] I want to argue that all four of the excised passages contain either overtones or depictions of homoeroticism, some of it male homoeroticism. These absent spaces, then, may be seen as sites of bodies and bodily activities whose display must be, and was, limited and regulated. And not only are these "queer" bodies and activities present in some way in the deleted material but, more importantly, in certain passages they are brought into contact with heterosexual bodies and practices. In short, these "queer" spaces, had they not been deleted, would have been on the move within the published text, jostling the "normativity" of heterosexuality and further denaturalizing heterosexual practice. The thematic and structural linkages between the published and unpublished material reveal how the homoerotic content of the novel would have been advanced, overtly and covertly, by the inclusion of the unpublished material.

The first deletion is a section set at a corner of Bourbon Street before the ill-fated outing begins. It is positioned in the prologue to the book following a conversation involving Talliaferro and the writer Dawson Fairchild at a restaurant in which Talliaferro has discovered Fairchild dining with the brother of lesbian poet Eva Wiseman (Julius, called "the Semitic man") and several other men, including the poet Mark Frost (called "the blond young man"). After dining with them, Talliaferro asks that Fairchild spend some time with him that evening to advise him, perhaps on his never ceasing efforts to find a woman, though he does not say so. Fairchild refuses, saying that he and Julius Wiseman "are spending the evening together" (44). The expurgated section begins with Fairchild's standing on the corner of Bourbon Street with Julius Wiseman and laughing at Talliaferro and "the blond young man" as they retreat toward Royal Street, "Mr. Talliaferro pacing sedately yet intently beside the other's tall ghostly figure" (ts 47). As they pass from view, Fairchild "chuckle[s] heavily" and Julius swats a mosquito on the back of his neck. Fairchild begins the conversation with Julius by saying, " 'the race . . . is playing out' " (ts 47). What follows is a conversation about American politics, the unnaturalness of art, and art as perversion. Julius says, " 'Art is against nature. Those who choose it are perverts' " (ts 48).

The least sexually explicit of the four deletions, this passage nonetheless seems rife with homoerotic questions: Does Ernest like Dawson? Does Dawson like Julius? Why is Dawson laughing at Ernest and "the blond young man" as they walk down the street together? The passage, which also seems to link writing

with these hints of male homoeroticism, coded as "perversion,"
takes on added resonance when considered alongside the rather
obvious similarities of Dawson Fairchild to Sherwood Anderson,
whose friendship and mentorship Faulkner was in the process
of distancing himself from before and during the writing of
Mosquitoes.[45] In his characterization of Fairchild, Faulkner
seems to be observing and laughing at Anderson in a vein not
unlike Fairchild's humor at the expense of Talliaferro.

The second deletion, and the one most frequently discussed,[46]
extends a lesbian erotic scene in the book which occurs at 11
p.m. on the second day of the excursion. In the published
version, the two young women on board, Pat and Jenny, have
taken their clothes off and are lying naked in their shared bunk.
Pat strokes Jenny, asks her if she's a virgin, and tells her
she's got " 'a right sweet little shape' " (150). Interestingly, the
deleted passage directly follows another scene set an hour later
in which Eva Wiseman helps a tired and upset Mrs. Maurier
(who realizes she has failed in her resolve to have "a very nice
party" [155]) to her room. As she closes Mrs. Maurier's door,
Eva Wiseman thinks, "I wonder what happened to her?" (156).
What "happened to her," as we learn in the epilogue, is that
Mrs. Maurier at a young age was forced to marry "old Maurier,"
a plantation overseer turned owner who was "a cold, violent
man" (322–26). It's at this point that the deleted passage picks
up. It returns us to the two young women, Jenny and Pat, in
their shared bunk, and commences to describe explicitly and in
highly erotic language their sexual contact:

> . . . [Pat] put her hand upon Jenny's body, stroking it lightly and
> slowly along her side and her swelling hip falling away again. Jenny
> sighed her soft ineffable sigh and she turned also, breathing against
> the other's face. She made a soft wet sound with her mouth and put
> her arm across the niece's body. The niece raised herself slightly on
> her elbow, stroking her hand along Jenny's side. As the niece raised
> herself Jenny's arm slid further down her body, then it tightened,
> and Jenny spoke an indistinguishable word that wasn't Pete. The
> niece bent over Jenny in the dark. Her moving hand ceased in the
> valley beneath the swell of Jenny's thigh and she was quite motion-

less a moment. Then she laid her sober broad mouth against Jenny's cheek.

Jenny made again her drowsy moaning sound, and without seeming to move at all she came to the other with a boneless enveloping movement, turning her head until their mouths touched. Immediately Jenny went lax, yet she still seemed to envelope [sic] the other, holding the bodies together with her mouth . . . (ellipsis Faulkner's) (ts 204–5).

At this point Pat jerks away and accuses the working-class Jenny of kissing in a common way. Pat says that she will teach her how to kiss properly. As she proceeds with this undertaking, Eva Wiseman opens their door and watches them "with dark intent speculation" (ts 207). And here the scene, which has been framed by the lesbian presence of Eva Wiseman, ends. [47]

The third excised passage, which occurs the next morning, builds on the second. It is added onto a scene on deck in the published book in which Jenny's boyfriend Pete kisses her, and then asks, " 'What's the matter?' "—to which she answers innocently, " 'The matter with what?' " (177). In the deleted passage which would have been part of this scene, however, Jenny tells Pete exactly what's the matter: she doesn't like the way he kisses anymore because " '[i]t's not refined' " (ts 235); i.e., not the way *Pat* has taught her to kiss, though she doesn't tell him this. In the missing passage, Pete becomes very angry, grabs Jenny's arm, and accuses her of " 'fooling around with that old bird' " (ts 236). He won't tell her who "that old bird" is, but warns her to watch her step; he's watching her. To which she responds, " 'Oh, you mean Gramma' " and then tells him he may kiss her if he does it " 'refined' " (ts 237).

Both of these deleted passages are closely tied to the published text and, had they not been cut, would have escalated the gender trouble which already is brewing on several different fronts, not just in the "queer" spaces of the lesbian erotic scenes, which also occur in the book between Eva Wiseman and Jenny, but also in the interplay *between* homosexuality and heterosexuality. This interplay occurs both in terms of character-

ization and structure. For example, in the second deletion Eva
Wiseman, whose poems were first quoted in the novel and then
later published by Faulkner as his own and whose ambiguous
gender identity is manifested in the interplay between her two
names and references to her as "Mrs. Wiseman," seems to be
taking up the position of the male gaze (which permeates the
book) as she watched Pat and Jenny engaged in lesbian sexual
activity, just as she observes Jenny's body at several points in
ways similar to the men on board. As Wittenberg has pointed
out, "[in] the textual oscillations of *Mosquitoes*, Eva seems
alternatively located in the masculine, bisexual, and feminine
positions, a subversive and challenging figure."[48] This is even
more true in the deleted passages. While "Mr. Talliaferro"
moves back and forth between male and female groups but
seems most comfortable with women, "Mrs. Wiseman" seems
most at home with male company and man talk. (The final
deletion especially emphasizes her strong footing on masculine
turf.) Although she and her brother have been linked to certain
New Orleans figures,[49] her intellectual demeanor, her lesbianism, her identity as a modernist poet, even the fact that she
doesn't wear the right kind of garters, are more reminiscent of
Gertrude Stein. Likewise, Pat Robyn, Mrs. Maurier's niece,
becomes even more of a bisexual figure, as she goes (or I should
say would have gone) directly from the deleted scene in the
bunk with Jenny to shipboard for a midnight tryst with David
West, the steward.

My point is this: had these two deletions remained part of the
text, the engagement *between* homosexuality and heterosexuality, and the part parody plays in that engagement, would
have been *performed* structurally through interlocking scenes.
Although Eva Wiseman spends a good bit of time above board
thinking of "Jenny's soft body" (251), the female-female erotic
scenes in the published book are compartmentalized, literally—
they take place in the bunk (Jenny and Pat), or in the room
(Jenny and Eva)—and structurally—they are set off from other
action. However, the deleted scene with Pat and Jenny in the

bunk, as I have said, comes directly on the heels of Eva Wiseman's speculations on Mrs. Maurier's life, which, we will learn later, was ruined by a bad marriage. And had that same scene remained, Pat would have gone straight from kissing and fondling the nude Jenny to her meeting with David. Even more obviously, when Jenny compares Pete's kiss to Pat's and finds the former lacking, she brings queer space above board, and thereby calls into question the naturalness of heterosexuality. And Pete's jealousy of "Gramma," who seems to be Eva Wiseman, serves to punctuate this questioning and escalate its disruptive effect.

The final major deletion, which, as I mentioned, is itself missing a page in the Garland facsimile, launches still another highly speculative inquiry into the construction of sexuality, sexual practice, and the institution of marriage. It extends a discussion in the book between Dawson Fairchild and Julius Wiseman about the comical nature of the logistics of heterosexual intercourse, so comical, in fact, Fairchild argues, that " '[t]here'd sure be a decline in population if a man were twins and had to stand around and watch himself making love' " (185). These two are also making fun of the institution of marriage. As Julius puts it, " 'it's the marriage ceremony that disfigures our foreheads' " (185). Piecing together the deleted passage in the Garland Edition with its missing page in the original typescript at the Alderman Library reveals this rather raucous conversation as becoming even more explicit. Eva Wiseman asks, " 'How about women?' " and Fairchild replies, " 'Oh well, there wouldn't be so much of them in sight. And anyway, its [sic] your backside that is ridiculous, that gives you away' " (ts 247).[50] In response to this comment, Mrs. Maurier makes "an indistinguishable shrill sound." And Mark Frost the poet says, " 'But the population need not suffer [should marital sex be discontinued]. Someone would invent a mechanical contrivance to do the work' " (ts 247–48). To which Fairchild speculates about how to make, copyright, and market " 'an instrument, a small one [women] could carry in their vanity cases' " and then adds,

" 'But not too small' " (ts 248). He concludes, however, that
" 'the old orthodox way' " is still best. As Fairchild puts it,
" 'what was good enough for my fathers is good enough for
me. Hey, Talliaferro?' " The passage closes with Eva Wiseman
saying, " 'Shut up, Dawson. . . . I want to talk some,' " as he
continues to drone on (ts 248). At this point the published text
picks up, with the women changing the subject to a safer
topic: music.

This deletion, as it supplements the conversation it would
have followed in the published book, is rife with gender trouble.
There is an attempt to show marriage and marital sex as performances that can be easily parodied. The amusing depiction of
the missionary position, however, ironically (and paradoxically)
places the man in a homoerotic pose, in which he is observed
by his male double or "twin." There are dildoes in women's
vanity cases which they may use, instead of men, for sexual and
reproductive purposes; a well-placed gibe at Ernest Talliaferro;
and a final assertion of dominance by Eva Wiseman. Even the
reassertion of "the old orthodox way" is couched in such a
humorous context that it is impossible to take seriously. Again,
queer space is layered over heterosexual practice, and the result
is unsettling, not only to Mrs. Maurier, who is horrified at
such talk, and the editors at Boni & Liveright, who, from all
indications, shared her view, but also to notions of sexuality as
either "natural" or fixed.

Here I want to return to the question which the title of my
paper implies. *If* Ernest does like Gordon, *if* the implications of
these four deletions to what is already a gender-troubled text
are fully pondered (which I don't claim to have done here), then
what does Faulkner's apologetic February 18 letter to Liveright,
that the results of the deletions were, after all, "not very
important," mean? There remains the very remote possibility
that Faulkner biographers and textual historians are wrong, and
that Faulkner himself deleted the passages, and his letter refers
to other deletions made by Boni & Liveright. However, as I've
said, the supposition offered by Blotner, who quotes Ben Was-

son as saying the book had been badly cut by the publisher, and others is that these four passages were indeed excised. Regardless, however, of who made the deletions, their expungement strongly suggests that Faulkner found the terrain, especially the male homoerotic terrain, of the queer abject treacherous footing for the successful male writer in the U.S. In this sense, Martin Kreiswirth's statement that Faulkner wrote *Mosquitoes* before he found out that an artist's work had to have a *design*, and Blotner's observation that if *Mosquitoes* were an apprenticeship novel, "it gave signs of *mastery*" (my emphasis) to emerge in Faulkner's later fiction, indeed may carry unintended double meanings.[51] Instead of taking, if not center stage, at least part of the stage, as it did in this second novel, "gender trouble" would later turn into a pesky, persistent but unnamed mosquito-like presence in Faulkner's work—always there, known by its sound and its bite, but more elusive, buzzing about in other arenas of sexual "trouble," especially incest and miscegenation, disguising itself as only a Mississippi mosquito can do, until the moment of the bite.

This is certainly not to say that disruptions of gender and sexuality do not occur in Faulkner's fiction which followed *Mosquitoes;* clearly what John Duvall calls "the power of Faulkner's texts to de-stabilize cultural polarization of masculinity and femininity"[52] is readily apparent in *The Sound and the Fury, Light in August, Absalom, Absalom!, The Unvanquished,* and *The Wild Palms,* to mention but some of the most obvious. It could be argued, in fact, that much of the power of such scenes as those between Quentin and Shreve in the Harvard dormitory room derives from their underlying homoerotic elements. But I do believe that the *bite* of gender trouble in Faulkner's other work—that is, the parody of the idea of heterosexuality as origin, as well as depictions of *explicit* same sex eroticism—may have been mitigated by his experience with *Mosquitoes*.[53] What Faulkner may have found out was that too much gender trouble could and would bite the hand that fed the artist, and when that hand was raised to slap, the queer culprit had better vanish fast. Or at least go underground.

And Faulkner figured rightly. As a multiversioned text with what seems to be a history of prepublication censorship, *Mosquitoes* tells a story of the regulatory powers of compulsory heterosexuality—certainly not, I would hasten to say, the only regulatory powers at work in the artistic domain, but surely among the most damaging. It is a story with a kinship to several stories which would follow its publication: in the twenties, the obscenity trial of Radclyffe Hall and the banning of her lesbian novel, *The Well of Loneliness*, which was published a year after *Mosquitoes;* and in the 1980s and 1990s, multiple attacks on government funding of gay and lesbian writers and artists—in short, international, national, and local efforts to censor and censure any art or literature that makes gender, or sexuality . . . trouble.

In her 1993 book, *Bodies That Matter*, Judith Butler attempts to understand the extent to which "sex" is "a constrained production, a forcible effect." She wonders "how what has been foreclosed or banished from the proper domain of 'sex' . . . might at once be produced as a troubling return . . . an enabling disruption."[54] It seems to me that, in terms of literature and literary study, this reproduction of meaning, these enabling disruptions, continue to emerge in certain kinds of readings of certain kinds of texts. These are texts which both perform and parody fixed notions of sexuality and whose "queer" spaces and "queer" people "break the sequence" in one way or another. Like *Mosquitoes*, such texts require a particular form of rereading that could be called "stirring up trouble." By "stirring up trouble," I mean any attempt to retrieve and reactivate in a text the gender trouble that has been banished through outright censorship, as I believe was the case with *Mosquitoes*, or foreclosed through the more subtle but equally coercive "regulatory fictions" that both shape and disfigure cultural and literary constructions of sexuality. Whether Faulkner intended all this trouble I've been stirring up I can't say. What I can say is that its bite is unmistakable.

NOTES

1. Virginia Woolf, *A Room of One's Own* (New York: Harcourt Brace Jovanovich, 1929), 84–86. *A Room of One's Own* is based on two lectures delivered in 1928.

2. I'm indebted to Adrienne Cannon of the University of Virginia Alderman Library special collections department for her assistance with materials for this essay, and to Noel Polk, Ruth Salvaggio, Judith L. Sensibar, and Judith Bryant Wittenberg for useful suggestions and information.

3. Judith Butler, *Gender Trouble* (New York: Routledge, 1990), 136.

4. Judith Butler, *Bodies That Matter* (New York: Routledge, 1993), 3, 22.

5. Eve Sedgwick, *Tendencies* (Durham: Duke University Press, 1993), xii.

6. Michael Millgate, *The Achievement of William Faulkner* (New York: Vintage, 1963), 70.

7. Later in his treatment of the novel Millgate himself turns to a discussion of its lesbian material. See Millgate, 70–71.

8. William Faulkner, *Faulkner in the University*, ed. Frederick L. Gwynn and Joseph L. Blotner (Charlottesville: University of Virginia Press, 1959), 257. Faulkner's statement about *Mosquitoes* was: "In that case I'll agree with Mr. Cowley [Malcolm Cowley who called *Mosquitoes* a very bad early novel] because I was still learning my craft, but I think that some of the book, some parts of it, are funny, but as a book it's—if I—I think that the writer feels that if he could write it over again it would all be better. That one, if I could write that over, I probably wouldn't write it at all. I'm not ashamed of it, because that was the chips, the badly sawn planks that the carpenter produces while he's learning to be a first-rate carpenter, but it's not a—not an important book in my list."

9. Adrienne Rich, "Compulsory Heterosexuality and Lesbian Existence," in *The Signs Reader*, ed. Elizabeth Abel and Emily K. Abel (Chicago: University of Chicago Press), 139–68.

10. I hedge this statement only slightly, following Blotner, Millgate, Edwin T. Arnold, and others, who state that four significant segments of *Mosquitoes* were cut in the editorial process at Boni & Liveright. See note 36.

11. To make such a distinction, I'd hasten to add, is not to accept Meryl Altman's assertion that "we must decouple homosexuality from gender-bending" in analyzing *Mosquitoes* (or other texts) ("The Bug That Dare Not Speak Its Name: Sex, Art, Faulkner's Worst Novel, and the Critics," *Faulkner Journal* 9 [Fall 1993/Spring 1994 (published Fall 1995): 26]). It seems to me that homosexuality and homoeroticism, by their very existence in the world and the text, inevitably "bend" binary constructions of gender based upon the presumption of heterosexual vectors of desire, and, more importantly, make the dynamics of gender production less transparent and hence less powerful.

12. Karen Ramsay Johnson, "Gender, Sexuality, and the Artist in Faulkner's Novels," *American Literature* 61, 1 (March 1989): 5, 1.

13. Frann Michel, "Faulkner as a Lesbian Author," *Faulkner Journal* 4, 1 & 2 (Fall 1988/Spring 1989): 5–18.

14. Lisa Rado, " 'A Perversion That Builds Chartes and Invents Lear Is a Pretty Good Thing': *Mosquitoes* and Faulkner's Androgynous Imagination," *Faulkner Journal*, 9 (Fall 1993/Spring 1994 [published Fall 1995]): 26.

15. Michel Gresset, *Fascination: Faulkner's Fiction, 1919–1936* (Durham: Duke University Press, 1989), 98–102. In what is for me a disturbing analysis of "perversion," Gresset believes that, for Faulkner, evil "signals a *perverted* relation between two

beings" and argues that in *Mosquitoes* "Patricia and Jenny avoid being branded with perversion only because of their youth" (102). Jenny, according to Gresset, "envelops and ensnares her victims," while Patricia is "the tomboy, the nonwoman, the epicene": "The irony—and of course the ultimate perversion—is that between these two a serious, truly sexual relationship is established" (98). In a similar vein, Joel Williamson's discussion of homosexuality in Faulkner's work hinges on the idea that homosexuality was "[a]n obvious surrogate for sex in the socially prescribed pattern" and that characters in the early stories who were experimenting with homosexuality were young people moving toward heterosexual personalities (*Faulkner and Southern History* [New York: Oxford University Press, 1993]), 389. In earlier assessments of the novel, lesbianism and bisexuality are linked to sterility (Edwin T. Arnold, "Freedom and Stasis in Faulkner's *Mosquitoes*," *Mississippi Quarterly* 28, 3 [Summer 1975]: 292, and Mary M. Dunlap, "Sex and the Artist in *Mosquitoes*," *Mississippi Quarterly* 22, 3 [Summer 1969]: 191).

16. Judith Bryant Wittenberg, "Configurations of the Female and Textual Politics in *Mosquitoes*," *Faulkner Studies* 1, 1 (1991):1–2.

17. Williamson, 214–15.

18. Shari Benstock, *Women of the Left Bank: Paris, 1900–1940* (Austin: University of Texas Press, 1986), 52.

19. William Faulkner, *Selected Letters*, ed. Joseph L. Blotner (New York: Random House, 1977), 24.

20. Joseph Blotner, *Faulkner: A Biography* 1 (New York: Random House, 1974), 417.

21. David Minter, *William Faulkner: His Life and Work* (Baltimore: Johns Hopkins University Press, 1980), 65.

22. For example, see Williamson, 279.

23. Michel, 16–17.

24. To my knowledge, Richard P. Adams is the only critic to venture an opinion that there may be male homosexuality in the novel in the suggestion that David West the steward may be homosexual since he is attracted to Pat Robyn's boyish body. That would make Gordon gay as well, of course, since he is also attracted (as Faulkner certainly seemed to have been) to that same figure. See Adams, "The Apprenticeship of William Faulkner," *Tulane Studies in English* 12 (1962): 114.

25. William Faulkner, *Mosquitoes* (New York: Boni & Liveright, 1927), 9. Subsequent references will be cited in the text.

26. Judith Bryant Wittenberg, *Faulkner: The Transfiguration of Biography* (Lincoln: University of Nebraska Press, 1979), 53.

27. Michael Zeitlin, "Faulkner in Nighttown: *Mosquitoes* and the 'Circe' Episode," *Mississippi Quarterly* 42, 3 (Summer 1989): 305–8.

28. Gary Harrington, *Faulkner's Fables of Creativity: The Non-Yoknapatawpha Novels* (Athens: University of Georgia Press, 1990), 39.

29. Wittenberg, "Configurations," 3.

30. Minter, 65.

31. Butler, *Gender Trouble*, 77.

32. Ibid., 31, 138.

33. Wittenberg cites this final passage as "a new female assault on the codified repressiveness," thereby allowing "[t]he gender questions posed by the text ultimately [to] remain open" ("Configurations," 17).

34. Michel senses the same discomfort with male homoeroticism and, as I noted earlier, believes that Faulkner appropriates the feminine position so as to distance male homoerotics (16–17).

35. Butler, *Bodies That Matter*, 241.

36. See my essay "*Mosquitoes*' Missing Bite: The Four Deletions," *Faulkner Journal* 9 (Fall 1993/Spring 1994 [published Fall 1995]): 31–41, for a further discussion of the textual history of the deletions and for full publication, for the first time together, of the four deletions.

37. In his 1984 one-volume biography, Blotner is more explicit, saying that Phil

Stone "added punctuation and corrections and passed [Faulkner's typescript] on to Sallie Simpson in his office for final typing. Faulkner added the last touches and sent the parcel off to Boni & Liveright" (Blotner, *Faulkner: A Biography* One-Volume Edition [New York: Random House, 1984], 188). In his February 18, 1927, letter to Horace Liveright, which apologizes for his initially negative response to the deletions, Faulkner explains, however, that punctuation problems in the manuscript were "due to my typewriter, a Corona, vintage of 1910" (*Selected Letters* 34). Perhaps he meant that his typist was unable to decipher his punctuation in working from draft to draft. The extant typescript published by Garland was obviously typed on a faulty typewriter, with a ribbon in need of replacement, especially in the second half of the book. Often punctuation marks, such as commas, periods, or quotation marks, are very difficult to decipher. The typescript also contains handwritten insertions. The Garland typescript, then, certainly seems to be the one Faulkner completed in Pascagoula and gave to Phil Stone and Sallie Simpson for final typing. What must remain in some question is its relation to the final typescript sent to Boni & Liveright. A comparison of the Garland typescript to the published volume reveals many additional less substantive changes in wording and punctuation, as well as the four major deletions. Arnold has found, in fact, more than 10,000 variants between the surviving typescript and the published text ("William Faulkner's *Mosquitoes:* An Introduction and Annotations to the Novel" [Diss. University of South Carolina, 1978, xxvii]). There is consensus, however, that the longer passages were cut without Faulkner's knowledge during the editorial process. Blotner cites Ben Wasson as saying the book had been badly cut, and Faulkner's letter to Liveright makes it clear that Boni & Liveright had made certain important deletions which surprised and disgruntled him initially.

38. See Blotner, *Faulkner* [1974], 1: 512–24 for a discussion of the textual history of the novel.

39. The deleted passages occur as follows: first, at *Mosquitoes* (Prologue, Section 8), top of p. 45 a new Section 8 is inserted in typescript, pp. 47–48; second, at (second day, end of 11 p.m. section) p. 156 an extension of the Eleven O'Clock section is inserted in typescript, pp. 204–7; third, at (third day, 10 a.m.) p. 177, an extension of Ten O'Clock section is inserted in typescript, pp. 235–38; fourth, at (third day, 1 p.m.), p. 185, in the middle of the One O'Clock section after the words "Mr. Fairchild," a section of dialogue is inserted in typescript, pp. 247–48 (p. 247 missing from Garland typescript). Edwin T. Arnold mentions all but the first of these in *Annotations to William Faulkner's* "Mosquitoes" (New York: Garland, 1989), 87, 94, 99–100. In his dissertation he mentions all four of the deletions (Arnold, "William Faulkner's *Mosquitoes,*" xxxii–xxxvi).

40. Blotner, *Faulkner* [1974], 1: 431.

41. Faulkner, *Selected Letters*, 34; Blotner, *Faulkner* [1974], 1: 511–23; 539–41.

42. Faulkner, *William Faulkner Manuscripts Four: "Mosquitoes": The Ribbon Typescript and Miscellaneous Typescript Pages*, ed. Joseph Blotner *et al* (New York: Garland, 1987). The original typescript is at the Alderman Library, University of Virginia. Subsequent references will be cited in the text of this essay. The unpublished material is from *Mosquitoes by William Faulkner*. Copyright 1927 by Boni & Liveright, Inc. Copyright renewed 1955 by William Faulkner. By permission of Liveright Publishing Corporation.

43. In the published typescript there are two pages designated 246, which are identical, and p. 247 is omitted.

44. In his introduction to the typescript, Blotner writes: "Faulkner's galley proofs must have revealed that four good-sized passages had been deleted, all relating to sexual matters, none shocking to a contemporary reader but probably daring in the American literature climate of 1927" (Introduction, ts, ix). See also Millgate, 71; Blotner, *Faulkner* [1974], 1: 540.

45. Blotner, *Faulkner* [1974], 1: 516–17.

46. Blotner, Millgate, and Michel quote segments of this passage.

47. Blotner finds this sequence, which he summarizes briefly but does not quote

fully in either the one- or two-volume biographies, "suggests the experimentation of children rather than overt lesbian behavior" (*Faulkner: A Biography* [1984], 184). This passage, however, seems to belie that assessment.

48. Wittenberg, "Configurations," 12.

49. Blotner, *Faulkner* [1974] 1: 517–19.

50. Blotner quotes this passage only approximately in the biography (*Faulkner* [1974] 1: 540).

51. Martin Kreiswirth, *William Faulkner: The Making of a Novelist* (Athens: University of Georgia Press, 1983), 99; Blotner, *Faulkner* [1974] 1: 522.

52. John N. Duvall, *Faulkner's Marginal Couple: Invisible, Outlaw, and Unspeakable Communities* (Austin: University of Texas Press, 1990), 131.

53. Millgate believes, instead, that the sexual themes in *Mosquitoes* reflect "Faulkner's early attempt to tackle problems which he dealt with much more successfully in later novels" (71).

54. Butler, *Bodies That Matter*, 23.

Selling a Novel: Faulkner's *Sanctuary* as a Psychosexual Text

JAMES POLCHIN

Published in February of 1931, William Faulkner's sixth novel, *Sanctuary*, provoked extraordinary public interest. Faulkner wrote in the introduction to the Modern Library edition that the novel was "a cheap idea, because it was deliberately conceived to make money."[1] Many critics have since disregarded such intent, and Faulkner himself had the introduction removed from subsequent printings.[2] Yet, whatever the significance of this statement, the evidence is clear that *Sanctuary* was a novel that sold. As Joseph Blotner notes in his biography of Faulkner, by March, "*Sanctuary* had sold 3,519 copies—almost as many in three weeks as *The Sound and the Fury* and *As I Lay Dying* had together since publication."[3] Two months later, the novel had sold over seven thousand copies. *The Nation* magazine noted in its review of *Sanctuary* that "from almost every point of view 'Sanctuary' is a better book than either 'As I Lay Dying' or 'The Sound and the Fury.' "[4] The *Saturday Review of Literature* devoted more space to *Sanctuary* then it had to any book review since the magazine's founding, stating that the novel is a "prime example of American sadism."[5]

The success of *Sanctuary* reflects a drastically changing American culture during the 1920s and 1930s, underscored by an intense interest in psychology. The new psychology of the period based itself on Freudian theory, focusing on both psychosexual behavior and the importance of proper childhood mental development. The case history became central to the changing sexual norms of the culture as a means of understanding the "self." What Faulkner creates in *Sanctuary* is a psychosexual plot that catered to the interests of the culture. More importantly, I will argue, Faulkner creates two veiled cases of homosexuality, positioning Popeye as the true example of psychopathic inversion next to the more socially respectable Horace Benbow's repressed homosexual desire. The novel's ending with the "case" history and death of Popeye, and Horace's return to his wife provides for a closure of "normal" sexual relations.

*   *   *

John Chynoweth Burnham has pointed out that "by the 1920s Freudian terminology had entered the American vocabulary . . . Freudian psychology was a much more titillating subject than [the Victorian notions of] Darwinian evolution, and borrowings from it were soon evident in motion pictures and popular literature, as well as in the works of critically acclaimed writers. It soon was influencing millions of Americans who had hardly heard of Sigmund Freud."[6] Psychology's focus on the psychosexual aspects of a person's life captured a great audience during the twenties, when sexual roles were shifting and sexuality was not so stable.[7] In an article entitled "The Feminist Future," published in 1928, Miriam Allen de Ford asserted that "we are at this very time in the midst of a transition period between masculine and feminine dominance."[8] She continued by alluding to the malleability of one's mind and personality: "continued research tends to emphasize the enormous importance of acquired characteristics, of traits produced by environment."[9] Psychology fueled an interest in the self and in doing so, an examination of how one's sexual self is formed—particularly in a period of shifting sexual boundaries.

To this end, numerous books on psychology emerged during the decade. In an article published in *The New Republic* in February of 1922, H. M. Kallen reviewed two such new psychology texts. "Everybody who is anybody, or wants to be, has a 'psychology' today," wrote Kallen, "and makes knowing remarks about other people's."[10] He continued in this skeptical tone, criticizing the results of such books: "Speculation and dogmatizing about the patterns and processes of the conduct of men has a contemporaneous vogue the terms of which are symptomatic. Men have ceased to be clear in their hearts about their own motives and actions, and have become suspicious of those of their fellows."[11]

By the end of the decade, psychology was making its way into areas of science and criminology, producing books with such titles as *Principles of Abnormal Psychology, The Psychology of Youth, The Psychology of Personality,* and *Archives of Psycho-analysis.*[12] A 1927 review of these four books by E. Boyd Barrett reflected the same skeptical tone evidenced by Kallen. "In ever increasing numbers," wrote Barrett, "books are appearing under the title 'Psychology' which, whatever their merits as literature, have little or no claim to be regarded as science."[13] These books based themselves on a pseudoscience offering more of a "self-help" approach to the use of psychology for the reader. As Barrett noted, in *Principles of Abnormal Psychology* the author claims "that the book is replete with practical suggestions bearing on personal and mental hygiene."[14] Following in the Freudian vein, these books relied on the case history as a means of exemplifying problems with the "self." Yet Barrett suggested that the apparent deluge of such books was catering more to the desires of the marketplace than to the mental hygiene of the society. "Perhaps the popularization of the theories and findings of the New Psychology has reached a saturation point," wrote Barrett in reference to the pseudoscientific grounding of psychology, "and we are feeling the need for more substantial and plain, if less tempting, food. It is certainly somewhat trying to be reminded in every new book on psychology of the abnormal characteristics of pyromaniacs and homosexuals. It reminds one too vividly of the Coney Island show booths with their monster men and women."[15] Barrett's comments reveal the nature of many popular psychology texts that exposed deviant sexual and social behavior. While such books were meant "to give practical advice," their content was undoubtedly part of their "market value."[16]

The very rise in psychological books and interests in theories of the self reflect an increased desire to categorize "normal" and "deviant" behavior, particularly in the area of sex.[17] Such interest evolved, in part, from the wider availability of sexologist publications by Krafft-Ebing, Havelock Ellis, and Magnus Hirschfeld. The new psychology, and its earlier predecessors, infiltrated the areas of sociology and criminology, as historian Estelle Freedman notes, becoming a means of "measuring normalcy and defining deviance."[18] Thus, the behavior of a person became a signifier of his "mental hygiene." Rape and homosexuality were two similar "disorders" that were the focus of much research by criminologists and psychologists alike. A person's history, particularly the childhood, emerged as a major influence on his or her mental health. While many books focused on improving the mental health of children, other books dealing with criminology relied on psychology, believing that poor mental hygiene, "if not the cause of crime, was highly correlated with it."[19] From such ideas, the concept of the male sexual psychopath was born. This sexual psychopath, Freedman points out, "provided a boundary within which Americans renegotiated the definitions of sexual normalcy. Ultimately, the response to the sexual psychopath helped legitimize less violent, but previously taboo, sexual acts while it stigmatized unmanly, rather than unwomanly, behavior as the most serious threat to sexual order."[20] By 1931, the year *Sanctuary* was published and two years after the stock market crash, control over masculinity was paramount, for the man's traditional role as breadwinner was seriously undermined. Male sexual deviancy was viewed as a threat to social and gender order. Thus, as Freedman notes, the psychopath was "perceived as a drifter, an unemployed man who lived beyond the boundaries of familial and social controls."[21] The homosexual, then, fell in the center of this emerging conceptualization of male sexual deviancy. His position in society evolved from side show "monster" to "psychopath." In each perception, "deviant males were thought to

attack children, thus simultaneously threatening sexual innocence, gender roles, and the social order."[22]

*   *   *

The degree of influence of this rising tide of new psychology on
Faulkner is difficult to measure. What is sure is his exposure to
both the traditional modes of theory and the more popularized
versions. His involvement within the intellectual circles of New
Orleans, New York, and Paris undoubtedly exposed him to the
contemporary discourse of ideas. As Blotner notes, in the library
talk at Sherwood Anderson's home Faulkner would have heard
"a great deal of talk about art, about Freud."[23] However, Phil
Stone, remarking to Carvel Collins in 1954, claimed that "the
truth is that the literary group in New Orleans . . . wer [*sic*] to
Bill a comedy group and he paid very little attention to anything
they said."[24] Faulkner's feeling toward the literary group is less
important than the fact that he was exposed through such circles
to the emerging ideas in popular psychology and, most likely,
society's ever-increasing interest in the deviancy of the "self."

What Faulkner clearly was aware of, and influenced by,
were the French and English "Decadents." Writers such as
Baudelaire, Rimbaud, and Verlaine influenced the young Faulkner. More importantly, he owned a copy of Oscar Wilde's
Salome, illustrated by Aubrey Beardsley, which undoubtedly
had some influence on his early work. Faulkner's *Marionettes*,
for example, an early play written about 1920, "left no doubt,"
claims Blotner, that Faulkner was "probably quite as familiar
with the work of the English 'Decadent' as he was with that of
his French colleagues."[25] On his trip to Paris in 1925, Faulkner
wrote his mother about his visit to Père Lachaise cemetery,
stating: "I went particularly to see Oscar Wilde's tomb."[26] The
fact that Faulkner respected Wilde and his work underscores
the young writer's interest in a certain sexual decadence. Such
a decadence marked the twenties, particularly within literary
and intellectual circles where figures such as Swinburne and
Wilde appealed to so many.[27] For Faulkner, Wilde's life and
work probably provided a means of creative social criticism.

Wilde's plight as the persecuted homosexual and outcast of Victorian England may have served as a model of the effects of repressive social morals. Wilde is in essence the first homosexual "case" of the modern period. As Havelock Ellis remarked: "The Oscar Wilde trial . . . with its wide publicity, and the fundamental nature of the question it suggested, appears to have generally contributed to give definiteness and self-consciousness to the manifestations of homosexuality."[28] For Faulkner, awareness of both the plight of Wilde as homosexual, and the emerging discourse of psychosexual and psychopathic male deviancy, came together in *Sanctuary*. The tragic homosexual figures in the novel point both retrospectively to Wilde's oppression and prospectively to the threat of the psychopath. Such a combination catered to the eager tastes of the American public, and created a novel that, like many of the new psychology books, did "make money."

*   *   *

The first chapter of *Sanctuary* presents both Horace Benbow and Popeye within the lush milieu of "the jungle."[29] Horace's excursion to bootlegger Goodwin's still comes after leaving his wife. He enters the novel and the wilderness as a nameless, delinquent husband who encounters a world of illegal and immoral production—qualities in opposition to his role as a respectable town lawyer. His meeting with Popeye is fraught with a masked sexuality as both men engage in an erotically charged "cruising," foregrounded by a two hour stare between Horace and the "queer" Popeye (4). As Horace bends to drink from the spring, he sees "the broken and myriad reflection of his own" image, emphasizing a splintered self (3). This image is followed by the "shattered reflection of Popeye's straw hat," bringing Popeye and Horace within the same mirrored state of a fragmented being (6).

Popeye emerges from the woods looking like "stamped tin," and having little to do with the natural (4). "His face had a queer, bloodless color, as though seen by electric light" (4). His "doll-like hands" and "face of a wax doll" bring together both feminine and nonhuman qualities (5). He is in many ways the very opposite of the natural environment. His constant smoking creates a haziness to his face like a "mask carved into two simultaneous expressions," underscoring a duality to his existence which becomes more evident in his "case" history at the end of the novel (5).

Popeye may have been based on the real person of Popeye Pumphrey, of whose notoriety in Memphis during the twenties Faulkner was most likely aware. As Blotner writes, Pumphrey was a "paradoxical figure: a handsome man never seen with girls, a temperate bootlegger, the grandson of an Arkansas attorney general, yet one who 'has just been different from other children,' beginning a long criminal record in early youth."[30] What Blotner does in this description of Pumphrey is what Faulkner does with Popeye: both place his handsomeness and lack of association with women within a framework of illicit/immoral behavior. In other words, the veiled presence of homosexuality becomes part of Popeye's strange (and threatening) being which would have catered to the feelings about male sexual deviancy of the time; and, apparently for Blotner, writing in the 1970s, the association between homosexuality and criminality/immorality is also strong. Why, I would ask, does a handsome man's lack of interest in women present a paradox to his being?

What emerges then in the initial chapter of the novel is the coming together of the illegal, unnatural Popeye, and the misdirected Horace who is searching for the illicit. The silence of the scene underscores a certain level of sexual tension between the two, broken only occasionally with such phrases as Horace's suggestive, "You've got a pistol in that pocket, I suppose" (4). Perhaps the strangest part of this scene is their sustained staring, "facing one another across the spring, for two hours" (5). While critic John Irwin does claim that Popeye serves "as Horace's antithetical double, as a dark mirror image whose physical impotence reflects Horace's spiritual impotence,"[31] he goes on to elucidate Horace's desire for his sister

Narcissa and stepdaughter Little Belle. Irwin's use of the myth
of Narcissus serves to foreground his discussion of Horace's
heterosexual love. However, Narcissus sees in the water his
own feminized version of himself and falls in love with it. Thus,
in such a reading, Horace sees in the "doll" face of Popeye a
version of himself, in opposition to his "broken" image in the
stream, and becomes deeply fascinated, even erotically charged
by the image of Popeye. Later, when he recounts his experience
to Aunt Jenny, he remembers the phallic pistol, associating it
with Popeye's body: "You could feel the pistol on him just like
you knew he had a navel" (113). Horace's discussion with
Tommy about Popeye, in which Tommy refers to Popeye as "a
case," (22) is especially tinged with such fascination—although
more reserved within the manly community of the still. Referring to Tommy's assertion that Popeye is "skeered of his own
shadow," Horace replies, "I'd be scared of it too . . . if his
shadow was mine" (21–22). The irony of this statement is that
Popeye is his shadow, the darker side of his sexual self—the
feminized, unnatural man. As the chapter makes clear, Horace
exhibits both fascination and disgust for Popeye, emphasizing
his threatening quality within the public domain, but staying
with him (staring at him) for two hours in the privacy of
the jungle.

Popeye and Horace never meet again, but the effect of their
encounter remains strong as each plays out his homosexual
desire through Temple Drake's body. Popeye's violent rape of
Temple starts the novel's movement—a movement from country
to city, from natural to social. Popeye says to Goodwin just
before the rape, "I'm clearing out . . . I'm getting out of here"
(102). Her rape then signifies Popeye's brutal appropriation of
the proper social role to "get out" of the country and into the
city. When Popeye and Temple stop at the gas station, for
example, "they appear . . . as decorous as two acquaintances
stopped to pass the time of day before entering church" (147).
Temple allows a certain level of respectability for the psychopathic drifter, Popeye. Her rape and the corruption of her

innocence represent a further appropriation of social power by Popeye to achieve a certain status—namely heterosexuality. There is no eroticism about the presentation of the rape or its subsequent effects on Temple. Rather, the act merely shows the true force of Popeye's violence moving the novel forward into the city and, ultimately, into the interest of Horace Benbow.

Horace also relies on Temple's body as a means to affirm his status as successful lawyer. If he fails in his defence of Goodwin he loses a certain male authoritative position as both defender of justice and hero of the public good. Thus, his search for, and consequent questioning of, Temple at Miss Reba's whorehouse underscores his attempts at maintaining his role. As Temple recounts to Horace her emotional state during her stay at Goodwin's she asserts an image of transexuality as a defense against male sexual violence: "Then I thought about being a man, and as soon as I thought it, it happened. . . . I could feel the jerking going on inside my knickers ahead of his hand and me lying there trying not to laugh about how surprised and mad he was going to be in about a minute" (231). Her fantasy of turning into a man suggests a dual sexual identity outwardly evidenced in her name: "You got a boy's name" Miss Reba says upon meeting her (153). More importantly, she does not simply see herself as the representation of a man, but actually becomes a man, exhibiting the external organs of the male. Her confessional tale acts as a psychological case of psychosexual inversion that grounded so many discussions in the popular psychology texts and confession magazines of the time.

Ultimately, Horace uses her case to project himself into the rape scene. Returning home from interviewing Temple, he sees the picture of his stepdaughter, Little Belle, and the scent of honeysuckle "filled the room and the small face seemed to swoon in a voluptuous languor, blurring still more, fading, leaving upon his eye a soft and fading aftermath of invitation and voluptuous promise and secret affirmation" (234). The "fading" image of Little Belle leads to a "secret affirmation" that propels

him to the bathroom, and a projection of himself into his erotic
imaginings of Temple's rape:

> He opened the door running and fumbled at the light. But he had
> not time to find it and he gave over and plunged forward and struck
> the lavatory and leaned upon his braced arms while the shuck set
> up a terrific uproar beneath her thighs. . . . [S]he watched some-
> thing black and furious go roaring out of her pale body. She was
> bound naked on her back on a flat car moving at speed through a
> black tunnel. . . . The car shot bodily from the tunnel in a long
> upward slant, the darkness overhead now shredded with parallel
> attenuations of living fire, toward a crescendo like a held breath.
> . . . (234–35)

Like the rape scene, the narrative structure of this scene creates
an ambiguity as to the exact nature of the action. Irwin argues
that "as the image of Temple lying on the corn shucks merges
with Horace's feelings for Little Belle, Horace's vomiting becomes a kind of perverse ejaculation, expressing at once his
forbidden desire and his revulsion at this desire."[32] Yet the
narrative structure of this scene moves from "he" to "she" in
the same sentence, merging the image of Horace with Temple.
While he may be envisioning the scene in his mind, Horace is
also projecting into the scene, just as the reader is moved
from Horace's bathroom to the rape. The scene presents a
sadomasochistic image of bondage ending with the suggestion of
ejaculation. The phallic "car," moving from the "black tunnel,"
appears in a "long upward slant" that is followed by thin streams
of "living fire." This "crescendo" of a climax culminates with a
"held breath." Thus, like Temple Drake's story of her rape in
which she creates her physical and mental state as a man,
Horace projects himself into a female position in his own
recollection of the rape. For Horace, the image evolves as an
erotically charged act of anal intercourse. The shift in the
narrative structure underscores his attempt at enacting male-
male desire.

Critic Joseph Urgo claims that "Horace has found Temple's
story as erotic as it is criminal. He has also discovered a

potentiality within himself which places him in collusion with a rapist."[33] Such an understanding, like Irwin's and many others, relies on a heterosexual vision. Why must Horace simply project himself into the role of the rapist? His meeting with Temple did not reveal any hint of desire for the bedridden, college debutante. His desire for Little Belle is a means of coding a sexual deviancy in Horace. His interest in his stepdaughter reflects a belief common in psychology, which Faulkner and his readers would have known, that homosexual desire was immature and undeveloped desire. Writing in 1924, psychologist David Seabury relies on the Freudian theory of sexuality, claiming that in childhood development it is "*normal* that after seven years . . . there is both individuality and some capacity to respond to the opposite sex."[34] Without such development, writes Seabury, "normality in sexual relations is seldom possible."[35] Thus, Horace's development is thwarted by a certain deviant sexual appetite for Little Belle, just as Popeye's brutal rape of the childlike Temple reflects his own deviancy. While Popeye is certainly the homosexual psychopath, threatening "sexual innocence, gender roles, and social order,"[36] Horace signifies a less violent image of homosexual desire. After the scene in the bathroom, Horace writes to his wife the next morning asking for a divorce, with a "feeling quiet and empty for the first time since he had found Popeye watching him across the spring" (274). His desire for a divorce brings about the feeling and memory of his first meeting with Popeye, not the image of Little Belle. In fact, divorce would further separate him from contact with his stepdaughter, putting into question his true sexual interest in her.

Popeye also projects himself onto Temple. His bringing Red to the whorehouse to have sex with Temple while he watches reflects his own desire of projection into the female form. Dianne Luce Cox argues that "Popeye's decision to bring Red to Temple is motivated by his hope that he can visually 'learn' the potency to act out his hostility."[37] But Popeye has not had problems "acting" out his hostility earlier. Cox views Popeye's actions as a means of becoming potent, when he could very well be seeking a sexual connection with the virile Red. Like Horace, Popeye uses Temple Drake to project his own self into a sexual relationship with a man. Many critics overlook such a reading, assuming instead a solely heterosexual vision. On the contrary, Temple Drake provides Horace and Popeye with a means to be both masculine and feminine, through each man's outward roles and internal imaginings.

Ultimately, Horace does lose the case and comes to suffer ignominy in the courtroom and in the home after his return to his wife. The town's revenge against the convicted Goodwin manifests itself in burning him to death, followed by an implicit threat to rape Horace: "Do to the lawyer what . . . he did to her" (311). The eroticized sodomy Horace imagined with Popeye indirectly becomes a brutal punishment against him by a vengeful town. His failure in the court case, his lack of masculine authority, connects his deviancy with that of the rapist. Thus, his deviant desire evolves as the threat of a brutal sodomization against him by a vengeful culture wanting to replace order and protect its innocence.

While Horace returns to the familial environment, Popeye leaves Memphis, becoming a drifter once again. The final chapter presents the "case" of Popeye from his childhood with his pyromaniacal grandmother and absent father—the former explaining his eerie skill with matches and the latter his lack of a masculine role model. We begin to see clues to Popeye's psychopathic behavior emerge in a psychoanalytic examination of his childhood. In tracing Popeye's development, Faulkner relies most heavily on his contemporary readers' interest in the psychosexual deviant. When Popeye is still a boy, the doctor explains that "he will never be a man, properly speaking. With care he will live some time longer. But he will never be any older than he is now" (323–24). Thus, Popeye's case history exhibits the fundamental element of inversion, that of immature sexual desire. His unnatural desire is, as Miss Reba says, "against nature" (269–70). Faulkner presents Popeye as both the "pyromaniac and homosexual," harkening back to E. Boyd

Barrett's 1927 comments on the character of popular psychological books. Once arrested, Popeye becomes the ambivalent prisoner who is ultimately convicted of murder with little evidence against him. As his lawyer protests, "Do you want to hang? Is that it? Are you trying to commit suicide?" (330). Ultimately he does hang, and his case follows two traditions: the homosexual as psychopath and the tragic homosexual. From Oscar Wilde to Jeffrey Dahmer, these two singular images of homosexuality have prevailed in the cultural consciousness throughout the twentieth century. The reader wants Popeye to die, just as the town wants to punish Horace violently as a means of controlling his behavior in the courtroom and the familial realm.

The final scene of Temple Drake in the Luxembourg Gardens reestablishes "normal" social and sexual relations in the novel. The psychopath has been hanged. The errant husband has returned to his wife, holding back deviant desires, fearful of brutal retribution. Horace's final act in the novel, ironically, is to lock the back door of the family home at his wife's request, securing his place in the world of domestic desire. Temple Drake sits in the cultivated gardens of Europe, recovering from her lost innocence in a different country. Temple's face, reflected in her compact, looks "miniature sullen and discontented and sad" (333). The novel thus moves from the "jungle" outside Memphis where two men flirt with their homosexual desire, to the manicured gardens of the "Old World" where a woman in a "smart new hat" attempts a recovery from the brutality of the psychosexual deviancy which took away her youth.[38]

*   *   *

In his review of *Sanctuary* in February 1931, John Chamberlain writes in the *New York Times Book Review* that the novel lacks a consideration of "moral ideas," but, Chamberlain assures, Faulkner shows "promise of continued growth."[39] Thus, the novel's focus on male sexual deviancy is viewed as immoral and immature—both terms constantly used to describe homosexual behavior. *Sanctuary* emerges from a culture obsessed with the abnormal and immoral aspects of life. The deviancy of self was ultimately the greatest popular appeal of the novel. The increasing need to categorize "deviant" behavior, especially aberrant male behavior, foregrounds the novel. How we read the nature of desire in *Sanctuary* depends upon numerous social conceptions of sexuality and how such desire has been understood by readers from the 1930s to today. Ultimately the novel reflects the ways in which cultural narratives come to construct our values and desires.

NOTES

1. Joseph Blotner, *Faulkner: A Biography* (New York: Random House, 1974), 337.
2. See William Faulkner, *Sanctuary, The Corrected Text* (New York: Vintage Books, 1987), 337. In the "Editor's Note" Noel Polk reprints the original introduction which Faulkner did not want included in later printings by Random House.
3. Blotner, 685.
4. Clifton Fadiman, "Reviews," *Nation* 132 (15 April 1931): 422.
5. As quoted in Blotner, 685.
6. John Chynoweth Burnham, "The New Psychology: From Narcissism to Social Control," in *Change and Continuity in Twentieth-Century America: The 1920s*, ed. John Braeman, et al. (Columbus: Ohio State University Press, 1968), 335.
7. For a discussion of the shifting social and economic aspects of the period see Stanley Coben, *Rebellion Against Victorianism: The Impetus for Cultural Change in 1920s America* (Oxford: Oxford University Press, 1991). For a background of American psychoanalysis in the early twentieth century see C. P. Oberndorf, *A History of Psychoanalysis in America* (New York: Grune & Stratton, 1953).
8. Miriam Allen De Ford, "The Feminist Future," *New Republic* 56 (18 September 1928): 121.
9. Ibid., 123.
10. H. M. Kallen, "Is Minding Behaving?" *New Republic* 29 (1 February 1922): 285.
11. Ibid.
12. Published the same year as *Sanctuary*, Frederick Lewis Allen's *Only Yesterday: An Informal History of the Nineteen Twenties* reveals that ideas of psychoanalysis "fertilized a bumper crop of sex magazines, confession magazines and lurid motion pictures, and that in turn had their effect on a class of readers and movie goers who had never heard and never would hear of Freud and the libido." (New York: Harper & Brothers, Publishers, 1931), 100.
13. E. Boyd Barrett, " 'Psychology' or Science," *New Republic* 52 (16 November 1927): 343.
14. Ibid., 344.
15. Ibid., 343.
16. Ibid., 344.
17. For an analysis of the (dis)use of psychoanalytic theory to sexual behavior see Jonathan Dollimore, *Sexual Dissidence: Augustine to Wilde, Freud to Foucault* (Oxford: Clarendon Press, 1991).
18. Estelle Freedman, " 'Uncontrolled Desires': The Response to the Sexual Psychopath, 1920–1960." *Journal of American History* 74 (June 1987): 90.

19. Ibid., 88.

20. Ibid., 87.

21. Ibid., 89.

22. Ibid.

23. Blotner, 396.

24. Susan Snell, *Phil Stone of Oxford: A Vicarious Life* (Athens: University of Georgia Press, 1991), 168.

25. Blotner, 296.

26. Ibid., 451.

27. Burnham, 334.

28. As quoted in Claude J. Summers, *Gay Fictions: Wilde to Stonewall* (New York: Continuum, 1990), 19.

29. William Faulkner, *Sanctuary*, The Corrected Text (New York: Vintage Books, 1987), 6. All subsequent quotes will be noted parenthetically in the text.

30. Blotner, 607.

31. John Irwin, "Horace Benbow and the Myth of Narcissa," *American Literature* 64 (September 1992): 546.

32. Irwin, 560.

33. Joseph Urgo, "Temple Drake's Truthful Perjury: Rethinking Faulkner's *Sanctuary*," *American Literature* 55 (October 1983): 442.

34. David Seabury, *Unmasking Our Minds* (New York: Boni and Liveright, 1924), 376 (emphasis added).

35. Ibid.

36. Freedman, 89.

37. Dianne Luce Cox, "A Measure of Innocence: *Sanctuary*'s Temple Drake," *Mississippi Quarterly* 34 (Summer 1986): 315.

38. "*Sanctuary* . . . is a radical novel," argues John Duvall, "one that calls into question the structures of community. If one assumes that community is built upon the orderly unions of women and men in family units, then *Sanctuary* presents a disturbing message." *Faulkner's Marginal Couple: Invisible, Outlaw, and Unspeakable Communities* (Austin: University of Texas Press, 1990), 60. Within my own reading, the "disturbing message" transcends Duvall's focus on heterosexual unions to the novel's presentation of the ultimate disruptive force of homosexuality.

39. John Chamberlain, "Dostoyevsky's Shadow in the Deep South," *New York Times Book Review* (15 February 1931): 9.

Narcissa's Love Letters: Illicit Space and the Writing of Female Identity in "There Was a Queen"

MICHAEL E. LAHEY

"Letters which, like a *Deus ex machina*, intervene in events, expedite them, call them forth, converge with them. . . . That which the letter gives to read is the possibility of love as the condition of its impossibility, as it allows the letter to become possible. And draws out a love in which no one retrieves himself."

—EVE MEYER, "Letters, or the Autobiography of Writing"

In "There Was a Queen" (1933) Faulkner explores fantasy elements of the erotic as they are captured in Byron Snopes's anonymous letters to Narcissa Benbow before her marriage to Bayard Sartoris. These letters secretly arrived for Narcissa thirteen years before the action of the story despite a protective warning from Aunt Jenny Du Pre, who believed only one and not eleven had been mailed. Yet Narcissa kept, even cherished, the letters with a mixed sense of curiosity and distance. The action of Faulkner's story revolves around the recovery of these letters, first and accidentally by the FBI twelve years before and then in the present moment by Narcissa herself, long after their theft by their hopeful then angered author when he first learned of Narcissa's marriage to Bayard. In this story, so intensely focused on the private and erotically imagined and imaginative space of a young woman, a particular space from the past that threatens now to become public through the letters' exposure, Faulkner raises several issues that bear on gender roles, the creation of personal identity, and the establishment of social space. Particularly striking is the way in which Faulkner has several competing versions of Narcissa collide to destroy any single notion of her in a particular female role. Faulkner presents Narcissa alternately as the good mother, honorable Sartoris widow, white town trash, vulnerable sexual subject, tenaciously private individual, and alleged whore. Most importantly, however, Faulkner suggests that in Narcissa's unusual experience with the recovery of the letters there is an emergent hope for resistance to masculine control of private and public female space, private and public female identities.

In the story Faulkner plays with available notions of feminine identity as they are privately and publicly imagined for, but not by, Narcissa. Faulkner demonstrates how, like the imagined space captured in the love letters themselves, female identity in the world of the story is imagined and written by men, with women serving as screens onto which identity is projected.[1] The conflict in the story arises from Narcissa's previous attempt both to accept and to defy social impositions on her evolving identity. Indeed, the story focuses on the authority, development, and possible meanings of the two texts still struggling after twelve years to claim a legitimacy within Faulkner's: the supposedly illicit body of love letters and the female imagination of Narcissa. By not once but twice breaking the patterns of identity assigned her, in secretly receiving and keeping the letters and in negotiating sexually with an FBI agent for their return, Narcissa changes forever her world and the range of roles she is willing to play in it.

On the whole, critics have overlooked or underestimated "There Was a Queen," particularly its exploration of the balance between possibility and failure in the area of privately imagined identity. Melvin E. Bradford's "Certain Ladies of Quality: Faulkner's View of Women and the Evidence of 'There Was a Queen,' " for example, overlooks all the social complexities and erotic confusions underlying Narcissa's position in the story and

instead resorts to vilifying her. Bradford even positions the
unnamed FBI agent, who had found the lost or discarded letters
at the scene of Byron Snopes's bank robbery, as Narcissa's
victim, rather than seeing the strong possibility that matters
may be the other way around: "And, with the same monstrous
calm with which she betrayed her brother to Eustace Graham
[in *Sanctuary*], she tempts the agent to violate his oath of office
with the promise of the Memphis assignation."[2] Bradford's
reading of the sex-for-letters bargain thereby casts Narcissa as
solely responsible for the arrangement, the moment of her
prostitution, while overlooking the ambiguity with which Faulkner depicts the agent, who, as Narcissa tells Aunt Jenny, " 'had
had them [the letters] twelve years, working on the case. . . .
He hadn't sent them to Washington yet, so nobody had read
them except him. . . . You don't understand yet, do you? He
had all the information the letters could give him but he would
have to turn them in to the Department anyway.' "[3]

Besides dismissively referring to the letters, which one should
not forget are Narcissa's private property, as her "disgraceful
treasures" (133), Bradford fails to do some obvious questioning
about the agent's treatment of the eleven letters. This critic
therefore misses the importance of Narcissa's position as a
vulnerable woman in Faulkner's text, a woman made vulnerable
by a circulating text of letters. Why, for instance, after twelve
years are the letters still in the agent's personal care and not
part of a more official file? Why, knowing their content and not
needing to prove his possession of them to anyone outside his
department, least of all to Narcissa, does he carry them with
him from Washington to Jefferson? And why is a collection of
anonymous love letters addressed to Narcissa still supposedly
considered material evidence in a bank robbery where the
identity of the perpetrator was revealed long ago? In the unlikely event that Washington officials are still considering, if
they ever were, Narcissa as somehow a crucial party or even in
shady cahoots with Byron because of their link through the
letters, the twelve-year time lapse to question her on the matter

would indicate that their investigation is inexplicably lagging. In short, Bradford's article does not take up the strong possibility of sexual coercion—the agent's of Narcissa, not Narcissa's of him—that these questions raise. In addition, Bradford does not address the insidious implications of the letters for Narcissa or for the ideas and possibilities of womanhood in the story. After all, an entirely imagined but lasting impression of Narcissa as either erotic subject or object or both—a representation that becomes socially dangerous to her—has been written and conjured without contact or exchange and while only in very limited circulation threatens to change forever the conditions of her life through the force of representation, more particularly, through the reception of that representation. At stake in this neglected Faulkner story, then, is a woman and her sense of herself, her security, and her position in the world. And all these concerns are defined along, but dangerously pitted against, the possibilities of and for erotic imagining, of male and female self-imaginings and imaginings of each other.

Like Bradford, Philip Castille condemns Narcissa as seedy and illicit for keeping the erotic letters which she has no role in authoring, nor any control over the audacity or accuracy of their male-created images of her as sexual woman. And while Castille promisingly states, or rather announces, that "I believe that the movement of 'There Was a Queen' is fundamentally affirmative,"[4] that Aunt Jenny's fatal stroke at story's end signals the passing of the old Southern order to the new, to Narcissa, in fact, as new head of the Sartoris house, this critic puzzlingly reverses or at least undermines his position by his own express attitude toward the letters and Narcissa's possession of them: "[i]n this instance her narcissism has gone beyond self-love to become self-arousal. The erotic gratification that she received from the letters is indicated by her admission of her rereading of them, which ceased only when they were stolen from her room" (311).

Here in Castile's view, women have to make admissions to erotic gratification, admissions to self-arousal, and only the crime of break and entry into Narcissa's home and the theft of private belongings can put a stop to her equal or greater crime of rereading the letters. Castille further confuses his overall evaluation—his declaration of the story's affirmative value—and, worse, misreads the shifting levels of Faulkner's story when he praises Narcissa for her ability to confront "the reality of ordinary life on its own ground, away from the Sartoris sanctuary, and in its own terms, in a hotel bedroom. She is a character who copes" (314). For Castille, then, ordinary life on its own terms includes sexual barter with the FBI in Memphis hotels to recover stolen personal items, and apparently it is a tribute to the new Southern social order and to Narcissa in particular that all parties involved can cope with these arrangements. Castille thereby misses the story's clear indication that Narcissa is being sexually punished, both by the actual barter with the agent and by the fear, motivating her barter, that the letters will become part of the public domain. And this punishment comes precisely for having allowed herself, through Snopes's unsolicited writing, an erotic space of self-imagining years before, for helplessly having the resurfacing letters stand now as her unspoken admission to the great social guilt of female arousal.

Unlike Bradford and Castille, Ron Buchanan reads the story with an awareness of Faulkner's bleak positioning of Narcissa, who, as an upper-class Southern woman is already necessarily torn between a space of female erotic imagining and a space of social positioning. That is, Buchanan perceives how these spaces are inevitably, fatally counterposed in the world of Faulkner's story. Buchanan also convincingly argues against the unfavorable assessments that Narcissa receives from most critics who overlook Faulkner's earlier presentation of her in *Flags in the Dust*, where she "demonstrates an awakening sexuality which external events thwart."[5] Buchanan points out Narcissa's emotional and psychological background as orphan and sister who must assume the role of mother to her brother, Horace, although seven years his junior, and argues that these circumstances may have caused her to suppress part of her identity as developing woman in order to assume prematurely a maternal role, without thereby experiencing the psychological and explorational development of adolescence (449–50). Buchanan further argues that, through the love letters, Byron Snopes awakens within Narcissa "that sexuality which she had ignored in favor of her maternal responsibilities. . . . For once in her life Narcissa has someone who desires her sexually, as a woman and not as a mother, and she finds herself both flattered and intrigued by the suggestive overtones of the notes" (451). Outlining the many male abandonments and absences that have imparted a sense of loss to Narcissa's view of the world, Buchanan observes that all the men who may have somehow meaningfully influenced Narcissa's sexual identity "no longer inhabit her world" (457), with John Sartoris, her unrequited love, dead in the war, Byron Snopes, her phantom lover in the letter, run away to Texas, and Bayard Sartoris, her husband, killed in a plane crash the day of their son's birth. Buchanan concludes that "[t]he maternal instinct wins out by default, but not before Narcissa has experienced her moment as desired female" (457).

Continuing on from Buchanan, but differently, I would argue that Narcissa's sexuality is not merely thwarted by outside events but is punished in the later "There Was a Queen" for having threatened to emerge before marriage, across class lines, and with its own supporting erotic material in the earlier *Flags in the Dust*, punished for flourishing even conceptually in a space that writing temporarily creates for her. Although questions immediately—glaringly—arise about the validity as female erotica of the male-created erotic images in the letters, Narcissa's initial exposure to them appears to be proposed by Faulkner as possibly liberating, a time of positive imaginative expansion in her own personal development. As Kathy Myers remarks in "Towards a Feminist Erotica," women have only recently begun "to understand the ways in which images work to construct our own experience of our sexuality. Rather than running away from the powers of the imagination and fantasy, we have to reappraise the role of representations in structuring our needs and desires."[6] In Narcissa's case, however, her attempted construction of and participation in an emergent sexuality become negative, dangerous, punishable, when the representations that she has tentatively allowed, though not authored, threaten to be used against her.

Since "There Was a Queen" depends so much upon its characters' differing personal responses to the erotic images and impressions in the Snopes letters (whatever those images are), the vexed question of what is appropriate or inappropriate sexual conduct and representation disruptively enters the world of Jefferson. The question is all the more vexed for the way the story stretches ideas of appropriateness across shifting spaces of the public and the private, spaces in which identity usually alters drastically, especially for Faulkner's female characters.[7] Clearly, Byron Snopes intended his letters to be the honest declaration of a privately expressed desire that he hoped would become mutual; his explicit writing begins an anonymous courtship. Narcissa's retention and attentive perusal of the letters suggests that they represent or represented something meaningful to her own energies and imaginings, though, significantly, their anonymity contributes to their quality of fantasy rather than a decisively anticipated reality with their author. Aunt Jenny Du Pre's response to Narcissa when the young woman informs her of having received the first letter, however, best captures the delicate, dangerous, and contradictory split between private and public identity for Faulkner's young Southern middle- or upper-class women. As Aunt Jenny summarizes, " 'no lady would permit herself to receive anonymous love letters, no matter how badly she wanted to' " (739).

In Jenny's advice, a further division thus opens up among the categories of the public and the private for female identity, whereby any young woman is also held socially accountable for public impressions of her private identity, and so the private exists only as it is imagined in the public and exists best, according to Aunt Jenny's standards, when absolutely nothing can be imagined. The conception of the private here is in danger of no longer really existing, then, but rather than becoming a void is expanded upon as a public space individually but not ever personally held. Aunt Jenny, in fact, would have the private, the personal imaginary, completely emptied, and to safeguard against the potential content of this dangerous space would implement strict punishment if certain thoughts were publicly knowable, accessible to social controls. In response to Narcissa's refusal to show the initial letter to Colonel John Sartoris, Jenny's brother, because of what he or anyone else might think of it, Jenny replies, " 'Well, I'd rather have the whole world know that somebody thought that way about me once and got horsewhipped for it, than to have him keep on thinking that way about me, unpunished. But it's your affair' " (736). For Jenny, since there is no genuine private space socially encouraged in a young woman's life, there can be no meaningful and complex division between desire and duty, no conceivable quarrels or productive tensions within individual identities that are arranged as outer and inner. Instead, there is only discernible continuum.[8]

Yet the acknowledgment in Jenny's advice that Narcissa or any other woman might want—"even badly"—to receive anonymous love letters ironically (and poignantly) demonstrates the older woman's full awareness of the existence and needs of the hungry space that we call the personal, particularly the erotic personal, though this space remains too socially unpredictable for nurturing in the Sartoris world, for any acknowledgment beyond denial. In Jenny's words to Narcissa there thus surfaces the dual attitude toward female identity that her culture at once promotes and refuses to acknowledge for the assigning of social and sexual values: confident denial of the validity or social importance of female erotic life and troubled awareness of the potentially disruptive energy that private female imaginations can hold for the world of social relations.[9] So while Jenny and Narcissa's exchange regarding the letters and notions of womanhood clearly holds the promising form of an instructional moment between two women, an older and a younger woman, the only wisdom it finally offers is caution against jeopardizing the supposedly necessary social structuring of female identity, ladyhood, rather than conveying any real learning about awakening sexuality and its difficult negotiation in a Faulknerian world that always requires heavy personal concessions to social forms. Searching for answers to questions of possible female identities and experiences, Narcissa receives a warning not to search, "no matter how badly she wanted to."

The supposedly illicit space that the series of letters creates is not only figured as threatening rather than educational, however. The wild, imaginative space of the letters is also contrasted in the story to the protected, cultivated, and civilized space of the garden, above which Aunt Jenny sits for her comfort and her meditations on the Sartoris history (727) and in which "she and the younger woman who was to marry her nephew and bear a son, had become acquainted" (735). The garden is further mentioned frequently in the story as a place that both nourishes and preserves "the quiet of womenfolks" (727). This enclosed space of stability and tradition, and also of the sanctity of a prescriptive Southern womanhood, clearly becomes challenged by the open, or rather semi-permeable, spaces of the outlaw male-written eroticism and, significantly, of the unscripted female fantasy that the letters threaten to open up. The garden as an enclosed space in which women are to exist happily self-enclosed is further suggested in Narcissa's name, both a flower and the mythic name for a limiting and lethal self-involved identification. Against this restricting propriety and sterile self-involvement, the letters can be seen to represent an unwalled zone of imaginative energy that exists in consciousness, yet not in the Sartoris world of physical, sexual, and social ordering.

While the garden and the letters represent the supposed opposites of a sacred and a "profane" space in the story, they are also significantly similar in that they are both privileged spaces. Both spaces are highly particularized, luxurious, and affirmative of the individuals who inhabit them. In "Of Other

Spaces," Foucault discusses how utopias—a highly defined type of privileged space—are unreal spaces but how, in all cultures, there are "counter-sites, a kind of effectively enacted utopia in which the real sites, all the other real sites that can be found within the culture, are simultaneously represented, contested, and inverted. Places of this kind are outside of all places, even though it may be possible to indicate their location in reality."[10] I read such countersites as emotionally and psychologically "elsewhere," though they also have spatial location. As examples, Foucault offers the mirror, where "I am over there, there where I am not" (24), and the honeymoon trip, where a young woman's real or symbolic deflowering takes place elsewhere, in a symbolic "nowhere . . . without geographical markers" (25).[11]

Faulkner's inclusion of the garden and the erotic letters in his story thus creates a violent collision of these countersites, these two privileged and differently necessary spaces—one cultural, one personal—of elsewhereness where ideas of the inner self are nourished and reconstituted. The story posits, through Jenny's eventual stroke and Narcissa's sexual sacrifice in order to recover and destroy the letters, that the female embrace of one of these countersites destroys the possibility of the other, according to cultural codes governing Southern womanhood. In fact, one can read the story as Faulkner's specific interrogation of the cultural and sexual politics, and not just emotional poetics, that swirl around the making of individual countersites, most especially female ones. For while the narrator refers to the initial letter that Narcissa showed to Jenny twelve years before as "anonymous and obscene; it sounded mad" (735), Narcissa obviously felt it was important enough to lie about burning it. Further, her greatest reservation when she first informs Aunt Jenny of that initial letter is more complex than any sense of offense at the material. Rather, Narcissa seems threatened not by the writing itself, which probably involves many speculative images and versions of her and her phantom lover in their fictional countersite, but by an outer world knowing that such a "communication" is occurring, that such a site imaginatively

exists for her: " 'But can't you see I just can't have any man
know that anybody thought such things about me' " (735).
Significantly, her concern is that others can discover what one
man in particular thought, while her attitude toward that one
anonymous man himself and his production of an illicit writing
for and of her remains unstated, except as can be inferred from
her decision to hide this letter and those that follow in several
places, eventually in her lingerie drawer. The obvious steps that
Faulkner takes to show that these letters are meaningful to
Narcissa in her private world and private way set up the sense
of violation that she experiences not at their arrival but at their
theft, their threatened entrance into a public world where the
materials of an erotically constituted countersite, now partly her
own eroticism, threaten to become commodity mass consumed:
" 'So they were in the world. They were somewhere. I was
crazy for a while. I thought of people, men, reading them,
seeing not only my name on them, but the marks of my eyes
where I had read them again and again. I was wild' " (739).

While "There Was a Queen" explores both the potentially
liberating and potentially reductive power of images of the
erotic, depending entirely on their mode of circulation and
consumption, the story also explores the question of locating
authorship in the construction of these powerful images, and so
locating the possible origins of the construction of our feelings
about ourselves and others. The question of how one's identity
becomes influenced, authorized, or written by another or others
is pertinent to Faulkner's shifting use of Snopes's letters. Moreover, presumptuous claims to both authoring and authorizing
identities define virtually all the other influences, such as family,
cultural hierarchy, gender codes, and the power of the historical
past, that seek to guide or shape Narcissa over her life. Certainly
Faulkner's story is concerned with competing types of authorship, with the claims that both authorized and outlaw forms of
authorship make on their subject and readers and the claims of
validity that they seek to make for themselves. The story seems
most concerned, however, with the conflict between cultural

male and personal female attempts at types of authorship, as expressed through Narcissa's awakening sexual consciousness becoming a site of struggle between the Sartoris (male) tradition for women and Narcissa's own inclinations and curiosities. The space that Faulkner creates for the presence but, notably, unstated expression of a female erotic imagining therefore sets in motion a struggle for control over the interplay and regulation of male and female artistic acts and sexual acts, acts of writing and reading and acts of becoming.[12]

The temporarily anonymous authorship of the letters is significant to the struggle over the male and/or female creation of a female identity in the story in that Narcissa seems able to claim—and, the implication is, to transform—the imaginative world they represent as her own expansive space without requiring the identity or anything further from their author. Since her name alone appears on the letters and the declarations are limited to a world of written and imagined representation, the letters can be seen to shift, or at least become challenged, in their sole authorship derived only from Snopes's words as opposed to a shared or even transferred authorship in their ongoing reading and engagement in Narcissa's unexpressed thoughts. While we have here an erotic imagining offered as male creation through male control of language, we also have the complicating, even redeeming, aspect of a willful female looking, of a possibly powerful and transforming female gaze. And the presence of a female erotic gaze in "There Was a Queen" becomes significant if it signals the inevitable movement towards a female voicing, that absence which Faulkner makes so conspicuous in this story, as he does in his other texts of desire and sexual regulation, of female silence and silenced females: *Sanctuary*, *The Hamlet*, "A Rose for Emily," and especially *The Sound and the Fury*.

If the question of whose text these letters are and whose they become hinges partly on their viewer's participation in, and not solely on the origin of, their creation, then Faulkner challenges an exclusive and exclusionary male control of female erotic

representation. Furthermore, by positing Narcissa's desiring
look at the writing and images of desire, Faulkner suggests the
bankruptcy of such images, and of attitudes toward erotic images, if they cannot accommodate the female gaze and encourage the erotic mind and voice of those whom they seek to
represent.[13] Faulkner's story thus questions not only the control
over but the authenticity of any and all representations of
desire. For how much of a claim could Snopes make to Narcissa's
erotic initiation and even sexual identity through the power, or
at least presumption, of his writing? Conversely and problematically, to what extent could Narcissa claim to have forged her
own identity when the letters are a record of his and not
her fantasies? Locating the author and identifying his or her
generative power—to create both texts and identities—thus
entails identifying the reader as either a type of participating
and/or revising coauthor, a writerly reader, or else merely
the constructed viewing subject. In Narcissa's case, Faulkner's
refusal to disclose to us the extent, method, or intensity of
her participation in the letters' imaginatively constituted world
leaves open all questions of collaboration, as well as that close
engagement's possible effects on Narcissa's thinking about
herself.

The questions and role of dubious authorship, as well as the
possible source of control in the expression, interpretation, and
even brandishing of images, shift violently in Faulkner's story,
however, as a circuit of changing modes of consumption is set
up. As private communication, the letters are arguably as much
Narcissa's acts of creation through reading as Snopes's through
writing. Once stolen, however, the letters enter a space where
ownership and erotic identity become jeopardized and subject
to the possibility of other readers, other readers' interpretations.
Faulkner suggests the complications around such delicate trans-
actions—of erotic and proprietal urges, authorship, female identity, and misreading—in the circumstances of and motives for
the theft. Snopes, after all, steals from Narcissa his letters to
her, thereby forming his own strange and transgressive channel

of outpouring and return. Here his energies as "lover," now expended without success (if we narrowly take encounter as the goal of erotic energies), have been symbolically reclaimed, even as hers are re-expanding into the new, socially authorized space of marriage: " 'Then you remember that night after Bayard and I were married when somebody broke into our house in town; the same night that book-keeper in Colonel Sartoris' bank stole that money and ran away? The next morning the letters were gone, and then I knew who had sent them' " (739).

Although a spontaneous act occurring when Snopes seeks to leave a final and hostile letter,[14] the theft indicates that Snopes felt there was a meaningful co-ownership of these quietly received letters that Narcissa has suddenly forfeited, leaving him sole and pained proprietor of an empty space. While letter-writing as a form always requires absence and separation, Snopes has chosen to see instead connection, genuine communication. The problem, of course, is that he also sees possession, and here his attempted outpouring of eroticism shifts to blank aggression, the theft standing as a deliberate act of power. As a self-dramatizing statement, the theft represents his desperate claim to the authorship of, and so authority over, the erotic text in Narcissa's possession, and thus to both real and imagined erotic moments and erotic meaning in the life of the woman written to, and of, up to the point of her marriage. Looking in Narcissa's lingerie drawer where the letters are concealed, one private space enclosing another, Snopes in *Flags in the Dust* "chose one of the soft garments. . . . He . . . put the other letters in his pocket, and he stood for a time with the garment crushed against his face" (300). Apart from being an expression of strained sexual sorrow and repossession, the theft is also his attempt to abolish for her, because it has now evaporated for him, the world the letters made, the countersite that he felt held their connected but not ever joined energies. The theft, then, may be seen as a genuinely anguished but dangerous claim to ownership of the inner life of another, a spontaneous psychological violation that makes insistent a male claim to all female space, justifying in a territorial male consciousness all invasions and especially those where there has been sharing.

Other changes in space and circulation in the story threaten notions of female identity and security. Narcissa's greatest fear once the letters enter what she believes will be a circuit of mass consumption, of pornographic availability, is that men will be able to see " 'the marks of my eyes where I had read them again and again' " (739). Her chief concern here is that men can actually read *her* reading—" 'the marks of my eyes' "—and not only read *about* her. Narcissa's fear indicates that her own participation through repeated viewing, and thereby collaboration, becomes her occasion for public shame and not any feared objectification at the initial level of Snopes's representation. Faulkner thus suggests that Narcissa's society, as constituted by men, will readily accept and participate in any possible objectification of her through the rendered images and fantasies of the letters, but will consider astonishing and pornographic her own acceptance of or participation in attempts to explore representations of the possibilities for female erotic life, even her own. Paradoxically, Narcissa fears that her anonymous audience can most objectify her through an anonymous author's representation if she is perceived—detected—to play a role in her own erotic representations. And here, what was to Narcissa perhaps an acceptable representation, in at least the fantasy space of the letters, threatens to be used against her in the world, even against her will: " '[i]t was like I was having to sleep with all the men in the world at the same time' " (740). Narcissa becomes violated not through image or writing itself but through her sudden lack of control over its reception, the shift to a public space defined as exclusively male, where female erotic impulse is translated—retranslated—through a lens of appropriation rather than shared celebration. Feeling both prostituted and raped—" '[i]t was like I was having to' "—Narcissa enters helplessly into a tangle of violation and misrepresentation that Diane Roberts sees operating systematically throughout Faulkner as part of Faulkner's "project of discrediting the belle," the

South's great cultural icon.[15] For Roberts, the social anxieties around Narcissa's forbidden erotic fascination with the letters captures the central Southern, but also generally male, contradiction of cultural capitulation to "a symbolic order that demands dominance over its young women's bodies" (22) while the individuals comprising that social whole recognize that "the virgin/whore opposition is unstable" (25). According to this account, the logic of enforcement of particular female identities and the cultural construction of femininity are undercut in the realization that such roles are indeed roles. Nonetheless, Narcissa's feelings of helplessness in becoming publicly accessible through a writing that previously addressed her alone and her engagement with fantasy hinge on the dismantling of her private female space for its conversion to a contradictory, reductive, and dangerous, because falsifying, public one. This conversion, from fantasy's engagement to exposure's social cost, supports the dichotomy of the reputable and the disreputable woman and stabilizes the unstable opposition.

In effect, then, the not one but two versions of Narcissa that the writing appears to create—the woman written to, who receives and reads the letters secretly, and the woman written about, the represented—are set against each other rather than seen as possible and sustaining extensions of one another. The social and gender codes operating in Jefferson declare that the presence of erotic hopefulness, curiosity, and experimentation in the private female space threatens to discredit the woman who must, as a condition of white Southern womanhood, always feel that she is inhabiting a public sphere. In this social and psychic division, rather than view the supposedly two Narcissas as complements who enrich the life of each other, her society is conditioned to read female identity as though one role, the public or the private, one the authentic, the other a forgery. Accordingly, the shaky status and embattled integrity of disreputable authorship which begins with and in Snopes's writing is cast onto Narcissa in her social reality when the letters resurface with the FBI agent. And this shift is important: she is now

implicitly credited, or rather quasi-criminalized, with having
authored a subversive outlaw identity of herself for having had
an erotic one authored of and for her. The social and family
tensions that have been continually topping themselves up in
the course of the story—not least of which includes the Sartoris
cook Elnora's insistent assertion that Narcissa is " '[t]rash. Town
trash' " (729)—finally break open, with the framework of social,
familial, and cultural female identities assigned to Narcissa in
the present moment unable to accommodate or absorb this
previous intensely personal one: that of erotically charged and
developing woman, written to and of, perhaps herself writing
(as well as writing her self) through acts of imagining, acts of
reading and rereading.

If Faulkner's story explores the authority of competing spaces
for the realization and expression of womanhood, then the cost
of that competition between spaces and identities becomes
most dramatized at story's end. The public quality of Southern
womanhood, especially important to the cultural and historical
identity of the Old South, is subsumed not into the New South,
another cultural ordering, but into the culturally defiant notion
of personal female identity. Faulkner figures the painful and
violent relinquishing of cultural authority over particular spaces
and assigned female identities through Aunt Jenny's stroke
when Narcissa reveals the existence of the eleven letters and
the sex-for-letters exchange with the agent. In his description of
Elnora's sudden and intuitive exit from the dining room upon
sensing Jenny's death in another room, Faulkner indicates that,
in contrast to Narcissa, the story's two other female characters
may accurately be seen as *willing* social actors in a social space:
"her long silent stride carried her from sight with an abruptness
like that of an inanimate figure drawn on wheels, off a stage"
(743). Here, with Aunt Jenny's wheelchair movements metaphorically attributed to Elnora, Faulkner superimposes these
female characters onto one another at the precise moment of
their shared crisis of social identity occasioned by the letters
and the letters' use for sexual exploitation in the life of the

female member of the next generation. The narrative fusion of Jenny and Elnora emerges on the basis of their shared commitments as proud Sartoris women, though of different races, to the cultural ideal that their lives have been lived on a type of political stage, their performance of cultural and family female identities their coveted role: as Elnora declares, " 'Born Sartoris or born quality of any kind ain't *is*, it's *does*' " (732). Now pulled "inanimate," however, as if "on wheels," the dramatic enactment of femaleness as public identity moves "off stage," surrendering to private possibilities and risks in private female identity.[16]

Over the story, then, Narcissa's sense of herself and not any assigned and imposed identities is the vital hope that emerges from the action. In fact, Narcissa's sense of herself is only finally asserted at the story's end when she retrieves the letters at considerable cost to herself and to the Sartoris sense of tradition, both the Sartoris women's sense of it and that tradition's sense of Sartoris women. Of course, Narcissa survives the FBI agent's use of the letters as sexual capital: " 'And that's all. Men are all about the same, with their ideas of good and bad. Fools.' She breathed quietly. Then she yawned, deep, with utter relaxation" (741). More importantly, Narcissa seems to have resisted the insidious implication, generating much of the story's tension, that since the erotic letters are supposedly part of a criminal investigation they are therefore somehow criminal in themselves, thereby insinuating a type of criminality onto her inner life and onto female eroticism generally. In such a confusion, personal and policeable spaces and identities threaten to shift and blur dangerously, whereby the inner and imaginative space of female countersite is nearly pushed into a category with the criminal: superimposed and, since similarly socially unauthorized, seeming legitimately punishable. And such a reckless fusion between outer claims and inner imaginings would reductively return us to Aunt Jenny's social vision of horsewhipping for thinking: " 'thinking that way about me, unpunished.' "

Throughout the story, however, Narcissa the private reader has been at risk and not a vanished phantom writer.

Finally, Faulkner plays with these blurred and blurring notions of authorized and illicit spaces through his positioning of the FBI agent as both specialized law enforcer and likely sexual opportunist and blackmailer, as in fact a type of erotic plagiarist for using unethically and for his own purposes the writing of another.[17] But even in depicting this sudden appearance of ambiguous institutional force and demand, Faulkner's edgy story works to resist this constant fusion, imposition, and public expansion into the personal even as it chronicles its happening. Despite the multiple threats of such collapsings, the story may be read as a type of celebration, with Narcissa strong and astute enough to keep separate these eliding categories, despite an ongoing pressure that begins twelve years before with Snopes's erotic writings and their theft in *Flags in the Dust* and ends only here with their strange recovery in "There Was a Queen."

NOTES

1. For an interesting discussion of woman as screen "on which a man projects his fantasies," see Robin Sheets's summary of some of the problems posed by pornography as well as by many of the attempts to analyze it in "Pornography and Art: The Case of 'Jenny,' " *Critical Inquiry* 14:2 (Winter 1988): 318.

2. Melvin E. Bradford, "Certain Ladies of Quality: Faulkner's View of Women and the Evidence of 'There Was a Queen,' " *Arlington Quarterly* 1 (1967): 133.

3. William Faulkner, "There Was a Queen," *Collected Stories* (New York: Random House, 1950), 740. While Narcissa's further statement that " 'I asked him if he would make his final decision in Memphis and he said why Memphis and I told him why' " (741) would seem to fuel Bradford's assessment of her willful whoring, attention must also be given to the agent's dubious presence in Jefferson in the first place, his motives in contacting Narcissa, and, indeed, his willingness if not to manipulate, either directly or passively-aggressively, the exchange, then to agree to it. Moreover, the precarious social conditions swirling around the possible exposure of the letters sufficiently empties Narcissa's position of the brash and utilitarian agency with which Bradford wishes to read her. In fact, Faulkner's great irony in the story is that to preserve public standing, Narcissa has no choice but to prostitute herself privately: "I knew I couldn't buy them from him with money" (741). This hypocrisy, clearly, is not hers, but her society's.

4. Philip Castille, " 'There Was a Queen' and Faulkner's Narcissa Sartoris," *Mississippi Quarterly* 28:3 (Summer 1975): 308.

5. Ron Buchanan, " 'I Want You to Be Human': The Potential Sexuality of Narcissa Benbow," *Mississippi Quarterly* 41:3 (Summer 1988): 447.

6. Kathy Myers, "Towards a Feminist Erotica," in *Looking On: Images of Femininity in the Visual Arts and Media*, ed. Rosemary Betterton (London: Pandora, 1987), 195.

7. I am thinking most especially of Joanna Burden in *Light in August* and Joe

Christmas's trouble with negotiating female public and private identities in his near disbelief that the woman who is his "demon" lover at night goes briskly about her business in the day in what to him seems an endless procession of clean calico dresses. In this example, Faulkner pushes back on Christmas, and certainly onto male readers too, the social and sexual dichotomies often imposed on women.

8. In "Within the Plantation Household: Women in a Paternalist System," Elizabeth Fox-Genovese observes that in the antebellum South, in contrast to the North, "the household retained a vigor that permitted southerners to ascribe many matters—notably labor relations, but also important aspects of gender relations—to the private sphere. The household structure and social relations of southern society had multiple and far-reaching consequences for all spheres of southern life. And it had special consequences for gender relations in general and women's experience in particular." Fox-Genovese thereby observes an enforced and necessary continuum for Southern female space and experience operating between public and private identities and duties: "Effectively, the practical and ideological importance of the household in southern society reinforced gender constraints by ascribing all women to the domination of the male heads of households and to the company of the women of their households" (*Society and Culture in the Slave South*, ed. J. William Harris [London: Routledge, 1992], 50–51). Aunt Jenny's notion of female space would thus be markedly and historically different from Narcissa's, since the younger woman does not feel herself responsible for or constrained by the idea of the Southern household as a publicly political or extended economy.

9. The places Narcissa seeks to hide the letters—her purse, bra, and lingerie drawer—in *Flags in the Dust* suggest the scarcity of any private female space in her world. And, notably, two of these locations are on her person, while the third, by its intimate associations in a world so concerned with female propriety, can be seen as a close extension of her person.

10. Michel Foucault, "Of Other Spaces," trans. Jay Miskowiec, *Diacritics* 16 (1986): 24.

11. It is interesting that Foucault's examples of the mirror and honeymoon trip as countersites are also important aspects of Faulkner's story. Narcissa's name suggests the centrality of mirrors, of sites of self-regard, and while usually bearing negative connotations, the act of self-regarding (and so self-reconstituting) takes on positive and necessary meaning in Foucault's figuring of personal countersites. The idea of the honeymoon trip is central to "There Was a Queen" in that the theft of the letters—the shift from private space to the possibility of a public consumption—occurs just prior to Narcissa's and Bayard's honeymoon, thereby robbing Narcissa of the joy and security of that voyage into Foucauldian countersite with her husband. Here, as one of Narcissa's countersites is jeopardized—in the danger of the letters' going public—the other two of the garden and the honeymoon trip are also immediately put at risk. The letters further constitute "countersite" in that epistolary time is "other" time, a consensual present that signals and signifies across time and space, creating its own special temporal moments. For a detailed and provocative discussion of the presences and absences that letters—their writing and reading—create and destroy, see Eva Meyer, "Letters, or the Autobiography of Writing," *Discourse: A Journal for Theoretical Studies in Media and Culture* 10:1 (Fall/Winter 1987–88).

12. Susan Stewart has insightfully and energetically written on the problems of controlling, containing, and commenting on representations of sexuality by analyzing the Final Report of the 1986 Attorney General's Commission on Pornography: "The task of the Meese Commission is to define the forms of aberrant sexuality, to suggest means for the control of the field of representation, and to establish scenes . . . whose actuality and legitimacy are shaped in 'the real.' . . . Once again, therefore, the commission's task is the task of all pornography—to invent a realism that will convince us that our fantasies are inevitable and realizable" (*Crimes of Writing: Problems in the Containment of Representation* [New York: Oxford, 1991], 246).

13. As Susan Stewart points out, "We cannot transcend the pornography debate for we are in it. But by writing through it, by examining its assumptions, we can learn a

great deal about the problem of representing desire and the concomitant problems of a cultural desire for unmediated forms of representation" (236).

14. William Faulkner, *Flags in the Dust*, ed. Douglas Day (New York: Random House, 1974), 300.

15. Diane Roberts, "Ravished Belles: Stories of Rape and Resistance in *Flags in the Dust* and *Sanctuary*," *Faulkner Journal* 4:1 and 2 (Fall 1988/Spring 1989): 26.

16. Narcissa's break with tradition in naming her son Benbow, her maiden name, rather than John or Bayard in the longstanding Sartoris pattern, further demonstrates the movement towards a private mothering identity embraced off the grand stage of family identities enacted as public identities. The implication that Narcissa will be a different type of mother than the Sartoris women before her and therefore raise her son differently also indicates a hope for transformed masculine Sartoris identities realized through the expanding female personal space in the story.

17. The notion of the agent as an erotic plagiarist taking over the writing of another raises a number of interesting points in a story concerned about authority, legitimacy, and authorship. That the agent reads another man's erotic response to and imaginings of a particular woman and apparently becomes erotically moved enough by the image of this male-written representation of the woman to seek her out indicates some of the complications with representations of desire in the story and generally. The agent, in fact, would be responding erotically to another man's erotic response, that written representation. Faulkner thus portrays a layering of and exchange between two masculines before reaching even a dubiously possible feminine at the represented level, and here the questions of false conjurings, containment, and deferral in writing also become mixed up with homoerotic transfer.

Miss Rosa as *"Love's Androgynous Advocate"*: Gender and Narrative Indeterminacy in Chapter 5 of *Absalom, Absalom!*

ANDREA DIMINO

In describing the unique power of *Absalom, Absalom!*, often considered Faulkner's masterwork, critics have explored many facets of Faulkner's narrative, including voice and structuration. Philip M. Weinstein, for example, considers *Absalom, Absalom!* "the pivotal novel in Faulkner's career" in terms of establishing his "signature" voice.[1] For Stephen M. Ross, the novel's over-powering "plenitude of voice," its "highly charged oratorical style," is linked to the patriarch Thomas Sutpen.[2] Using Bakh-tinian terminology, Ross points to a "monological 'overvoice' " that overwhelms the individual differences between the novel's listeners, speakers, and events—the potential "dialogism" of a work of fiction (79). This overvoice is not literally Sutpen's, but is rather "a discursive re-presentation of Sutpen's symbolic role," his "authority as 'father' in the novel" (79–80).[3]

In the context of the "politics of narration," Richard Pearce also sees in *Absalom, Absalom!* a complex reaffirmation of the power of patriarchy:

> Sutpen's failure and the deauthorization of his story occur within the central, white male storyline, which turns black people and women into marginal characters, which persists despite Rosa's attempt to tell another story, and which must be told in the language of which Sutpen is the symbolic source. The discourse does contain the seeds of its own deauthorization, but it is nonethe-less capable of marginalizing and co-opting voices that oppose it.[4]

As critics continue to probe the ways in which gender informs Faulkner's work, however, some questions have been raised about the degree to which a patriarchal voice and storyline dominate *Absalom, Absalom!* Minrose Gwin, for example, asks whether Faulkner wishes to silence the voice of Rosa Coldfield in the novel, or whether, as a reflection of his artistic "bisexuality," he is "writing her silence as the hysterical symptom of the Old South's patriarchal narrative of mastery."[5] Robert Dale Parker is more willing than previous critics to advance strong claims on Miss Rosa's behalf:

> Rosa's voice gives *Absalom, Absalom!* so much of its sumptuous eloquence that, despite her lonely pitifulness, Rosa comes close to something like Faulkner's own fierce ideal, to the voice of *Absalom, Absalom!* itself. Critics often link Quentin's yearnings to Faulkner's own youthful angst. But Rosa is every bit as close as Quentin to Faulkner's novel-writing, language-fashioning self.[6]

In order to explore the challenge to patriarchy that Miss Rosa embodies in *Absalom, Absalom!*, it is necessary to complicate further an already complex subject. I want to argue in this essay that the character whom critics and readers call "Miss Rosa" is not actually a single entity; the conventional character in chapter 1 is transformed, in chapter 5, into an indeterminate narrative voice that spurs us to consider the degree to which gender is blurred and problematized in the novel. My use of the term "indeterminacy" follows Timothy Bahti's definition of indeterminacy as the undecidability of interpretation, which is linked to the lack of interpretive closure.[7]

I have chosen, then, to read chapter 5 "against the grain" of the current critical consensus. As we grapple with the novel's difficulty and with its exhilarating energy, we find that some narrative units or passages act as particular markers for the reader, signaling a need for active interpretation; Miss Rosa's second narrative, chapter 5, seems to me a unit that signals most urgently for special interpretive effort. We encounter in this chapter elements that are resistant to conventional interpretation to a degree that makes for a special openness of form, for a lack of closure in the reader's experience with the text.

As they construct a tentative model of narrative voice and structure, readers of *Absalom, Absalom!* quickly perceive that most of the story is told by male narrators: Miss Rosa narrates in chapter 1, Mr. Compson in 2–4, Quentin and Shreve in 6–9. At a point roughly midway in the novel, however, chapter 5 is set apart from the rest in a number of respects. Its main mark of difference is its orthography: the entire chapter, except for one page at the end, is set in italics.

We can start by asking some basic questions: who narrates chapter 5, and when, and where? The most obvious answer is that Miss Rosa Coldfield narrates in her house on a hot September afternoon in 1909. The chapter appears ostensibly in her voice, even though there are some significant changes in style, including vocabulary, structure, and rhythm, compared to chapter 1. If we consider that practically the entire chapter is set in italics, we might conclude, on the basis of Faulkner's use of this convention elsewhere in the novel, that we are hearing Miss Rosa's unspoken thoughts as she and Quentin sit together. The last page of the chapter, the only one *not* in italics, confirms this basic description. Since the chapter ends with Miss Rosa telling Quentin that something is hidden in the Sutpen house, the narration must be taking place in the afternoon. They go to the Sutpen house on the evening of the same day.

Quentin and Shreve's later use of some facts and turns of phrase from this chapter indicates that Miss Rosa must have said some of these words aloud during their long conversation, which lasts "from a little after two oclock until almost sundown."[8] But clearly the monologue is too impassioned, too sensuous, and too personal actually to have been spoken by a gentlewoman like Miss Rosa. Noting the "farfetched intensity and eloquence" of the chapter, Robert Dale Parker calls this "Rosa's unspeakable monologue, so as to indicate the abstract, impossible sense in which she speaks what cannot be spoken" (63). Since there are direct references to chapter 5 in Quentin and Shreve's collaboration in chapter 8, there is no doubt that some kind of oral narration has occurred.[9] But it is not too far-

fetched to assume that Quentin has intuited, or created, some
of the statements in Miss Rosa's monologue, since he treats the
Sutpen story in a similar fashion later in the novel, and since
the style of chapter 5 is similar enough to Quentin's style of
narration in later chapters. This new voice—an expansion and
blurring of Miss Rosa's identity—could be called "Miss Rosa" in
quotation marks, and I shall refer to the voice in this way.
(When I refer to Rosa as simply a character in the story, there
will be no quotation marks.) The novel's first chapter has already
told us that the voice of Miss Rosa is in a significant sense a part
of Quentin's consciousness: he is "not a being, an entity," but a
"commonwealth" (12).

I want to emphasize as well another important melding of
narrative voice that for many readers might go unnoticed: Miss
Rosa's key phrase in chapter 5, "*a summer of wistaria*," first
appears in the voice of Faulkner's third-person narrator at the
beginning of chapter 2: "It was a summer of wistaria. . . . The
twilight was full of it" (178, 34). We should consider, then, that
the third-person narrator is included in the complex dialogism
of chapter 5.[10] Robert Dale Parker's term "unspeakable monologue" also draws attention to the ways in which the chapter
insists on its identity as writing, stirring us to ask about the
connections between "Miss Rosa" and her creator. Though
Rosa's limitations as a character, her bitterness and frustration,
may distance us from her, the power of her voice in chapter 5
has given rise to new readings of *Absalom, Absalom!*

Finally, we can add the voice of the reader to this complex
dialogic interaction. In his suggestive discussion of reading as
performance, Warwick Wadlington stresses the mental (and
sometimes physical) "voicing" that takes place as readers enact
the text's multiple roles: "The model of the text I will propose
is that of a script or score to be performed by readers in an
enacted creation and regeneration of persons fundamental to
human being."[11] For Wadlington, reading is not simply a cognitive act, but is part of what we do in order to create ourselves,
to become persons within a particular culture. The concept of

voicing reminds us that Faulkner's texts recruit our bodies as well as our minds; the diversity of "gendered" bodies and cultural scripts that we as readers bring to a novel like *Absalom, Absalom!* compounds the elements of indeterminacy (Wadlington 44). We, too, are part of "Miss Rosa." In discussing the indeterminacy of "Miss Rosa's" voice, then, I have emphasized what Stephen M. Ross calls the *"principle* of dialogue" at work in the novel.[12] In spite of the tendency for the novel's driving rhetoric to override differences in narrative voice, the multiple genders of "Miss Rosa's" voice in chapter 5 evade the fixity of patriarchal naming. With textual elements that cannot be pinned down, with the voicing of countless readers, "Miss Rosa" is ever in flux.

If we do not consider chapters 1 and 5 separately, if we stop at the deduction that Miss Rosa narrates chapter 5 on the September afternoon in 1909 with some possible imaginative embellishment from Quentin or from the third-person narrator, we may be left with an interpretation that relegates Miss Rosa to her role as a flawed narrator of the Sutpen story. For some readers she remains in large part a gender stereotype, the frustrated spinster who turns Sutpen into a demon because she does not know some important humanizing facts about Charles Bon and about Sutpen's past. Moreover, as Donald Kartiganer suggests, her insistence on Sutpen's demonic quality justifies her estrangement from life, permitting her to remain frozen, a "crucified child" (*Absalom, Absalom!* 4).[13]

This view is compelling as a psychological portrait of the character Miss Rosa. But an important new perspective emerges when we highlight narrative voice and when we focus on the novel as, above all, a powerful meditation on the human experience of time. In the last analysis the novel's temporality is oriented toward the present, an orientation that makes it problematic to lump together chapters 1 and 5 as "Miss Rosa's narrative." In spite of the novel's obsession with the past, its suspended meanings, evasions, and omissions, *Absalom, Absalom!* plays out a compelling urge to actualize time in the present. In his major novels Faulkner consistently envisions this action as a communion or confrontation between self and other, almost always between a man and a woman or between two people (or, as in the case of "The Bear," two creatures) whose gender identities are undeveloped or ambiguous. In part by transforming narrative conventions, Faulkner spurs this hunt for the present in the reader, stimulating the necessity not just for active interpretation—an alertness toward, and an appreciation of, the novel's complexity—but for endless interpretation and rereading. For Faulkner's characters, the urge toward the present remains an imperative in spite of being all but impossible. Miss Rosa herself both longs for and fears such an actualization within chapter 5, as she reveals her abortive love for Charles Bon, whom she never even meets, and her troubled attachment to Sutpen, the man she thought she would marry. Once we conceive of "Miss Rosa's" voice as indeterminate, we can recognize how chapter 5 serves as the pivot of *Absalom, Absalom!*. The chapter provides a crucial transition between the passive and internally divided Quentin of chapters 1–4—the Quentin who simply parrots Miss Rosa's words in the novel's first italicized passage (5–6)—and the Quentin who eventually dares to re-create the Sutpen story with Shreve in the second half of the book. The chapter transforms Quentin into someone who can reshape the Sutpen story creatively, which is both a psychological breakthrough for Quentin and a process of historical transformation of the story. In an important sense, chapter 5 does not merely anticipate the achievements of Quentin and Shreve in their narrative collaboration; it makes the achievements possible. Exploding beyond the boundaries set by the previous chapters, chapter 5 breaks significant new ground in terms of the key themes, issues, and images of Quentin and Shreve's re-creation. In all of these instances, the blurring of gender identity plays a significant role.

Chapter 5 is self-reflexive in its insistence that human communication can take place in unconventional ways, and that voices are not "owned" by atomized individuals—a perception that Faulkner's readers can extend to the gender identity of narrative voices. When Miss Rosa confronts Clytie after Henry's murder of Charles, she *"cried—perhaps not aloud, not with words,"* and this may in fact be the way in which her chapter 5 monologue itself is communicated to Quentin (174). At the end of the confrontation, Rosa hears the word " *'Clytie,'* " and insists that it was *"the house itself speaking again, though it was Judith's voice"* (176).

There are also a few particularly striking uses of words in chapter 5 that set up strong resonances within the text and point to the possibility of shared narrative voices, to the novel's significant dialogism. It is "Miss Rosa," for example, who ostensibly introduces in chapter 5 the vivid word "meat," in the phrases *"the male-furrowed meat," "mammalian meat,"* and *"the ravening meat"* (181, 182, 204). At the very least this is an extremely incongruous word for a gentlewoman to use, and the sexual reference would be scandalous if it were spoken aloud. The word later appears, conspicuously, in Quentin and Shreve's narrative. As in chapter 5, it is found in an italicized passage representing a complex sharing of consciousness, in the phrase *"the old mindless sentient undreaming meat"*: the roommates are reliving Bon's announcement to Henry that he will try to marry Judith, and the word "meat" is later echoed by Henry when he speaks to Sutpen (436, 442).

As another example of shared vocabulary, "Miss Rosa" also speaks of the *"might-have-been which is the single rock we cling to above the maelstrom of unbearable reality"* (186). The image of the maelstrom is repeated strikingly in Quentin's recounting to Shreve, in chapter 7, of Sutpen's conversation with Grandfather Compson during the Civil War, when Sutpen is searching for the flaw in his design. The image seems to come from Quentin's grandfather; Sutpen rides away

> as if (Grandfather said) . . . even while riding he was still bemused in that state in which he struggled to hold clear and free above a maelstrom of unpredictable and unreasoning human beings, not his head for breath . . . but his code and logic of morality. (343–44)

If the image is in fact created by Quentin's grandfather, its appearance in chapter 5 suggests that Quentin's consciousness is indeed operating within "Miss Rosa's" monologue and that his voice has melded with hers.[14]

Up to now critics have tended to relegate "Miss Rosa's" narrative to a sealed compartment in the novel—a critical version of Miss Rosa's own claustrophobic *"corridor"* (179). In working toward a new sense of chapter 5 as a dynamic force in the novel's structure, we need to reconsider as well some of the chapter's strongest themes, which are vitally linked both to Quentin and Shreve's ability to collaborate and to some of the most important issues in the story they tell. As she describes her existence in a temporal limbo from her childhood to Sutpen's death, Miss Rosa returns with intense emotion to the question of human connections and alienation. Only once in her narrative does she experience a link that is intensely real: when Clytie's hand stops her from running to the room where Charles Bon lies dead, Miss Rosa feels a *"touch of flesh with flesh which abrogates, cuts sharp and straight across the devious intricate channels of decorous ordering. . . . let flesh touch with flesh, and watch the fall of all the eggshell shibboleth of caste and color too"* (173). The passage has important ramifications for the Sutpen story; this is, of course, the touch of flesh that Bon seeks from Sutpen and never receives, for Sutpen has patterned his design on an analogy with a system of landholding based on a particularly oppressive "decorous ordering" that includes strict boundaries of race and gender.[15] Unlike the character Miss Rosa in chapter 1, "Miss Rosa" is able to question the "decorous ordering" that constitutes Sutpen's patriarchal world. In such contexts as these, we are able to see the indeterminacy and blurring of gender in this voice as an element in a political struggle.

For Miss Rosa, however, the *"touch of flesh"* with Clytie brings not just a powerful reality but also the threat of an overpowering and troubling bond: Clytie's hand *"held us, like a fierce rigid umbilical cord, twin sistered to the fell darkness which had produced her"* (173). Both in the image of a sinister "umbilical" connection and in the reference to Sutpen (the *"fell darkness"*), this passage foreshadows Quentin's anguished perception in chapter 7 of Sutpen's primacy and of the burden of filiation, in a broad cultural sense as well as in the sense of family relationships (326). The reader perceives, as Miss Rosa does not, what a liberating transgression a "touch of flesh" with Clytie could represent—not only in transgressing boundaries of race and class, but also in asserting the value of bonds between women, relationships that are considered irrelevant by patriarchs like Sutpen.

It is Sutpen's furious dynastic design that ultimately denies Miss Rosa the supreme connection that she seeks, the connection to Charles Bon. After Henry Sutpen shoots Charles, she is forced to channel her being into a narrative that tells, among other things, of her belief in love and of her claim to the sexual *"urge"* that Charles's death has transformed into narrative desire (179). In a strangely ironic and blackly humorous way, the reading that I am proposing casts Miss Rosa in the role of what I would call (with tongue partly in cheek) a "heroine of narrative." I am referring, of course, to the character Miss Rosa created by the indeterminate voice I have called "Miss Rosa." Like other Faulkner characters she is part sublime poetry, part grotesque—as Minrose Gwin persuasively shows, with some of the attributes of a hysteric, but with an overtone of eloquence in her voice, and a vein of outrageous Faulknerian humor underlying her creation.[16] To see such a character as a "heroine of narrative," we need to examine a major theme in chapter 5, the transgression of gender boundaries. This transgression is significantly related to the chapter's other key themes: the creative transcendence of love, the possibility of change, and finally the assertion of creativity and autonomy.

The narration of chapter 5 reclaims for the Sutpen story the meanings that readers will find in a crucial episode of Miss Rosa's youth, her summer of wistaria. She lives out this summer *"not as a woman, a girl, but rather as the man which I perhaps should have been,"* becoming *"all polymath love's androgynous advocate"* (179, 182). Miss Rosa's transcending of gender boundaries reemerges later in the novel, just before the height of Quentin and Shreve's collaboration in narrating the story. At this point the roommates, too, are associated with shifts in gender and with virginity; they look at one another "almost as a youth and a very young girl might out of virginity itself" (374). The dissolving of gender boundaries involves two processes, connection and change, that are related in other ways to the poetic force of "Miss Rosa's" narrative voice and to Quentin and Shreve's achievement of narrative power. Uniting with the world in a *"living marriage,"* the adolescent Miss Rosa breaks out of her past existence in a womblike *"corridor";* the desire to narrate about love helps Quentin and Shreve bridge the cultural and psychological distances that separate them (179). These changes can occur because all three characters believe in what "Miss Rosa" calls *"a metabolism of the spirit as well as of the entrails, in which the stored accumulations of long time burn, generate, create and break some maidenhead of the ravening meat"* (204). In an important sense, Quentin and Shreve's narrative "novitiate" has included "Miss Rosa" as a mentor.

"Miss Rosa's" ultimate accomplishment, simply put, is the power to alter time through narrative. Faulkner's portrayal of this process highlights two aspects of her power at different times. The first aspect is a poetic vein of creativity linked to the imagining of Charles Bon's face; the second is the sheer power to control narrative by changing plots and by giving birth to—or killing—characters. The fact that Miss Rosa never actually sees Bon's face, but only a photograph, threatens to plunge her back into the shadowy unreality that marked her childhood; to a certain extent Miss Rosa shares Mr. Compson's frustration about abstractions or symbols that will not emerge, or cohere, in the world of flesh and blood, the world of the present. Rather than retreating to Mr. Compson's cynicism, however, Miss Rosa claims a prerogative—her own narrative power:

even before I saw the photograph I could have recognised, nay, described, the very face. But I never saw it. I do not even know of my own knowledge that Ellen ever saw it, that Judith ever loved it, that Henry slew it: so who will dispute me when I say, Why did I not invent, create it? (183)

Like Faulkner himself, who spoke of creating, "like God," "a cosmos of my own," "Miss Rosa" dares to think that *"if I were God"* she would invent Bon's face (183).[17] As I have noted, "Miss Rosa" has in a sense given up the love of Bon, and accepted instead the love of words, and the power of words to shape human experience.

If the poetic passage about Bon's face emphasizes both creativity and power, "Miss Rosa's" recounting of her actions after Bon's death recalls the crude power, described in strongly gendered terms, that she shares with some other female characters in Faulkner's works: women's power to wrench male narratives out of their linear path of chronology and causality, and their power to annihilate men's existences retroactively.[18] Together with Judith and Clytie, Miss Rosa insists on acting as if she still lived *"in that time which [Henry's] shot, those running mad feet, had put a period to and then obliterated, as though that afternoon had never been"* (196–97). The three women retroactively erase Henry's killing of Bon:

No, there had been no shot. That sound was merely the sharp and final clap-to of a door between us and all that was, all that might have been—a retroactive severance of the stream of event: a forever crystallized instant in imponderable time accomplished by three weak yet indomitable women which, preceding the accomplished fact which we declined, refused, robbed the brother of the prey, reft the murderer of a victim for his very bullet. (197)

The power that Miss Rosa assumes—to disrupt the *"stream of event"*—is analogous to the reader's power to reshape infinitely, through the operation of memory and anticipation, interpretive focus, and heightened attention, the linear "stream" of fictional narratives as well. If we concentrate on this shaping power, we see that chapter 5 is not superseded by the subsequent narrative that Quentin and Shreve create; it transforms and is transformed by what comes after. As long as the reader seeks to reanimate the voice of "Miss Rosa," the voice has not been silenced.

Unlike Miss Rosa's narrative of Sutpen as demon in chapter 1, which is in large part superseded by later constructions of the Sutpen story, the insights of chapter 5 crystallize truths about Miss Rosa's life whose particular kind of intensity makes them, in a sense, timeless. By the time Quentin and Shreve's narrative collaboration begins, in chapter 6, Miss Rosa herself has, to use Faulkner's repeated phrase, "vanished" into death. Yet the content of chapter 5, torn loose from its moorings in chronology, remains as a dynamic legacy on which Quentin and Shreve can draw. It represents the part of Miss Rosa that can most connect with other people, that reaches beyond the bounds of her own identity and of her finite existence in time.

The indeterminate voice and italic form of chapter 5 thus foreshadow in an important way the changing relation between Quentin and Shreve at the height of their narrative collaboration in chapter 8, where the narrator "might have been either of them and was in a sense both: both thinking as one, the voice which happened to be speaking the thought only the thinking become audible, vocal" (378). At the climax of the collaboration the narrative shifts to italics, for the roommates have entered the story in Carolina 46 years earlier; both of them take on the existences of both Henry Sutpen and Bon, "compounded each of both yet either neither" (439).[19] In forging their narrative coalition, Quentin and Shreve have retreated from what Judith Butler would call "identity politics," based on a reification of identity.[20] As they move through the narrative they now bring into play a "variable construction of identity" that includes even a shift in gender (Butler 5).

Thus the blurring of gender and the indeterminacy of "Miss Rosa's" voice work to energize two key aspects of *Absalom, Absalom!:* the narrators' struggle for creative freedom and the related struggle with Sutpen as the symbol of patriarchal power. Chapter 5 challenges the particular mode of existence that

Thomas Sutpen seeks to impose on his family and on his descendants, a patriarchal mode that decrees a certain model of human identity. This challenge helps to alter the way we conceive of the writing and reading of fiction, and is also significantly related to Faulkner's depiction of psychological and social issues. Sutpen's patriarchal design—itself an imitation of a conventional planter's life—requires subsequent generations to repeat the experience of an earlier model, Sutpen himself. It also polarizes the world by race and gender, so that Charles Bon and Milly Jones's female baby (Sutpen's illegitimate daughter) must be excluded from the design.

In contrast, chapter 5 uncovers the creative possibilities of Miss Rosa's otherwise *"barren"* youth, overcoming the sentimentality of phrases like the *"short brief unreturning springtime of the female heart"* (179). This youthful possibility links her to the Shreve and Quentin of chapter 8, whose "heart and blood of youth" enable them to overcome the barriers between them—"not individuals now yet something both more and less than twins" (367)—and to enter into the lives of Henry and Charles. Affiliation, not exclusion, is the social mode of "Miss Rosa's" chapter 5.[21]

Instead of enduring what she describes as the ghostly heterosexual marriage of patriarchy, Miss Rosa inhabits, as I have noted, *"a world filled with living marriage like the light and air which she breathes"* (180). This "living marriage" anticipates the famous phrase in chapter 8, the "happy marriage of speaking and hearing" that crowns Quentin's collaboration with Shreve, a marriage that enables them to move freely in the Sutpen story (395). The marriage thus crystallizes an attitude diametrically opposed to Sutpen's rigid search for the fault in his design and to Sutpen's arrogant proposal of marriage to Miss Rosa, *"a decree . . . like a sentence . . . not to be spoken and heard but to be read carved in the bland stone which pediments a forgotten and nameless effigy"* (205). The image of the stone carving contrasts, moreover, Sutpen's rigid mode of existence and rigid use of language to Faulkner's concern about liberating modes of writing.

Finally, the blurring of gender and "Miss Rosa's" indeterminate voice have important consequences for narrative structuration. These elements help to trigger the novel's most dynamic and most radical destabilizing of form. To use Robert Dale Parker's wonderful phrase, applied to a different part of the novel, chapter 5 becomes an "unidentified flying narrative" (149). For the indeterminacy of "Miss Rosa's" chapter works strongly as an antilinear and "antisequential" force, allowing the reader to be "lost" in the text—or as "Rosa" herself puts it, to sever or disrupt the narrative's *"stream of event."* To "privilege" the end of the book is to follow an established cultural pattern, a convention of reading: such a path would lead us to focus on Quentin, and to a lesser extent on Shreve, in our summation of the novel's meaning.[22] But we can make the interpretive—and political—decision not to close off our engagement with the book when we reach the last line. Chapter 5 endlessly problematizes our shaping of *Absalom, Absalom!,* drawing us back into the text, inviting us to question rigid conceptions of gender and of identity, and to join our voices to the "Miss Rosa" who speaks of the *"metabolism of the spirit."*

NOTES

1. Philip M. Weinstein, *Faulkner's Subject: A Cosmos No One Owns* (New York: Cambridge University Press, 1992), 141.

2. Stephen M. Ross, "Oratory and the Dialogical in *Absalom, Absalom!,*" in *Intertextuality in Faulkner,* ed. Michel Gresset and Noel Polk (Jackson: University Press of Mississippi, 1985), 79; hereafter cited in the text.

3. In Bakhtin's view, the dialogism of a work of fiction stems from the social nature of language itself. There is "within the arena of almost every utterance an intense interaction and struggle between one's own and another's word . . . a process in which they oppose or dialogically interanimate each other" ("Discourse in the Novel," in *The Dialogic Imagination,* ed. Michael Holquist [Austin: University of Texas Press, 1981], 354). Since every word that an individual may use is already shot through with a complex history of social interactions, all utterances have the potential of blurring the distinction between self and other: "As a living, socio-ideological concrete thing, . . . language, for the individual consciousness, lies on the borderline between oneself and the other. The word in language is half someone else's" (293). At least potentially, then, language may be instrumental in problematizing or blurring gender distinctions within a patriarchal system.

4. Richard Pearce, *The Politics of Narration: James Joyce, William Faulkner, and Virginia Woolf* (New Brunswick: Rutgers University Press, 1991), 124.

5. *The Feminine and Faulkner: Reading (Beyond) Sexual Difference* (Knoxville: University of Tennessee Press, 1990), 71.

6. Robert Dale Parker, *"Absalom, Absalom!": The Questioning of Fictions* (Boston: Twayne Publishers, 1991), 22–23; hereafter cited in the text.

7. Bahti, "Ambiguity and Indeterminacy: The Juncture," *Comparative Literature* 38, 3 (Summer 1986): 209–23. Bahti's essay provides a useful perspective on contemporary theories of ambiguity and indeterminacy, treating such figures as Cleanth Brooks, Abrams, Empson, Culler, Rimmon-Kenan, Miller, Altieri, Ingarden, Jauss, Iser, de Man, and Hartman.

8. *Absalom, Absalom!, The Corrected Text* (New York: Vintage, 1987), 3; hereafter cited in the text.

9. When she goes to the Sutpen house after the murder of Bon, Miss Rosa feels that she must find a scene of mourning, *"else breathing and standing there, I would have denied that I was ever born"* (171). In chapter 8 Shreve envisions Eulalia Bon believing implicitly that her day of revenge against Sutpen " 'would have to arrive or else she would have to do like the Aunt Rosa and deny that she had ever breathed' " (370). Miss Rosa also speaks of *"a might-have-been which is more true than truth"* (178; see also 186); Shreve refers to " 'what the old Aunt Rosa told you about some things that just have to be whether they are or not' " (406).

10. Some similarities in the creation of metaphors also suggest that the voice of the third-person narrator penetrates and helps to meld the voices of the other narrators. For example, in chapter 5 "Miss Rosa" describes her love for Charles Bon—which she gives as a gift to Judith—in terms of a sudden sprouting: " 'there may come some moment in your married lives when he will find this atom's particle as you might find a cramped small pallid hidden shoot in a familiar flower bed' " (185). In another italicized passage in chapter 7, Quentin remembers—and possibly reproduces—a past narration of Mr. Compson's that describes Sutpen's shrewdness as *"suddenly sprouting and flowering like a seed lain fallow in a vacuum or in a single iron clod"* (347).

11. Warwick Wadlington, *Reading Faulknerian Tragedy* (Ithaca, New York: Cornell University Press, 1987), 28.

12. For Ross's treatment of "dialogical scenes," see 82–85.

13. Donald Kartiganer, *The Fragile Thread: The Meaning of Form in Faulkner's Novels* (Amherst: University of Massachusetts Press, 1979), 73–76.

14. The word "maelstrom" is also spoken by Mr. Compson in the third-person narrator's account in chapter 6 of Quentin's visit to the Sutpen graveyard with his father in the past. Mr. Compson describes Charles Etienne Bon's fury in terms of the reaction of Bon's wife, who is dragged through a " 'maelstrom of faces and bodies' " (258). This reinforces the word's links with the Compson family and brings the third-person narrator into the equation as well.

15. Bon thinks, " '*I will just touch flesh with him*' " (435). In chapter 7 Quentin describes Sutpen's shock when he first encounters such "ordering," arriving in a " 'country all divided and fixed and neat with a people living on it all divided and fixed and neat because of what color their skins happened to be and what they happened to own' " (276).

16. It is essential not to lose sight of this vein of humor in coming to terms with chapter 5. The flamboyant and playful exaggeration of "Miss Rosa's" voice simultaneously creates and parodies the celebrated Faulknerian "voice" of his major period. For an influential discussion of the role of parody as an agent of the dialogic, see Mikhail Bakhtin, "Discourse in the Novel," 271–75.

17. Interview with Jean Stein vanden Heuvel, *Lion in the Garden: Interviews with William Faulkner*, ed. James B. Meriwether and Michael Millgate (Lincoln: University of Nebraska Press, 1980), 255.

18. I discuss this topic in detail in "From Goddess to 'Galmeat': Narrative Politics and Narrative Desire in Faulkner's Novels," *Faulkner Journal*, forthcoming. For

example, in *The Hamlet* Eula Varner's sexual magnetism deflects the schoolteacher Labove's linear road to a law career (New York: Random House, Vintage International, 1991). Eula causes the entire narration of Labove's life to repeat itself, since the first version had omitted mentioning her power over him ("Eula," Chapter 1, 1, 105–40). Eula also annihilates Flem Snopes's existence retroactively when she is oblivious to him (163). Similarly, in *Light in August* Lena Grove interrupts the linearity of Byron Bunch's predictable and well-ordered life.

19. See Robert Dale Parker's treatment of the relation of italics to the merging of identities and to "perspectiveless explanation" in chapter 8 (*Questioning* 145–52).

20. See Judith Butler, *Gender Trouble: Feminism and the Subversion of Identity* (New York: Routledge, 1990), 4; hereafter cited in the text.

21. I argue elsewhere that this chapter helps us to perceive a "counterfamily" in *Absalom, Absalom!* Along with a number of the novel's characters, "Miss Rosa's" multiple voices fuel an antipatriarchal design that "is engaged in erasing the name of the father as its origin and center of power, substituting instead a complex series of fluid, dynamic, and temporary coalitions. In spite of the fact that many of its members also belong to the first Sutpen family, the counterfamily transgresses patriarchal boundaries and creates new forms of human affiliation"; see "Fathers and Strangers: From Patriarchy to Counterfamily in Faulkner's *Absalom, Absalom!*," in *Critical Essays on William Faulkner: The Sutpen Family*, ed. Arthur F. Kinney (Boston: G. K. Hall, 1996).

22. As a related example, in an essay that describes Miss Rosa as a "striking exemplar of [Lacanian] 'desire' " who links "narrative and loss," Deborah Garfield closes her argument with a scene that Quentin imagines at the end of the novel: Rosa goes to the Sutpen house to fetch Henry in December 1909, and Clytie burns the mansion down ("To Love as 'Fiery Ancients' Would: Eros, Narrative and Rosa Coldfield in *Absalom, Absalom!*," *Southern Literary Journal* 22, 1 [Fall 1989]: 69). For Garfield, drawing on the work of Roland Barthes, "Rosa has at last become one of the text's 'enemies,' consenting to the 'destruction of discourse,' the 'loss of verbal desire' "; she has chosen "the exclusive tyranny of closure over the dialectic between deferral and consummation which dominates her narrative and actions" (77). This is an intriguing view of the character Miss Rosa; but, as I have argued, chapter 5's "Miss Rosa" works against this kind of narrative closure.

Faulkner's "Greek Amphora Priestess": Verbena and Violence in *The Unvanquished*

PATRICIA YAEGER

In a recent article in the *New York Times* entitled "That Scitex Glow" we finally learned the glamour secret of the '90s. Someone has cracked the conundrum of how to take female beauty to the "next dimension." With the help of Scitex, a new computer retouching system, the terrible beauty of the fashion model can be changed so that her body surpasses perfection. "The skin is hairless and flawless. The whites of the eyes have the smooth finish of the inside of a robin's egg." Until recently the techniques for retouching were reserved for a few fashion photos: only the cover shot and a limited number of choice pictures "got the treatment." But with the revolution in computer technology the monolithic space of the female face can be fractured at will, broken into millions of microscopic squares called pixels, tiny fragments of the body that can be moved about at will. As the *Times* reporter explains, every published photograph can now be retouched; our flesh beguiled by

> image after image of young women with skin like milk, women without veins—anywhere—women whose underarms have never known hair. Their eyes are curiously flat because the sockets cast no shadows. And although sometimes the models are sitting with legs splayed, there is no dark between those limbs, no hint of (God forbid!) pubic hair. The poses may be suggestive, but they are sexless. The models do not seem to have gone through puberty. They are babies with breasts, so pure that they almost blend into the page until they are invisible and only their shining infant eyes

remain. It isn't until we come to a photo of a man in an ad for sunglasses that I realize all that's missing. "Look what men get away with!" says Lucy. There's stubble on his chin, a scar on his eyebrow, and although he's not old, there are lines. This flesh has moved. This face has a history.[1]

In Scitexized bodies what gets erased is not only the body's individuality and iconoclasm, but the body's experience: its connection to institutional power and to the chaos and unpredictability of the past. Composed from the lineaments of history, the male model's face has mobility, as if men's actions were the source of their power. But the Scitexized female body loses the impact of the political; Scitex eviscerates the way that the body is marked by the world and has the capacity to mark the world in return. Despite its baby doll smile, the Scitex face offers a secret turn on an aesthetics of torture—the female body cut apart and reassembled, its veins slashed, eyes flattened, sexuality gutted—with no afterimage, birthmark, historical signifier, or political referent announcing the defacement of the newborn (or never-born) female body in pain.

In this essay I want to ask how women's bodies can enter history, and how this entry might change both the body and the physical world. The surprise is that for the Southern heroines we'll encounter in this essay, entry into the historical world (the world of civic politics and flamboyant public action) demands the excision of beauty; history is made by grotesque female bodies that are scarred, marred, or mangled by their environments. The body that is excessive and risks a bizarre grandiosity—the hybrid body that blends dissimilar families or species—creates a voluptuous and disturbing category confusion; it mimics the prowess of the postmodern male model's invaluable flaws. Possessing stubble, scars, and creases becomes, in the glossy world of today's media imaging, the simulacrum for life lived in the public world. But if inhabiting the grotesque body is, for men, an index or antechamber to a life of significant action, for the irregular and powerfully blemished women who occupy Southern fictions grotesqueness may mean access to power, but inhabiting a marked body is also a sure path to social death: to ostracism, psychic exile, and sexual segregation.

Before turning to the grotesque characters who enact these dramas in William Faulkner's *The Unvanquished* we need to ask: what are the parameters of the grotesque body and why does it behave so powerfully? In Faulkner's *The Wild Palms*, in the scene where Wilbourne drifts precariously among "organless" mannequins while Charlotte decorates holiday windows for a Chicago department store, we find an uncanny example:

> He would have an evening paper and now for the next two or three hours he would sit on fragile chairs surrounded by jointless figures with suave organless bodies and serene almost incredible faces, by draped brocade and sequins or the glitter of rhinestones, while charwomen appeared on their knees and pushing pails before them as though they were another species just crawled molelike from some tunnel or orifice leading from the foundations of the earth itself and serving some obscure principle of sanitation, not to the hushed glitter which they did not even look at but to the subterranean region which they would crawl back to before light. [2]

Terry Eagleton defines the grotesque as a signifier that is "intrinsically double-faced, an immense semiotic switchboard through which codes are read backwards and messages scrambled into their antitheses." [3] In Faulkner's text the glittery codes of smooth, unblemished mannequin bodies are scrambled or read backwards through the oracular lowness of charwomen whose bodies are the quintessence of the grotesque. Low, earthy, menial, other: the eruption of these half-mole, half-human forms politicizes this passage, reminding the reader of everything the sanitized bourgeois code omits—namely, that the unblemished bodies carrying the dreams of high bourgeois life are always uplifted by working class women, capital's invisible laborers. Their blasphemous labor supports the smooth secrets of commodity fetishism—until the invisible bodies of these charwomen emerge from their hiding places to enact a swift mapping of economic power.

To see the grotesque as a "semiotic switchboard," a site

where background information is pushed into the foreground of readerly consciousness, suggests that the maimed, excessive, inordinate bodies that populate Southern fiction can also become a primary locus for reading the social, a place where the work of the body politic shines through the physical body. I'm suggesting a revisionary reading of the used-up trope of the Southern grotesque in which the grotesque body becomes a place for imaging the ways in which society superimposes itself upon bodies: carves itself into—and out of—human flesh. In forcing readers to confront subterranean class, race, or gender struggles, the grotesque mobilizes the pain of classificatory schemes that "function below the level of consciousness," moving what is out of sight into bodily cognizance.[4]

This works with extraordinary power in Charles Chesnutt's "Po' Sandy," a tale from his 1899 volume, *The Conjure Woman*. In this story a man's body is chopped to pieces and carved into an unexpected shape. Sandy's torn flesh is literally Scitexized; incorporated into the walls and floorboards of a plantation kitchen, his sinews lend strength to the foundations of antebellum history.

Sandy begins life as a "monst'us good" slave who is so hardworking that plantation owners come from miles around to purchase his bodily labor.[5] In this landscape of migrancy Sandy's master dispatches his prize slave on another Herculean errand, then sells Sandy's first wife and casually buys him another. Within this story's magical world the new couple ward off anxiety by falling in love until, by and by, Sandy is forced to go off-plantation again. As luck would have it, Tenie, Sandy's new wife, is also a conjure woman. To keep him from wandering she roots Sandy to the earth: " 'I kin turn you ter a tree,' sez Tenie. 'You won't hab no mouf ner years, but I kin turn you back oncet in a w'ile, so you kin git sump'n ter eat, en hear w'at's gwine on.' "(47). In Tenie's words the symbolic features of the grotesque body come to life. The political and sensual penury of Sandy's fate—his lack of voice, loss of control, and denial of human dignity—is mirrored in his newly hybridized body; he becomes a tree-man lacking hearing and vision. But Chesnutt uses Sandy's blindness to sharpen the reader's insight. In the next scene his master decides that this strong young tree will make a wonderful cookhouse. Here the tale told by the grotesque body becomes almost unbearable. As Tenie runs into the woods to see how Sandy is doing, she discovers his splintered remains: "W'en she seed de stump standin' dere, wid de sap running' out'n it, en de limbs layin' scattered roun', she nigh 'bout went out'n her min'. She run ter her cabin, en got her goopher mixtry, en den follered de tracker de timber waggin ter de sawmill. She knowed Sandy could n'lib mo'd'n a minute er so ef she turnt him back, fer he wuz all chop' up so he' da' be'n bleedst ter die. But she wanted ter turn 'im back long ernuff fer ter 'splain ter 'im dat she had n' went off a-purpose, en lef 'im ter be chop' down en sawed up. She did n' want Sandy ter die wid no hard feelin's to'ds her" (54). This sawed-up body, this marred, scarred, never-to-be-finished man-corpse-kitchen-tree, offers a violent semiosis. The historical world shaping this narrative literally turns the body inside out, killing Sandy while allowing us to read his entrails: to intuit the history of the outside world from the ruination of the inside. This open body doesn't take us toward the expected literary site of the grotesque, toward the merry subversions of carnival, but offers a peculiar window on the murderous, distorting power of a malign social order.

And herein lies the discomforting power of the Southern grotesque. For the foremost theorist of grotesque realism, Mikhail Bakhtin, even the ugliest grotesque is "gay and gracious," the bodily element "deeply positive." The stigmatized bodies of Bakhtin's carnival point of fertility, growth, abundance; degradation is the prelude to regeneration.[6] But the grotesques of Southern fiction suggest another politics altogether. Here the body's open orifices, its exaggeration and degradation, insist on a world of social violence in which terrible things happen to the body's boundaries. In Katherine Anne Porter's "The Witness" a former slave named Uncle Jimbilly becomes so grotesque through forced labor that "he was almost bent double. His hands were closed and stiff from gripping objects tightly . . . and they could not open altogether even if a child took the thick black fingers and tried to turn them back."[7] While Bakhtin stresses those inner parts of the body that are open to the outside world of growth and becoming, the gnarling of the Southern grotesque offers, instead, a regional index for measuring the intrusions of this world and its aggressions.

Faulkner's fiction has been praised in Bakhtinian terms for its organicism, its sprawling portrayal of the growth and becoming of Yoknapatawpha's colossal world. In the words of Malcolm Cowley: "each novel, each long or short story, seems . . . to have a subject bigger than itself. All the separate works . . . are like wooden planks that were cut, not from a log, but from a still living tree. The planks are planed and chiseled into their final shapes, but the tree itself heals over the wound and continues to grow."[8] But Chesnutt's story about a black man whose branches become the walls of someone else's history suggests the continued need to disturb this complacency, to displace critical celebrations of Faulkner's fictive largesse with another portrait in which we reenvision his grotesques as images that *lack* curative power, that helplessly and deliberately reopen the old wounds of a destructive body politic and prevent their healing over.

This means that the grotesque bodies in Southern fiction can evoke the corporeal attributes of giving testimony, of bearing witness to trauma. "The specific task of the literary testimony," Shoshana Felman argues, "is . . . to open up in that belated witness, which the reader now historically becomes, *the imaginative capability of perceiving history—what is happening to others—in one's own body,* with the power of sight (of insight) usually afforded only by one's own immediate physical involvement."[9] I want to explore the peculiar power of witnessing inherent in the Southern grotesque: the possibility that instead of offering the repetition of a degraded form, the mark of Southern degeneracy, this obsessive Southern trope provides an incredible mimetic device—a way of transferring history from the other "to one's own body." I will also suggest the ways in which Faulkner both enacts and evades this trope's critical power. Scitex and its photogenic lesions become an unexpected metaphor for the gender trauma at the heart of *The Unvanquished*.

How does a grotesque character like Drusilla Hawk, the heroine who dominates the last stories in *The Unvanquished*, transfer the weight of history from Faulkner's story to the reader's body? With her bloodlust and belief in the hyperscript of Southern honor, can she reliably bear witness to other people's traumas? To answer, we will need to explore two tendencies in Faulkner criticism—first, the inclination to dismiss *The Unvanquished* because it is neither a fiction at the pinnacle of Faulkner's design nor his most vigorous work. Not only is *The Unvanquished* lauded as slight Faulknerian fare, but critics remind us that this collection of stories is drab meat-and-potatoes writing of the *Scribner's/Saturday Evening Post* variety. Or, as Eric Sundquist argues in *Faulkner: The House Divided, The Unvanquished* is merely an "addendum to *Sartoris* primarily of veiled autobiographical interest."[10]

Indeed *The Unvanquished* is a tale half mutilated by the clichés of Confederate romance, as if in inventing a bildungsroman about the adolescence of the New Southern Man, Faulkner feels compelled to indulge in juvenile scenarios. The story opens with a disturbing portrait of two children who fire on the oncoming federal army and then scurry into hiding under Granny's skirts. The boys, Bayard and Ringo, connive against an entire army but cannot avoid a grandmother's wrath; their mouths are washed out with soap for minor blasphemy. On the road again, Bayard's swashbuckling father routs a passel of Yankees; meanwhile Granny and Ringo cook up a scheme to steal livestock and sell it back to the Yankees—not just once, but again and again. A generous schemer, Granny shares her pot of gold with poor local farmers, until she is killed by a renegade soldier.

In the midst of this romantic soup Faulkner forges an uneven story about black emancipation. At first Loosh, Ringo's uncle, enters *The Unvanquished* as an African American fall guy, providing a gloomy background for the Sartorises' heroics.[11] And yet Faulkner also recasts Loosh as critic of the very tropes of inertness or darkness that *The Unvanquished* employs to describe African Americans:

> "Loosh," Granny said, "are you going too?"
> "Yes," Loosh said, "I going. I done been freed; God's own angel proclamated me free and gonter general me to Jordan. I don't belong to John Sartoris now; I belongs to me and God."
> "But the silver belongs to John Sartoris," Granny said. "Who are you to give it away?"
> "You ax me that?" Loosh said. "Where John Sartoris? Whyn't he come and ax me that? Let God ax John Sartoris who the man name that give me to him. Let the man that buried me in the black dark ax that of the man what dug me free." He wasn't looking at us; I don't think he could even see us. He went on.[12]

Loosh's critique of the politics of blackness lasts but a moment. And yet his implosive insight suggests the cacophony of whiteness that *The Unvanquished* simultaneously explores and tries to ward off. At first Ringo, the slave child, and Bayard, the juvenile aristocrat, seem indistinguishable from one another; they are equally passionate about routing Yankees and equally bent on achieving emancipation. By invoking a child's confused politics as the deep background to this story—a politics in which the concepts of liberty, equality, and emancipation have a sudden potential to swing free of a propertied metaphysic— Faulkner is playing with fire.[13] But this hopefulness is always tempered by the story's dehumanization of the Africanist masses: "They were not singing yet, they were just hurrying, while our horses pushed slow through them, among the blank eyes not looking at anything out of faces caked with dust and sweat, breasting slowly and terrifically through them as if we were driving in midstream up a creek full of floating logs and the dust and the smell of them everywhere" (117). Although scholars have suggested the relative stability of slave populations at the end of the war, Faulkner depicts a migration of Biblical proportions: a set worthy of Cecil B. DeMille. The text seems to inhabit two places at once. That is, while the freedmen are cast as flotsam and jetsam to give the story an epic undertow, a gargantuan cast, these floating masses also offer a human backdrop for deriding the shallowness of Granny's quest for lost family silver. Riding helplessly over these "blank-eyed" bodies and snapping their bones, Granny ignores their plight and cries out for her property. The surprise of *The Unvanquished* is that Faulkner soon follows suit; he pursues the trail of still salable commodities, abandoning this tumultuous river of grief to follow Granny's fetishes.

Where Sundquist finds a failed narrative or autobiographical addendum in these nostalgia-fed stories, my preference is to describe *The Unvanquished* as a story in painful process, as a series of half-made maps that point toward an encrypted Southern world. Faulkner's story is struggling not only to be popular—it also struggles with a buried ethic, trying hard *not to know* what it knows, struggling *not to explore* the connections among gender, race, emancipation, and lost property that flood its most superficial plot lines. This suggests another route for exploring *The Unvanquished*, one that follows Toni Morrison's analysis of the complexity of any act of literary "failure"; her conviction that a failed text, even one that looks like an "addendum," may be encountering material it cannot control, trying simultaneously to address and to avoid topics buried, distorted, or sociologically askew within a region's political unconscious.

Not surprisingly, *The Unvanquished* is obsessed with burial—with the war's uncivil crypts. On the night his father comes home to tell the story of Vicksburg, Bayard is banished to his room but remains on the stairs listening to his father's tales, waking to dream again: "I was telling myself, 'They have already carried it out, they are in the orchard now, digging.' Because there is that point at which credulity declines; somewhere between waking and sleeping I believed I saw or I dreamed that

I did see the lantern in the orchard, under the apple trees"
(20–21). The buried object may be the family silver, but the
referent is also more elusive; the scene conjures up Loosh,
buried in the "black dark" of the Sartoris plantations, as well as
the defeated South, the already lost cause that is evoked once
again in the repulsive, elegiac portrait of Granny's grave—
draped with the amputated hand of the man who killed her. As
Morrison says in her analysis of another racially charged "failure," *Sapphira and the Slave Girl:* "Consider the pressures
exerted by the subject: the need to portray the faithful slave;
the compelling attraction of exploring the possibilities of one
woman's absolute power over the body of another woman . . .
the need to make credible the bottomless devotion of the person
on whom Sapphira is totally dependent. . . . These fictional
demands stretch to breaking all narrative coherence." Morrison
suggests that such disruptions occur when texts work unevenly
to repress "the bizarre and disturbing deformations of reality
that normally lie mute in novels containing Africanist characters" (23). I will argue that *The Unvanquished* is caught in just
such a melancholy bind, but that Faulkner finds a site for
communicating and containing this melancholy. He manipulates
the character of Drusilla Hawk—the increasingly grotesque site
of a white woman's body—to discharge this imponderable
tension.

In order to recover Drusilla's bizarre role in this novel, her
metamorphosis from androgynous warrior to "Greek amphora
priestess"—a vessel ritualizing and containing regional
trauma—we need to encounter a second tendency in criticism
of *The Unvanquished*. Critics who admire the novel's adventure-
someness often dismiss Drusilla's value as female protagonist.
She is described as a character warped, "embittered," "unsexed" who refuses "her proper nature and function."[14] Instead
of representing (as does her idealized, womanly companion,
Miss Jenny) "the nurturing and sustaining force on which a
society rests" (99), for Cleanth Brooks Drusilla's aristocratic
goodness is forever "perverted: she is dauntless, but in her

worship of honor and courage, she has forgotten pity, compassion, and even her womanhood. She is willing to send her stepson to his probable death . . . because she is utterly fascinated by some abstract conception of masculine honor."[15] True enough. But by focusing on the complex political fictions driving Drusilla's perversions, I will argue that Brooks is wrong to see her eccentricities as simply character driven. Drusilla is not only a magnificent heroine who refuses the confines of the moonlight-and-magnolia plot by swaggering onto the battlefields of a terrible war, but her grotesque ambivalence dislocates, deracinates, and questions the ordinary lacerations of gender. Drusilla plays a curious role in this narrative. At first she is a storyteller and soldier—someone hungry for a life of significant action who also possesses a talent for changing roles. But by the last story this role subsides and her body becomes a screen or symbol for the text's unresolved political issues. Like other women, both real and imagined, Drusilla's body becomes a "battlefield on which quite other struggles than women's own have been waged."[16] Drusilla may adopt the bloodlust and rapacity, the power for hunger, of an unreconstructed Southern world. But her body does not explode of its own accord; she becomes a site of transference for the most clichéd and intractable of her society's desires. She becomes, then, a somatic battlefield for the race and class struggles that mark Faulkner's understanding of the postbellum South. Caught in a tragic role in this ultimately romantic and comedic novel, she pays for these displacements with her sanity.

To rethink Drusilla's body in this epic way—as a battlefield for the derangements of local and national politics—suggests the need for a revised historicism, for fresh ways of approaching the body's relation to history. In his essay on Nietzsche and genealogy Foucault insists that historians need a new bodily vernacular. The body can no longer be scripted as a discrete personal entity; it is radically charged and reshaped—marked by its historical world. Transmuted by time, the body is a site inscribed by the "surface of events," a "volume in perpetual disintegration." For Foucault genealogy's new task "is to expose a body totally imprinted by history and the process of history's destruction of the body."[17]

How is it that Drusilla's disintegration, her "forgetting of womanhood," can also represent this lethal imprinting? Or, to ask the question another way, by focusing on Drusilla's disintegration, what will we learn about the body politics of Southern history? I will argue that Drusilla's body becomes a surface for exploding the most tragic narratives of Reconstruction, so that what is literally tattooed upon her flesh in "An Odor of Verbena" is the acrid death, the unremitting fragrance of assassinated carpetbaggers, African American apartheid, and lost voting rights.

Although feminist criticism has developed a set of categories to interrogate the interconnectedness of race and gender, to explore the ways in which diverse cultural categories get condensed or displaced onto one another, and although my initial examples of Southern grotesques have focused on the South's racial boundaries, the scope of this argument (this placing of epochal history upon a minor female character) surprises even me. To make Drusilla's body into a weighty synecdoche, to argue that her frame becomes a cipher for everything wrong with the postbellum South—this is not the argument I'd expected to make when I began writing this essay. Instead, I'd planned to zero in on Faulkner's troubles with gender and on my own readerly rhythms of anticipation and disappointment as I make my way through *The Unvanquished*'s final, magnificent story of Bayard's triumph and Drusilla's marginalization, as I scent, once again, that incorrigible olor of verbena.[18] Every time I read *The Unvanquished* I am enthralled and disappointed when I come to the end. If something vital drops away—an excision so aestheticized that it is almost invisible—what remains in the story's beautiful concluding paragraph, in Faulkner's paean to the powers of verbena, is a vestigial melancholy—a loss unnamed and impossible to mourn. What is this loss? The last story in *The Unvanquished*, "An Odor of Verbena," describes a new Southern man who invents a revivified ethic for his vengeance-ridden world. Bayard trades in an *Old Testament* code of retribution for a *New Testament* coda in which the strongest man can always run his opponent out of town by turning the other cheek. At first Drusilla Hawk seems destined to enter this new society as an androgynous character capable of redressing the gender asymmetries haunting the South. But instead Drusilla clings to a banished code of blood and honor; in the end she cedes both androgyny and the force of natality, of beginning again, to her cousin Bayard.

In tracking my own desire with its loops of disappointment and rapture (rapture at the mere fact of Drusilla's invention, rapture at the floral incantation tracing the rise of the new Southern man) I had hoped to devote this essay to a critique of *The Unvanquished*'s ending, to speak out against the transcendent poetry that naturalizes Bayard's ascent and Drusilla's supercession:

> I saw her open door (that unmistakable way in which an open door stands open when nobody lives in the room any more) and I realised I had not believed that she was really gone. So I didn't look into the room. I went on to mine and entered. And then for a long moment I thought it was the verbena in my lapel which I still smelled. I thought that until I had crossed the room and looked down at the pillow on which it lay—the single sprig of it (without looking she would pinch off a half dozen of them and they would be all of a size, almost all of a shape, as if a machine had stamped them out) filling the room, the dusk, the evening with that odor which she said you could smell alone above the smell of horses. (293)

The story's final, exalted paragraph offers a conclusion so saturated with beauty that it seems barely utterable. For when Bayard seizes symbolic control of verbena, Drusilla's flower, he is drenched with its powers of transformation. At this moment Drusilla disappears from the story without a demur, a mere prop in a world where men can freely appropriate feminine symbols, while women who confiscate the attributes of the masculine world are sent to the margins, becoming abnormal, freakish, crazed.

But in rereading *The Unvanquished* to prepare for this essay
I began to feel the pressures of another story—to feel that I also
have to bear witness to the incredible saturation of Drusilla's
body with regional politics: that is, with Mississippi's peculiar
brand of class and race trauma. In this augmented reading
verbena becomes more than a fragrant, abiding symbol of male
transcendence and courage, its scent vaulting above the rank
smell of soldiers and horses; it becomes more than an image of
female genital power, its scent increasing a hundredfold whenever Drusilla and Bayard start to kiss. Verbena is also associated
with language: with the verbiage of the ballot box and post office
and law school, with the power of verbalizing or seizing the
verb: that part of speech expressing both existence and action.
The question of *The Unvanquished* is not only who is allowed to
wear this bouquet—to abjure it, to crush it, to keep verbena
forever—but who owns the verbs that construct the meanings
of Southern culture? And what happens not only to Drusilla,
but to her black compatriots—to Ringo, to Louvinia, and to
Joby—when these verbs are ceded to Bayard, when the story's
dreams of gender and race metamorphosis fade?

To answer these questions we need to scrutinize Drusilla's
first appearance in Faulkner's novel, to look at a young girl still
free of the Southern grotesque, her body not yet burdened by
the weight of its own history. At first Drusilla's body, with its
shorn hair, men's clothing, and sleepless mirth, looks like a
body escaping from history. Why is her escape so evanescent?
We find a clue in Sundquist's analysis of Faulkner's uncanny
ability to "hold the myth of memory at a point of perilous
balance, neither endorsing it nor declaring it sheer fabrication.
In so doing, it brings into view the most conspicuous feature of
Faulkner's romantic mythologizing of the old South—that its
power depends on his straining to the very limits of coherence
those nostalgic legends of old Confederate times that were
being offered up in all seriousness by his contemporaries" (21).
Drusilla represents that point in the world of *The Unvanquished*
where this "perilous balance" keeps tipping over and straining

the limits of Southern ideology. In a world of hard facts her retrograde chivalry spills over into a gushing surrealism that both confirms and condemns "those nostalgic legends of old Confederate times." The scene where Drusilla guides Bayard to John Sartoris's open casket (as Bayard's animality takes over, and he starts to pant) is hypersaturated with the most florid conventions of vengeance-romance. "Drusilla and I turned and crossed the portico, her hand lying light on my wrist yet discharging into me with a shock like electricity that dark and passionate voracity, the face at my shoulder—the jagged hair with a verbena sprig above each ear, the eyes staring at me with that fierce exaltation" (270). Faulkner plays this scene for all it's worth. As Drusilla changes from vamp to vampire, from femme fatale to fatal priestess, she inhabits contradictory worlds. Her jagged aura cuts into Bayard's body, pressuring him to join in the story of vengeance as she presses the dueling pistols into his hands, calling to him with a "silvery ecstatic voice," "whispering into that quiet death-filled room with a passionate and dying fall: 'Bayard.' She faced me, she was quite near; again the scent of the verbena in her hair seemed to have increased a hundred times as she stood holding out to me, one in either hand, the two dueling pistols. 'Take them, Bayard,' she said, in the same tone in which she had said 'Kiss me' last summer, already pressing them into my hands, watching me with that passionate and voracious exaltation, speaking in a voice fainting and passionate with promise" (273). This passage seduces and burdens its readers from several directions.

First, Faulkner's prose is completely mesmerizing, a real Southern high. The hypnotism of these repeated words, these building cadences of verbena and violence, these stock figures pushed over the edge, catch the body up in an old, well-known story in which the South is reinvented as the fetish site for a lost nationalism, for chauvinistic dreams of vengeance and violation.

Second, this hyperbole serves as a reminder that all this exaggerated romancing, this prancing about the Southern coffin (with its voracious and passionately dormant corpse), is overdone; this is a story ridiculous, repetitive, obsessional. Here Faulkner offers a critique of regional romance; he satirizes the inflamed diction that drives the dithyrambs of Southern honor and ironizes Drusilla's version of the glorious adventures that lost the Civil War.

Third, even as Faulkner strains this plot to the limits of coherence, he also pushes Drusilla's character beyond the reach of facile critique. Her bizarre borderline behavior and shlock hysteria serve to remind us how very powerful these ghostly death rituals can be for their participants; her dream begins to inhabit us even as we stand outside its aura, in part because Faulkner's rhythms work so hard to mimic the surprising bodily states of those driven by the participatory magic of codes of Southern honor.

Finally, Drusilla strains the limits of social coherence because the rhythms emanating from her body enact a violent blending of cultural oppositions. Pierre Bourdieu suggests that the cognitive structures defining the social world are really "internalized, embodied" systems of classification that allow us to divide the world into hierarchies but "function below the level of consciousness and discourse" and therefore relieve us of the guilt of being undemocratic. "The agents in a given social formation share a set of basic perceptual schemes" that have the gloss of objectivity because they rely on a series of "antagonistic adjectives" that help us classify everyone we meet: "The network of oppositions between high and low, spiritual and material, fine and course . . . unique and common, brilliant and dull, is the matrix of all the commonplaces which find such ready acceptance because behind them lies the whole social order. The network has its ultimate source in the opposition between the elite of the dominant and the mass of the dominated" (468). Drusilla's grotesque body strains the myths of the Old South to their limit because she repudiates these embodied schemes; her hybridity—her body's androgynous doubleness—is a breathtaking refusal of conventional hierarchies. Faulkner tells us that her touch is light as "dead leaves," yet filled with electricity.

She is wise, but her mouth is empty and pale as a rubber ring. Her gender identity is completely bifurcated: the dueling pistols, closely cropped head, and participation in male codes of vengeance are at war with her yellow ball gown, flower-fragrant hair, and manipulation of the female codes of gyneolatry and sexual ecstasy. Her identity represents a collage of the dominant culture's images that will not come together. Is it any surprise that this body so overloaded with competing codes comes apart at the seams?

> There was no blood on her face at all, her mouth open a little and pale as one of those rubber rings women seal fruit jars with. Then her eyes filled with an expression of bitter and passionate betrayal. "Why, he's not—" she said. "He's not—And I kissed his hand," she said in an aghast whisper; "*I kissed his hand!*" beginning to laugh, the laughter rising, becoming a scream yet still remaining laughter, screaming with laughter, trying herself to deaden the sound by putting her hand over her mouth, the laughter spilling between her fingers like vomit, the incredulous betrayed eyes still watching me across the hand. (275)

As Drusilla's mouth, hands, and eyes careen apart, as laughter heaves out of her innards like so much sour milk, I'm reminded of Scitex's ability to fracture the female face into a million fragments to be resutured at will. I'm also reminded that Faulkner was burdened, at the time of writing *The Unvanquished*, with a task of literal resuturing. He agreed to help a local mortician reconstruct his dead brother's face after this brother died—catastrophically—while piloting Faulkner's private plane. Does this traumatic event (Faulkner's physical act of abetting this reconstruction and his lingering survivor's guilt) help to explain at least some of the biographical pressures driving *The Unvanquished*, especially the need to refabricate the story of the beautiful boy, the new Southern man? Is the portrait of Bayard's reconstruction, of his renovated perfectibility as the new Southern man partly driven by Faulkner's own history? *The Unvanquished* is deeply haunted by a reconstitutive urgency—as if the desire to bring a dead brother to life

merges with the creation of a beautiful youth who also partici-
pates in the novel's urgent need to create a utopian version of
the South as it might have been.

But if the shreds of biography intrude and add private pressures to Faulkner's fictional inventions of a renovated Southern
community, why should Faulkner displace this anxiety about
the splintering of a masculine body onto Drusilla? Why does
she become the matrix for both exploring and hiding an eviscer-
ated story of race and emancipation? We first meet Drusilla
Hawk as a comic heroine: a Beatrix or Rosalind who finds, in
the midst of war, an excuse for heroism and the pleasures of
cross-dressing. She saves her horse Bobolink from the Yankees
and tells Bayard and Ringo mesmerizing tales of a war she
finally joins. By "Skirmish at Sartoris," the penultimate story,
she is living out of wedlock with John Sartoris: wearing trousers,
doing men's work, and scandalizing matriarchs for miles around.
The plotting here is delightful, but also predictable. Drusilla's
irregular behavior and the text's delight in it offers Faulkner a
podium for satirizing the rigidities of Southern victorianism.
"Skirmish at Sartoris" begins with a series of letters from
Drusilla's mother to Granny and Mrs. Compson, letters written
with pokeberry ink on pieces of torn up wallpaper, suggesting
this world's lost anchoring points and the scrapping of its
standards of domesticity: *"[W]hen I think of my husband who
laid down his life to protect a heritage of courageous men and
spotless women looking down from heaven upon a daughter
who had deliberately cast away that for which he died, and
when I think of my half-orphan son who will one day ask of me
why his martyred father's sacrifice was not enough to preserve
his sister's good name"* (219). As Drusilla's mother rewrites the
war as a fable of gyneolatry or redeemed female honor, Faulkner
pokes fun at her melodrama; he cracks open the "romantic
mythologizing of the Old South" from yet another angle. When
Gavin Breckbridge is killed "at Shiloh before he and Drusilla
had had time to marry," Drusilla was to have become the
glorious bride of the Confederacy: "there had been reserved for

Drusilla the highest destiny of a Southern woman—to be the bride-widow of a lost cause." Against this buxom hysteria, Drusilla's choices seem wonderful: "Drusilla had been gone for six months and no word from her except she was alive, and then one night she walked into the cabin where Aunt Louisa and Denny were . . . *in the garments not alone of a man but of a common private soldier* and told them how she had been a member of Father's troop for six months, bivouacking at night surrounded by sleeping men" (220). She feels neither shame nor remorse, and when her mother demands that she and John Sartoris marry, Drusilla shows her proto-feminist colors; she is appalled by the idea of matrimony: " 'Can't you understand that I am tired of burying husbands in this war? That I am riding in Cousin John's troop not to find a man but to hurt Yankees?' " Ever mindful of appearances and anxious about the semblance of incest, her mother insists: "Don't call him *Cousin* John where strangers can hear you" (220).

What's amazing about Drusilla's demeanor early in the story is how ungrotesque, unburdened, and transcendent she seems; she's a woman who crosses boundaries without cost. The onus in "Skirmish at Sartoris" is on the ladies, who refuse to see a "thin sunburned girl in a man's shirt and pants" as anything human, as anything other than "a tame panther or bear" (221–22). When fourteen respectable women descend on Sartoris land to fabricate a wedding, they find Drusilla working in the log-yard, feeding the bandsaw along with Ringo and Joby, "her face sweat-streaked with sawdust and her short hair yellow with it" (225).

To understand the eventual grotesquing of Drusilla's androgynous body, we need to explore the twinning of Drusilla and her African American comrades at such a crucial moment—when what hangs in the balance is Drusilla's future identity, as well as the symbolic future of Southern femininity. Faulkner's text begins to ask what kinds of communities will spring to life when the war ends and the South reinvents itself. Working in the yard alongside two black male laborers was a role forbidden to young women in Faulkner's own world, with its paranoid rendition of the South's Afro-phobic romance, in which black men become the hallucinatory mirrors of a predatory white economy. In *The Promise of the New South* Edward Ayers records the voice of a middle Tennessee woman remembering that in her community girls were taught to sew, but not to cook "because we were never allowed to enter the kitchen. There was a prohibition because the Negro men on the place that didn't have families were fed in the kitchen. . . . You can't remember and maybe can't understand the horror that had grown up of any contact with a Negro man."[19]

In Faulkner's story the scenario is reversed. Instead of worrying about contamination from African American men, Drusilla feels violated by her racial and sexual cohort, by white women. Her history-marked body with its "dirty sweated overalls" and "sweat-streaked" face sets her apart; in search of protection she runs to Louvinia, another marked woman, who plays the complicated role of servant, sister, mother, and African American double.

At this very moment when the text starts to fill with a melange of potential communities, Drusilla seems to pair herself with Bayard; she begins "to run like a deer, that starts to run and then decides where it wants to go; she turned right in the air and came toward me" (226). But Drusilla changes course and races, anguished and half-coherent, to the former slave cabins, to Louvinia: "Her hand came out quicker than Drusilla could jerk back . . . then Louvinia was holding Drusilla in her arms like she used to hold me and Drusilla was crying hard. 'That John and I—that we— And Gavin dead at Shiloh and John's home burned and his plantation ruined, that he and I—We went to the war to hurt Yankees, not hunting women!' 'I knows you ain't,' Louvinia said. 'Hush now. Hush' " (227). What is happening to Drusilla's verbs? They begin to disintegrate when Faulkner starts riffing on that old, enticing theme: the long, ambivalent march toward the altar. By making Drusilla boyish, transgressive, and different, Faulkner also probes a deeper set of questions. Can a young girl refuse her expected roles, escape the confines of marriage? If this happens, can she also lay the preliminary foundations for social transformation, for a new peacetime society which neither fears blacks nor hunts women? At issue is Faulkner's profound if conflicted sense of the inadequacy of the roles allotted Southern women, and Drusilla's desire for a life of significant action—suggesting an urgent need for cultural change.

But a second plot opens up in the midst of the first, a story doomed, but equally bent on revolution. This story has been developing in fits and starts, from the ambivalent portrait of Loosh, who becomes an ironic if defeated critic of the culture that owns him, to the conundrum of who should own the ballot box in the South and who will protect the voting rights of African Americans. In fact, the chronicle of the ballot box momentarily derails the marriage plot, since John Sartoris and Drusilla Hawk ride into town to get married but end up killing carpetbaggers instead. This violent detour halts any dream of cross-racial or cross-sexual collectivity, since Faulkner presents this murderous expedition as the merriest of comedies. Jefferson, which had abjured Yankees forever, is now clamoring for the protection of federal troops. Since the town is off limits to Drusilla and Bayard, it is Ringo, "his eyes rolling a little," who slips away to bring Bayard some news:

> "Do you know what I ain't?" he said.
> "What," I said.
> "I ain't a nigger any more. I done been abolished." Then I asked him what he was, if he wasn't a nigger any more and he showed me what he had in his hand. It was a new scrip dollar; it was drawn on the United States Resident Treasurer, Yoknapatawpha County, Mississippi, and signed "Cassius Q. Benbow, Acting Marshal" in a neat clerk's hand, with a big sprawling X under it.
> "Cassius Q. Benbow?" I said.
> "Co-rect," Ringo said. "Uncle Cash that druv the Benbow carriage twell he run off with the Yankees two years ago. He back now and he gonter be elected Marshal of Jefferson. That's what Marse John and the other white folks is so busy about."

"A nigger?" I said. "A nigger?"

"No," Ringo said. "They ain't no more niggers, in Jefferson nor nowhere else." Then he told me about the two Burdens from Missouri, with a patent from Washington to organise the niggers into Republicans. (228–29)

And here, once again, we reach the matter of the verb—of Ringo's powers of action and speech. "Abolish" means to do away with, to bring to an end, exterminate, extinguish, eradicate, obliterate. Faulkner's little joke—that Ringo mistakes "abolition," the termination of slavery as an institution, for "emancipation," the freeing of African Americans for citizenship—has a devastating ring. Because Ringo, for all his stereotypic talk, is right; he has been abolished. Early in *The Unvanquished* Bayard explains that Ringo is the smarter of the pair; he masterminds Granny's mule scam and acts throughout these early stories as Bayard's equal. But when we reach "An Odor of Verbena" and Ringo attains manhood, he becomes Bayard's "boy." His verbena—his verbiage—disappears; like Drusilla he moves into the background of history.

Although Ringo's celebration of Cassius Q. Benbow's signature, his indomitable "X," becomes a site for profound melancholia—the reminder of the constant loss of speech, rights, recognition, and selfhood that African Americans endured without benefit of public mourning—for me the most wrenching moments of *The Unvanquished* occur in the peculiar racial schizophrenia of "Skirmish at Sartoris." When we witness Louvinia's holding and comforting of Drusilla, Louvinia is asked to mirror the depth and breadth of humanity itself. Greeting Drusilla's bewildered fierceness with her own body, Louvinia bestows the capacity for infinite comfort: "I knows you ain't," Louvinia said. "Hush now. Hush." But if Faulkner grants African Americans this vast and capacious humanity, he also perpetuates their social diminishment. In the midst of the white men's seizure of the ballot box, when even the most minimal power of inscription is stolen from the black community, Faulkner can only rehearse this disenfranchisement in the silliest and grimmest of plots; his white characters make offhand remarks about the "herd" of illiterate ex-slaves who hover behind the con men from Missouri: "the herd of niggers look like they had when I first saw them, with the Northern white men herding them together" (238). If these bodies are distorted by Faulkner's text, is it because even fantasied access to equality under the law creates such seismic difficulties for Faulkner that he can only invoke the civil rights of African Americans in inhuman terms? Ringo's "I done been abolished" is equal in force to the potent illiteracy of Cassius Q. Benbow's "X": both connote an ostracism from power. Oddly, *The Unvanquished* withholds every vestige of sympathy for this ostracism; Faulkner's text seems determined to ride over these voting men's bones with the nonchalance of Granny's wagon when it crushes black women and children en route to Yankee silver.

In describing this nonchalance, I don't want to grandstand about a fashionable need for Faulkner to adhere to the standards of political correctness: texts that wear their politics on their sleeves are rarely so interesting. In any event, we could pretend to be talking about *Bayard's* politics, since he's the nominal narrator of these stories. What I am trying to intuit is this text's political unconscious, to examine the ways in which the grotesque trivialization of African American's rights and humanity finally maps itself on Drusilla's body as we move from the matter of Drusilla and Ringo's lost verbs to the floral poetry that aestheticizes this loss at the story's end.

How is Ringo's fate tied to Drusilla's? We have seen that when Drusilla is forced to get married, when her healthy penchant for transgression and cross-dressing comes to crisis, she clings to her cross-racial family: to Ringo, Joby, and Louvinia. They, in turn, hope to hold the promissory notes of Reconstruction; they have a new (if halting and imperfect) access to narratives of empowerment and transformation. But this promised collateral comes to nothing; it falls apart with the rise and demise of Cassius Benbow's election for town marshal.

In a gender-based reading of *The Unvanquished* the story of the ballot box seems like so much fictive filigree, an apotropaic device designed to build suspense about Drusilla's wedding. The ballot box plot has little vivacity or depth; it turns upon the swashbuckling staples of adventure and bloodshed. But as uncertainty mounts about the best way to clobber those carpetbaggers and get Drusilla married, the text uses this very flatness to ward off its deepest concerns—namely, its uneven obsessions with social renovation, female emancipation, and desegregation. Who should own the power in Jefferson—which faction of white men? And what role will African Americans play in this drama? Will they gather the seeds of political power, achieve the right to make history? In answer, John Sartoris kills the two Burdens (a grandfather and grandson, those young and old carpetbaggers) and in the resulting carnival ambiance Drusilla is named voting commissioner; she seizes the power of black speech and cedes the ballot box to George Wyatt, as if to confirm the fact that "one's relationship to the social world and to one's proper place in it is never more clearly expressed than in the space and time one feels entitled to take from others, more precisely, in the space one claims with one's body in physical space."[20] The ballot box scene is precisely about this taking of space. Not only is the box itself carried to Sartoris's house, but George Wyatt does all the writing to "save some more time." He inscribes every ballot: "You needn't bother to count them," George said. "They all voted No" (241).

In this moment of negation the text's intimations of gender equality also fall apart, as if supporting new forms of oppression for African Americans must also result in new constellations of gender oppression. After the confiscation of the ballot box Drusilla is asked to act a new part in the Southern imaginary. The text ceases to celebrate her split, androgynous personality and invokes her pathology instead. In the midst of Reconstruction, the mapping of Southern social concerns onto women's bodies must begin all over again

Thus the failed wedding and failed election are shown to be, if not interchangeable, then interconnected. To change the structure of elective power is, after all, to change the structure of marriage as well. Equality between blacks and whites raises many socioeconomic specters, among them, the ghost of miscegenation. In this story Faulkner's bizarre substitution of one institution for another—of an election for a marriage—involves a series of parallel metaphors in which each institution comments upon the other. Once the ballot box has been safeguarded and her mother drums her into the house, demanding that John and Drusilla must at last see a minister, Drusilla's negative response echoes the naysaying of the white men around her: she "didn't move, standing there in her torn dress and the ruined veil and the twisted wreath hanging from her hair by a few pins" (240). In this moment Drusilla provides a new allegory of the ruined South: not as the bride of the Confederacy, but as the spouse of a mangled Reconstruction, as war's twisted aftermath.

Why has so much meaning migrated to Drusilla's body? To explore this migration I want to return to the theme of bearing witness, to Shoshana Felman's idea that "the artist's role is to demolish the deceptive image of history as an abstraction (as an ideological and/or statistical, administrative picture in which death becomes invisible) by bearing witness to the body." In describing the force of literary testimony, Felman cites Camus's eloquent epigram: "In a civilization where murder and violence are already doctrines in the process of becoming institutions," the artist becomes "freedom's witness" in testifying "not to the Law, but to the body" (96).

Faulkner adheres to this principle both gorgeously and imperfectly. "Odor of Verbena" is an immense testimonial to African American disenfranchisement and the female body's symbolic disintegration under the pressures of the post-Reconstruction South. But in the reinscription of lost voting rights as comedy and the displacement of this repressed tragedy onto the intensifying grid of Drusilla's body (beginning with her parodic role as voting commissioner) the story barely spoken in "Skirmish at Sartoris" explodes. The unverbing of blacks, the murderous insistence on white supremacy: Faulkner's text submits to an iterative Southern crisis that is elided even when it is expressed. What this elision produces within *The Unvanquished* is the magnificent pressure that becomes "An Odor of Verbena"—a story driven by its obsessive invocations of flowers, its magnificent fixation upon the odor of courage, and its use of these aesthetic images to heighten the story's heroic mood, glossing over its diminished ethos, its lost social ethic.

In this atmosphere of floral obsession, why does Drusilla's body split into two incompatible images: the unkempt, unruly, uncontrollable image of Drusilla as female grotesque (as a female body so covered with history that she must finally be jettisoned by Faulkner's story) and as the fragment symbol of verbena (an image that breaks off from Drusilla's body to be gathered up by Bayard himself)? I want to ignore the obvious answer: namely, that Drusilla herself is abjured because she represents the old order's appetite for violence and prejudice, and verbena is kept because it represents her earlier aura of metamorphosis. This is to refuse the suggestion that Drusilla reaps the fruits of her own immorality; history (especially Faulkner's history) is always more complex than this. Instead, I want to turn to Peter Stallybrass and Alon White's insistence that discourses about the body become especially prominent when social hierarchies start to change: "transcodings between different levels . . . of social reality are effected through the intensifying grid of the body. It is no accident that transgressions and the attempt to control them . . . return to somatic symptoms, for these are the ultimate elements of social classification itself."[21] In *The Unvanquished* the grotesque female body at first offers a surface for tracing the progressive pressures of political change. But in the final story Faulkner decides not to write about the female body in motion or process (with all the clamoring racial overtones, the pressures toward equality that this might imply), but the female body as it must be immobilized to become the site for the founding (and foundering) of a new social order.

After all, the prescient topic of *The Unvanquished* is Bayard's search for a new cultural geography where his father's verbs can be changed, where Bayard himself can speak differently but still become "The Sartoris." What obsesses me about this quest is not only the fact that this project is carried out by a semiprogressive white male, but that, in addition to the dehumanization of African Americans, this quest requires the unmooring and male reclamation of the exploded female's body parts. In saying that Drusilla becomes the text's quintessential split subject and that history is marked upon her body, I'm also describing my own self-splintering as reader—as someone so worked over by the violent stories that lead up to Drusilla's loss of verbena that I'm entirely prepared for that amoral, complex body made from monstrous, incoherent parts that greets us in Drusilla's most theatrical scenes. But if I'm ready for Drusilla to fall apart, nothing prepares me for the unifying vehemence of verbena, that rich aesthetic site that provides Bayard's story with a new coherence: verbena, that fragrant symbol of female sexuality so imbricated with language that it becomes something more intimate than a flower and more intimidating than a verb— perhaps the power of metaphor itself.

Since this floral image seems so pacific, delighting our senses in order to naturalize Bayard's transcendence, I want to disrupt this delight by returning to the equally serene surfaces of the Scitexized body—that process allowing women's images to be defaced and dehistoricized at will. The incantatory power of verbena is obsessive, ecstatic, and every bit as satisfying in Faulkner's story as those voluptuous female flowers gracing the pages of *Vogue*. I'm suggesting that an incredible fantasy is held forth in this story—one Faulkner hardly believed in, but may have longed for nevertheless. This is the fantasy that the South could erase its history and start again, could erase the scars of the past. But this fantasy simply deepens an old schizophrenia. Just as black men lost the power to vote, so Drusilla, in the moment she abjures verbena, loses her power of speech and becomes the laughing, crying hysteric of the story's final pages. But for Bayard, verbena and its transformative power are every-

where. He imagines its fragrance as "louder" than the two shots
his father fired to kill the Missouri Burdens. He sees two orange
blossoms burning against Redmond's coat when Redmond fires
at Bayard and misses. For him verbena "gathers all the sun"
and its "suspended fierce heat" until "I moved in a cloud of
verbena as I might have moved in a cloud of smoke from a
cigar." (283).

To understand the deliberately masculinized beauty of these
transformations we must look again at the ways in which traditional narratives of gender, nationality, and race are embedded
in Faulkner's story. Mary Jacobus suggests that "the body,
whether masculine or feminine, is imbricated in the matrices of
power at all levels" but that "the feminine body, as the prime
site of sexual and/or racial difference in a white, masculine
western political and sexual economy" offers a particularly vola-
tile site for defusing the consequences of social action. Drusilla's
body serves just such a function in Faulkner's tale. Focusing
on her derangements we are invited to forget the greater
derangements of the social order; focusing on her anxiety we
can ignore the text's still greater anxiety about ceding civic
rights to African Americans.

But we also need to remember that this is not a story that
centers on Drusilla or Ringo, but on Bayard and the role he will
play in the South's new ethic of intimacy. As Benedict Anderson
suggests, the novel offers a crucial technical means for "representing the kind of imagined community that is the nation."[22]
In the course of Faulkner's story Bayard not only comes to
represent a new body politic, he also invents a new narrative
for the South as subnation or region. In other words, *The
Unvanquished* is a narrative about failed nationality and the
compensatory invention of a new kind of imagined community.

But when Faulkner marginalizes these stories about violent,
unredeemed Southern women and the failed emancipation of
black women and men in order to chronicle the story of a
beautiful boy who masters a new set of moral norms (with the
power to transform the South's old-fashioned revenger's tragedy

into newfangled redemption), something extraordinary happens; the story itself begins to pant. By supercharging the narrative of verbena, by distracting the reader with a surfeit of floral hyperbole, Faulkner asks his readers to overlook the fact that this narrative is entirely race- and gender-bound. As Toni Morrison suggests, "national literatures, like writers, get along the best way they can. Yet they do seem to end up describing and inscribing what is really on the national mind. For the most part, the literature of the United States has taken as its concern the architecture of a *new white man*" (14–15). In providing this architecture and banishing the complexities of race and gender prejudice from his utopia, in focusing on Bayard's beauty, on his embodiment of the new American man, Faulkner constructs an illusion as delusive and dream-ridden as the Scitex glow.

Verbena becomes, then, a changed image as well as a charged one. It becomes the beautiful body of Southern possibility, perhaps even the New South's Scitexized norm. But its blossoms are, I would argue, so much more tellingly violent when Drusilla crushes them, and we remember that these mangled blossoms also contain her banished ardor as well as the voices of those African Americans who longed for the verb but were forced for so many years to abjure the ballot box. What I'm trying to describe is a series of structural displacements that unify *The Unvanquished* and seem motivated by the most utopian, but also the most malign, of political impulses. First, the trauma of African American disenfranchisement is mapped or displaced onto Drusilla's body in the scene where the ballot box is stolen and she becomes the ruined bride of the South; then Drusilla's, Ringo's, and Louvinia's loss of power is aestheticized or displaced onto the text's obsession with verbena. What results is an extraordinarily dense, condensed floral body that pretends to transcend its political antecedents. What gets lost, but what may also be desired in each of these displacements, is the egalitarian community that Bayard imagines at the very beginning of *The Unvanquished* when he hears Loosh's story of emancipation and runs to tell his grandmother that the Yankees

are coming: "they're coming to set us free." This "us" marrying
Bayard and Ringo, Louvinia and Granny, carries with it the
most poignant odor of all; it becomes a word so redolent that its
absence in verbena's final story must be fragrantly abjured in
order to be so flagrantly denied.

NOTES

I want to thank Yopie Prins, Jay Watson, and my students in English 239 for their
thoughtful contributions to this essay.
1. "That Scitex Glow," New York Times Magazine (July 10, 1994): 45.
2. William Faulkner, The Wild Palms (New York: Vintage, 1966), 120–21.
3. Terry Eagleton, Walter Benjamin or Towards a Revolutionary Criticism (London:
Verso, 1981) 145.
4. In Distinction: A Social Critique of the Judgement of Taste, trans. Richard Nice
(Cambridge: Harvard University Press, 1984). Pierre Bourdieu argues that "the schemes
of the habitus, the primary forms of classification, owe their specific efficacy to the fact
that they function below the level of consciousness and language, beyond the read of
introspective scrutiny or control by the will" (467). Additional references appear in
the text.
5. Charles W. Chesnutt, "Po' Sandy," in The Conjure Woman (Ann Arbor: University of Michigan Press, 1969), 41. Additional references appear in the text.
6. Mikhail Bakhtin, Rabelais and His World, trans. Helen Iswolsky (Cambridge:
M. I. T. Press, 1968), 19.
7. Katherine Anne Porter, "The Witness," in The Collected Stories of Katherine
Anne Porter (New York: Harcourt Brace Jovanovich, 1979), 340.
8. Malcolm Cowley, "Introduction to The Portable Faulkner," in William Faulkner:
Three Decades of Criticism, ed. Frederick J. Hoffman and Olga W. Vickery (New York:
Harcourt Brace Jovanovich, 1963), 99.
9. Shoshana Felman, "Camus' The Plague, or a Monument to Witnessing," in
Shoshana Felman and Dori Laub, M.D., Testimony: Crises of Witnessing in Literature,
Psychoanalysis, and History (New York: Routledge, 1992), 108. Additional references
appear in the text.
10. Eric Sundquist, Faulkner: The House Divided (Baltimore: Johns Hopkins University Press, 1983), 5. Additional references appear in the text.
11. In the final chapter of Playing in the Dark (Cambridge: Harvard University Press,
1992), Toni Morrison suggests a parallel structure in Ernest Hemingway's To Have and
Have Not: "Here we see Africanism used as a fundamental fictional technique by which
to establish [white] character" (80). In The Unvanquished (New York: Vintage, 1966),
Loosh enters the text as an Africanist double whose brooding, inhuman presence helps
to establish the parameters of Sartoris's flawed heroism. Both men appear out of
nowhere, both carry news of the fall of Vicksburg, both make their escape in "Retreat."
In each scene Loosh's dehumanization props up Sartoris's humanity. While Loosh
"stood there . . . in the fierce dull early afternoon sunlight, bareheaded, his head
slanted a little . . . like a cannonball (which it resembled) bedded hurriedly and
carelessly in concrete, his eyes a little red at the inner corners as Negroes' eyes get
when they have been drinking" (4), Sartoris rages off the page; he evokes dreams of
victory with "that odor in his clothes and beard and flesh too which I believed was the
smell of powder and glory . . . but know better now" (11).
12. William Faulkner, The Unvanquished (New York: Vintage, 1966), 85. Additional
references appear in the text.

13. Hearing about the Yankees' approach from the freedom-longing Loosh, Bayard and Ringo rush in to Granny and exclaim: "They're coming here! . . . They're coming to set us free!" (26).

14. Cleanth Brooks, *William Faulkner: The Yoknapatawpha Country* (New Haven: Yale University Press, 1963), 92. Additional references appear in the text.

15. Cleanth Brooks, *William Faulkner: Toward Yoknapatawpha and Beyond* (New Haven: Yale University Press, 1978), 335.

16. Mary Jacobus, Evelyn Fox Keller, Sally Shuttleworth, *Body/Politics: Women and the Discourses of Science* (New York: Routledge, 1990), 2.

17. Michel Foucault, "Nietzsche, Genealogy, History," in *Language, Counter-Memory, Practice*, ed. Donald F. Bouchard (New York: Cornell University Press, 1977), 148.

18. There was much talk at the Faulkner conference about verbena's lack of fragrance. Does this change the meaning of the story? I think not. The flower I was taught to call verbena during my own Southern childhood was incredibly fragrant. I'm assuming that Faulkner is referring to the same flower—by its common and not its botanical name.

19. Edward L. Ayers, *The Promise of the New South: Life After Reconstruction* (New York: Oxford, 1992), 18.

20. Pierre Bourdieu, *Distinction*, 474.

21. Peter Stallybrass and Allon White, *The Politics and Poetics of Transgression* (Ithaca: Cornell University Press, 1986), 26.

22. Benedict Anderson, *Imagined Communities: Reflections on the Origin and Spread of Nationalism* (London: Verso, 1983), 30.

Gender, War, and Cross-Dressing in
The Unvanquished

DEBORAH CLARKE

*I'd rather engage Forrest's whole brigade every morning
for six months than spend that same length of time trying to
protect United States property from defenseless Southern
women and niggers and children. . . . Defenseless! God
help the North if Davis and Lee had ever thought of the
idea of forming a brigade of grandmothers and nigger
orphans, and invading us with it*[1]

Are women defenseless damsels or consummate soldiers? The
role of women in Faulkner's work is always problematic, but
women's relation to war intensifies that situation in a particularly
intricate and complex manner. As Susan Schweik has observed,
"Wars have a way of revealing with special clarity how men as
well as women are both intensely and uneasily gendered."[2]
War, which sets up a system characterized by bifurcation and
polarization, seems to reorder the world through opposition.
But war, in fact, is a cross-dresser's dream. Civilians cross-dress
as soldiers; women cross-dress as men; boys cross-dress as men;
scared men cross-dress as heroes; homosexuals, these days,
must cross-dress as heterosexuals to maintain the Pentagon's
misguided assumption that there are no gays in the military;
enemies cross-dress as friends, infiltrating each other's turf; and,
in possibly the most tragic feature of war, especially civil war,
friends and even family cross-dress as enemies. Thus, despite
imposing a binary framework war also—somewhat paradoxically—opens up possibilities of transcending it, of finding an
alternative position, of mixing the categories.

Examining the binaries of race and gender, Faulkner reveals

their vulnerability to the pressures of war. Women may be ostensibly silenced by the rhetoric of war which, like combat, is generally controlled by men, but male absence from the home-front can transform defenseless creatures into active speaking subjects. Yet finding a discourse is not easy, particularly for the women of *The Unvanquished* caught between supporting the system which subordinates them and breaking free of that subordination. Consequently, Granny Millard and Drusilla Hawk wage war against both the Yankees and their own lack of power within the chivalric order, a battle in which they are joined by Ringo, whose defense of a slave-owning culture defies the framework of slavery itself. Ostensibly one of Faulkner's most military novels, *The Unvanquished* primarily examines not Colonel Sartoris, who rides in and out on his stallion Jupiter, playing a relatively minor role in the various military and nonmilitary struggles, but the ways in which "defenseless Southern women and niggers and children" deal with the war and the chivalric tradition which it attempts to uphold.

War, of course, has largely been viewed as a particularly male stronghold. Anne Goodwyn Jones notes, "if anything in our 'adult' culture has a history of establishing manhood in opposition to the feminine, it is war: war makes men."[3] Men fight; women wait. War grants men an authority of experience—both of combat and of representation—denied to women. Men write; women stay silent. One need recall only some of the most famous war poetry to see the pattern.[4] English Cavalier poet Richard Lovelace begins "To Lucasta" with the injunction to his mistress to be quiet: "Tell me not, sweet, I am unkind / That from the nunnery / Of thy chaste breast and quiet mind / To war and arms I fly." Then he ends it by insisting that she approve of all this: "Yet this inconstancy is such / As you too shall adore; / I could not love thee, dear, so much, / Loved I not honor more." Not only must she keep her mouth shut, she must love sitting there in silence or she loses everything. Several centuries later, Wilfred Owen, in a dedication—"To Jessie Pope"—often left off of many contemporary reprintings of his famous "Dulce et Decorum Est," directs his poem at a woman poet who has had the temerity to write about war. Jessie Pope wrote patriotic verse, but Owen does more than simply contest her glorification of war; he implicitly denies her the right to speak, by pointing to her lack of experience.

> If in some smothering dreams you too could pace
> Behind the wagon that we flung him in,
> And watch the white eyes writhing in his face,
> His hanging face, like a devil's sick of sin;
> If you could hear, at every jolt, the blood
> Come gargling from the froth-corrupted lungs,
> Obscene as cancer, bitter as the cud
> Of vile incurable sores on innocent tongues,—
> My friend, you would not tell with such high zest
> To children ardent for some desperate glory,
> The old Lie: *Dulce et decorum est*
> *Pro patria mori*.

The conditional "If" says it all: she was not there, so she has no authority to speak. Jones, drawing on Jean Bethke Elshtain's analysis of the war story, notes that such a story "self-decon-structs by insisting on the importance of the actual experience of war for the the production of manhood: a story is never enough, it tells its reader; you had to [will have to] be there."[5] Thus women are doubly excluded: from the experience and from telling the story.

Gender, then, appears to divide the combatants from the noncombatants, experience from spectatorship, voice from silence. But what of Faulkner, who spent much of his life lying about his war experiences? Clearly, he felt that his lack of combat duty unmanned him to a certain extent, and may have worried about being linked with the Jessie Popes. His belief in both the authority of experience and the gender division it gives rise to are implicit in a 1947 interview, when he noted, "War is a dreadful price to pay for experience. The only good I know that comes from a war is that it allows men to be free of their womenfolks without being blacklisted by it."[6] While the price may be high, he upholds the experiential definition of war, an experience relegated primarily to men, who enjoy unrebuked freedom from women. Faulkner's responses in interviews are often suspect, and the blatant misogyny of this statement, particularly when combined with his own lack of military credentials, simply doesn't hold up in his fiction where war seems to allow women to be free of their menfolks, though it rarely protects them from being blacklisted for it. While Faulkner's statement reveals a wry yearning for socially acceptable freedom from women, his fiction more often examines the ways that war both genders and ungenders human beings, and raises questions about who is freed from whom. He may have been inexperienced in combat, but his novels overflow with battles between the sexes, an arena in which he did have some expertise.

Even when he turns directly to war, Faulkner generally places greater emphasis on the impact and aftermath of war than on the battlefield. Possibly due to the untenability of his claim to combat experience, he examines most directly the experience of noncombatants and the inadequacy of gender to define both one's position in war and one's voice in response to it. In thus elevating the claims of the spectator—generally women and children—it may be that he vindicates his own unacknowledged feminine position. In so doing, Faulkner breaks the pattern—as he so often does—of other male modernists. Sandra Gilbert and Susan Gubar claim that "inevitably, in the aftermath of the emasculating terrors of the war [i.e., WWI], many men insisted that the ultimate reality underlying history is and must be the truth of gender."[7] But despite his Nobel Prize speech, in which he insists that writing, in the aftermath of World War II, be comprised of "the old universal truths,"[8] Faulkner's fiction rarely ascribes to any kind of absolute truth, particularly truth about the determinacy of gender. The stories of The Unvanquished, largely written some fifteen years after World War I, with World War II just beginning to hover on the horizon, rather reflect the ways that war strips away acknowledged truth about gender.

This is particularly true for the American Civil War, a war

that, especially in the South, broke down the binaries of gendered experience. As Sarah Morgan of Baton Rouge wrote in her Civil War diary,

> "*Oh!* if I was only a man! Then I could don the breeches, and slay them with a will! If some few Southern women were in the ranks they could set the men an example they would not blush to follow. Pshaw! there are *no* women here! We are *all* men!"[9]

Morgan moves from desiring men's opportunities to denying female identity, revealing the extent to which gender is deconstructed during wartime. And yet, it is women who are sacrificed: "there are no women here." However, this annihilation occurs only if one equates sex with gender—only if donning breeches and slaying the enemy necessarily entails a sexchange operation. Margaret R. Higonnet observes, "Wars may awaken our awareness of the ways sexual territory is mapped because they disrupt the normal division of labor by gender." Not only do women move into men's vacated peacetime occupations, they may also intrude into the ranks of the battle itself. Higonnet goes on to assert that "civil wars, which take place on 'home' territory, have more potential than other wars to transform women's expectations."[10] In the Civil War South, where the front lines often corresponded with the homefront, Southern women and children experienced war first hand, a situation which sometimes allowed women greater freedom to take on masculine roles and masculine language. Drew Gilpin Faust has noted women's expressed desires to participate in the war and concluded, "Without directly acknowledging such frustrations, Confederate public discussion of women's roles sought to deal with incipient dissatisfaction by specifying active contributions women might make to the Southern Cause and by valorizing their passive waiting and sacrifice as highly purposeful."[11] But Drusilla Hawk and Granny Millard content themselves neither with "passive waiting and sacrifice" nor with the specified contributions allotted to women, which rarely included mule-trading or cross-dressing. Aunt Louisa's horror that Drusilla has "unsex[ed] herself" (189) by fighting thus reflects Southern wartime ideology, and applies equally well to Granny Millard, a more formidable opponent than General Forrest.

In *The Unvanquished* Faulkner interrogates the conventional expectations of women's place in war. Women in the novel take two different approaches to war, yet each one adopts a kind of male persona. Granny Millard, in her vanquishing of the Yankee army, relies on—and manipulates—written texts and Biblical authority, while Drusilla reacts more with her body; she cuts her hair short, dresses as a man, and joins Colonel Sartoris's troop. In these varying responses, Faulkner tests the limits of gender and gendered discourse, examining the efficacy of men's texts and women's bodies in the war against a patriarchal system. While both women fight to uphold Southern chivalry, their modes of discourse seriously undermine the very system they set out to defend.

On the surface, Drusilla's cross-dressing marks her as male identified, unsexed, while Granny behaves more like a lady. Yet Granny's reliance on textuality reveals her dependence on what has often been identified as a particularly masculine form of discourse. Western tradition aligns women more closely with their bodies than with language. Women are physical, men figurative, creators. As so many feminist theorists have postulated, women's language tends to be tactile and literal, focused on the body. Margaret Homans observes, "For the same reason that women are identified with nature and matter in any traditional thematics of gender . . . women are also identified with the literal, the absent referent in our predominant myth of language."[12] Faulkner, however, is a prime example of a man who questions such paradigms. His male characters flounder amid the wreck of symbolic discourse, desperately trying to make words replace reality. Thus Quentin Compson kills himself because among other reasons virginity is not just a word; thus Harry Wilbourne finds his language inadequate next to Charlotte's drawings; and thus Reverend Whitfield can only "frame," not speak, the words of his confession, while Addie

Bundren knows that words are no good. Faulkner both reproduces and challenges this gendered linguistic split, and one often finds that women's silence and women's bodies hold greater sway than men's language.

The Unvanquished mixes these categories in curious and interesting ways. Granny, an avid supporter of the patriarchal system, relies on written texts to vanquish the Yankee army. While the misunderstandings behind her note from Colonel Dick provide an almost slapstick tone to her mule-trading—she demands the return of a chest of silver, her mules named Old Hundred and Tinney, and two slaves, which gets transcribed by the Yankee orderly as ten chests of silver, 110 mules and slaves (that equation is surely no accident)—Granny's participation in the procedure marks her reverence for justice and textual authority. Her note from Colonel Dick is legal; as she herself quickly points out, she "tried to tell them better. . . . It's the hand of God" (112). Associating the hand of God with the written hand of man firmly ensconces textual authenticity as akin to divine authority, and both are further affiliated with masculine power. But the Yankee orderly's comic mistake and the consequent blind obedience by the rest of the army to this text illustrate both the power of textual legality and its limitations. With nothing more than a "handful of durn printed letterheads" (122), Granny routs the Yankees so thoroughly that Ab Snopes wonders "if somebody hadn't better tell Abe Lincoln to look out for General Grant against Miz Rosa Millard" (123). The unquestioned authority of the masculine text can be effectively subverted by a woman who recognizes that fixed meaning can be manipulated, particularly in a system which does not question a lady's—or a Colonel's—word. Granny's appropriation of textual authority, for the sake of the Southern patriarchal system, places her in precisely the position which that system has denied her: in control of military men and military language.

But it is Ringo, an even more problematic supporter of Southern patriarchy, who first recognizes the full potential of the note, that it is a text with multiple applications. He, like

Granny, claims only to be fulfilling the letter of the law: "I never [said] nothing the paper never said" (114). His reliance on what the paper said—or never said—illustrates his understanding of the cultural reliance on textual legality, which he then goes on to exploit. Yet his dedication to the cause which has declared him legally nonhuman demands attention. Certainly his loyalties are less to the South than to the Sartorises; he has, in a sense, cross-dressed as a white Southerner. He looks at the pathetic band of escaped slaves who have just been handed over to them and remarks, "The main thing now is, whut we gonter do with all these niggers" (114). His inability to recognize his own affiliation to these slaves may result from his youth and the decent treatment he has apparently received from the Sartorises, but it also reflects a lack of self-awareness striking in one so intelligent. Ringo's racial identification is as unfixed as his legal racial status is fixed, creating the "third term" which Marjorie Garber, in her book on cross-dressing, identifies as a challenge to "binary thinking, whether particularized as male and female, black and white, yes and no, Republican and Democrat, self and other, or in any other way."[13] It is a fitting description of Ringo who, as Bayard says, has grown up in the family so that "maybe he wasn't a nigger anymore or maybe I wasn't a white boy anymore, the two of us neither, not even people any longer: the two supreme undefeated like two moths, two feathers riding above a hurricane" (7). But this is the Civil War South; the possibility of there being a third term is denied by the very terminology of the dichotomy: nigger vs. white boy. In fact, the possibility of transcending race also indicates that to deny race is to deny human identity; once Bayard admits the possibility of their being neither nigger nor white boy, he realizes that the next stage is "not even people any longer." Judith Butler has suggested that naming and labeling can constitute gendering of the individual self. "Such attributions or interpellations contribute to that field of discourse and power that orchestrates, delimits, and sustains that which qualifies as 'the human.' We see this most clearly in the examples of those abjected beings who do not appear properly gendered; it is their very humanness that comes into question."[14] In Faulkner's work, indeterminacy in either race or gender can question human identity; just as Drusilla's ungendering undermines her humanity, so here does the unracing of Ringo and Bayard challenge their existence as people. However, the power of the names, nigger and white boy, destroys the possibility implied in the "maybe" clause of Bayard's formulation; once those terms are employed, it is no longer possible to say, "maybe he wasn't," for in these circumstances Ringo *is* a "nigger" and Bayard *is* a white boy, labels which the South is fighting a war, in part, to preserve.

Yet just as the war reinforces the binary, it also challenges it both in the opportunities it provides Ringo to assert his intelligence and resourcefulness and in the ways that it explodes the binary system of slave and free, putting Ringo on a par with Granny. In fact, he one-ups Granny by not merely accepting the note but enforcing it to the letter, and then turns to her and very adroitly challenges her language. "Hah . . . Whose hand was that?" (114). If Granny's manipulation of the text can be ascribed to the hand of the Almighty, then Ringo's action is similarly inspired. But his comment reflects more than an attempt to escape punishment; it asserts an equality to Granny in its tacit acknowledgment that the hand in question is, in fact, Ringo's.

By placing himself within the divine scheme of things, Ringo breaks down the dichotomy of slave vs. free which has hitherto defined his life. He does, I would argue, set up a third term as an African American subject, living the identity which Loosh has movingly but less successfully asserted: "I done been freed; God's own angel proclamated me free and gonter general me to Jordan. I don't belong to John Sartoris now; I belongs to me and God" (75). Like Ringo (and Granny), Loosh redefines the binary of honesty vs. theft, replying to Granny's condemnation of his violation of private property when he betrays to the Yankees the location of the silver, "Let God ax John Sartoris who the man name that give me to him. Let the man that buried me in the black dark ax that of the man what dug me free" (75). This unanswered demand that the legality and authority of slavery be named questions the very notion of such authority, a challenge which Ringo duplicates in his subversion of the legal text; his actions on behalf of those who have enslaved him may mark the degree to which he has been co-opted by the system, yet also illustrate the system's failure in that he has the ability to exploit it. His manipulation of written texts, which he goes on to produce himself—"by now Ringo had learned to copy it so that I don't believe Colonel Dick himself could have told the difference" (127)—grants him a kind of subversive power, as he undermines the very discourse which defines his status. Still it seems poor compensation: discourse is one thing; slavery is another. As Audre Lorde has pointed out, it is difficult to dismantle the master's house by means of the master's tools.

While one might claim that Ringo's appropriation of the master's tools—writing and legality—reveals him as incapable of imagining any alternative, we can also read Ringo's active participation in this attack against the army which will liberate him as his claim to personal worth. The boys grow up playing together almost as equals, though Bayard notes that their arrangement is that "I would be General Pemberton twice in succession and Ringo would be Grant, then I would have to be Grant once so Ringo could be General Pemberton or he wouldn't play anymore." Despite the seeming equality of two boys who have "both fed at the same breast and had slept together and eaten together," they both realize that "Ringo was a nigger too" (7), and thus lesser than Bayard. In this war against the Yankees, however, Ringo plays the starring role. His superior intelligence ("Father was right; he was smarter than me" [125]) finally places him, if only briefly, ahead of Bayard. In fact, as Bayard rather resentfully notes, "he had got to treating me like Granny did—like he and Granny were the same age instead of him and me" (126).

Yet once the peculiar institution has been overthrown, Ringo loses position. As he himself announces, "I ain't a nigger any-more. I done been abolished" (199). He speaks more truly than he probably realizes. With the war now over, his lead over Bayard vanishes. In fact, by the time of John Sartoris's murder, Ringo has been reduced, even in Bayard's language, to "my boy" (213). He now, however, seems more attuned to racial difference and what it means, for after suggesting that they bushwhack Redmund, he continues, "But I reckon that wouldn't suit that white skin you walks around in" (218). By suggesting that Bayard's whiteness is merely a covering, something "you walks around in," Ringo again associates racial identity with a kind of cross-dressing. In this wonderfully subtle turn of phrase, Ringo aligns aberrance with whiteness and further suggests that this whiteness has been recently attained, something which desecrates Bayard's sense of self for, unlike Ringo's black skin, Bayard's white skin has gotten in the way of his family identity. "I remember how I thought then that no matter what might happen to either of us, I would never be The Sartoris to him" (215). Ringo, who has "changed even less than I had since that day when we nailed Grumby's body to the door of the old compress," is still caught in Colonel Sartoris's era. His unique individuality can only be asserted in the upheaval of war, which may explain his reluctance to accept the changing postwar standards, a change recognized even by Colonel Sartoris, who tells his son, "But now the land and the time too are changing; what will follow will be a matter of consolidation, of pettifogging and doubtless chicanery in which I would be a babe in arms but in which you, trained in the law, can hold your own—our own" (231). Postwar law, a different type of textuality from the divine authority which Granny and Ringo play at so deftly, demands different talents: formal study, an opportunity denied to Ringo. It is only during war that he can define himself as outside the binary. In fighting, he can find his way to a third term; in voting, there is no third term—nor even a second. Wash Jones's words in *Absalom* resonate here with an eerie force: "[T]hey mought have whupped us, but they aint kilt us yit."[15] As long as that "us" defines a white culture, with its attention now turned back to governing itself, there is no place within it for Ringo.

Rosa Millard's world, while closer to the border of the white male hegemony than Ringo's, nonetheless also has some nebulous boundaries in times of war. Like Ringo, Granny struggles to maintain a world order based upon the very dualities which she destroys through her behavior. Trying desperately to retain her sense of good and evil, she discovers that war not only provides the opportunity to transgress the boundaries of being a lady, but it also enables her to cheat in her Christian beliefs. In fact, her usurpation of masculine power is tied to her challenge to divine authority. It is not surprising that Granny should find herself caught in a Christian vacuum, for war, of course, violates the central tenets of Christianity. All may be fair in war, but little is Christian in war. Her struggles are revealed in the ways that she tries to manipulate her Christian beliefs by making what even she admits is a sin acceptable due to extenuating circumstances: the horrors of war. Her attempt to justify the means by the end offers a further implicit criticism of patriarchal authority, in its open challenge to God the Father.

> "I did not sin for revenge; I defy You or anyone to say I did. I sinned first for justice. And after that first time, I sinned for more than justice: I sinned for the sake of food and clothes for Your own creatures who could not help themselves—for children who had given their fathers, for wives who had given their husbands, for old people who had given their sons, to a holy cause, even though You have seen fit to make it a lost cause." (147)

Granny's complaint that God has "seen fit" to make a holy cause a lost cause suggests that God is not quite with it. The greater sin rests not with her but with God's inefficiency. Yet even in her concern for her lost cause, Granny focuses not on the men who died but on those who remain behind. She seems to be outraged not so much at defeat as at God's willingness to sacrifice the lives of "creatures who could not help themselves"—women, children, and the aged. God has been a bad Father in that He has ignored His obligations to the helpless.

Thus war reveals the tenuous hold which God has upon the world, the limitations of patriarchy itself. Granny's complaint echoes the lamentations raised by many Confederate women, as Drew Faust has demonstrated. Yet there are some significant differences. Faust cites Almira Acors's letter to Jefferson Davis: "I do not see how God can give the South a victory when the cries of so many suffering mothers and little children are constantly ascending up to him. . . . [I]f I and my little children . . . die while there [sic] Father is in service I invoke God Almighty that our blood rest upon the South."[16]

For Acors, the responsibility lies not with God but with the South, a charge which Granny Millard never quite recognizes. In her anger at this failure of patriarchal authority, Granny fails to see the implicit indictment of the Southern culture in which she is firmly entrenched. Interestingly, she omits any mention of the other "creatures who could not help themselves": slaves. When saddled with 110 former slaves, she sends them back to their masters with the injunction, "if I ever hear of any of you straggling off like this again, I'll see to it" (115). Regardless of whether she could or would make good her threat, she still refuses to acknowledge that slavery itself is at least as great a betrayal of Christianity as war. She retains the position of mistress, arbiter of justice, and ultimate authority. Thus her critique of God the Father suggests that the system would be improved by bringing in God the Mother, someone more attuned to the problems of women and children, but who still knows how to keep the slaves in line. And, not surprisingly, Granny herself seems the perfect candidate for the job. Yet shifting from a patriarchal to a matriarchal God does little to undermine the system. Granny may challenge the efficiency of Christian patriarchy, but she seeks to improve it, not overthrow it. Again, the structure of the binary—patriarchy versus matriarchy—leaves no space for a third term.

This Christian order is held in place largely by language, a power Granny clearly recognizes, as Bayard and Ringo get their mouths washed out with soap for swearing, for desecrating the sanctity of the word. However her assumption that she can knowingly sin and then attain forgiveness on the grounds that God has fallen short on the job marks a far greater challenge to the sanctity of the word and the text than the boys' curses. Her adherence to divine authority is tenuous at best; as Ringo says, "She cide what she want and then she kneel down about ten seconds and tell God what she aim to do, and then she git up and do hit" (93). Then, if what she does is a sin, she dares God to damn her for it. In qualifying the Biblical injunctions against lying and stealing, she challenges both Biblical authority and the fixity of linguistic meaning, particularly in the face of war. Yet even this potentially subversive response to Biblical textuality is based upon her belief in another patriarchal system: Southern chivalry, which should defend women and children. In being unable to imagine an alternative to chivalry, even though she herself lives one, she reveals the degree to which she remains firmly grounded in the patriarchal order. We need that third term to destroy the binary which, as Hélène Cixous would point out, is inevitably hierarchic. One of the elements in such standard oppositions as male/female or black/white is always more powerful. Thus, if we cannot break down the dichotomy we have not a binary but a unitary ordering.

In fact, Granny's dedication to chivalry and the binaries of gender it inscribes, literally kills her. While even the Yankee Colonel Dick is willing to protect Southern women and children, the outlaw Grumby is not. Granny's involvement in patriarchy has blinded her to its limitations. Living in a world highlighted by war's oppositions of north and south, black and white, she takes for granted another hierarchical system: class. Diane Roberts notes that Granny's "guerilla cunning fails to take into account the way the war itself has destroyed old verities of class."[17] The polarization of war causes her to idealize one side. If "Even the Yankees do not harm old women" (153), then she is surely in no danger from Southern men. She "still believed that what side of a war a man fought on made him what he is" (149), and so fails to realize that the same war which allows her not to be a lady also allows men not to be gentlemen. Once the laws of chivalry break down, women and children need to fend for themselves, yet the system which has placed them on pedestals has also denied them the means to do so. Granny, who wants to correct and perpetuate rather than overthrow the system, is ultimately victimized by it. As Mr. Compson says in *Absalom,* "we in the South made our women into ladies. Then the War came and made the ladies into ghosts."[18] War destroys the lady, and in so doing, betrays the woman behind the lady.

Drusilla Hawk, on the other hand, vehemently rejects the lady's role. Though her mother believes she has achieved the perfect destiny when her fiancé dies in battle, "to be the bride-widow of a lost cause" (191), and thus chosen but sexually pure, Drusilla has other ideas.

> "Living used to be dull, you see. Stupid. You lived in the same house your father was born in . . . and then you grew up and you fell in love with your acceptable young man. . . . But now you . . . don't have to worry now about the house and the silver because they get burned up and carried away, and you don't have to worry about the negroes . . . and you don't even have to sleep alone, you dont even have to sleep at all." (100–101)

Drusilla sees the war as liberation from domesticity and marriage, yet she fights to support the system which has imposed that domesticity upon her. Apparently unable to see beyond her immediate situation, she tries to become a man in order to preserve the man's world against which she rebels. Drusilla later claims that her aim was simply "to hurt Yankees" (191), but this brief statement lacks the power of her passionate condemnation of conventional female domesticity. While many Confederate women, in fact, expressed similar sentiments, and some few did fight, they were viewed, Catherine Clinton argues, as "gender traitors, impermissible patriots. Women dressing as men to serve as soldiers betrayed a fundamental tenet of Confederate faith."[19] To fight not only *like* a man but *as* a man defies the system which the men fought to uphold, to "protect," as Aunt Louisa puts it, "the heritage of courageous men and spotless women" (190). Drusilla's cross-dressing violates this binary of "courageous men and spotless women," illustrating Judith Butler's observation that drag may illuminate "the exposure or the failure of heterosexual regimes ever fully to legislate or contain their own ideals."[20] Cross-dressing exposes the ideals for which the South is fighting—stable racial and gender hierarchies—as a sham.

Not surprisingly, then, Drusilla's ostensible support of Southern patriarchy through her "manly" behavior in fact constitutes a more serious challenge to it than Granny's usurpation of divine patriarchal authority. Granny, who operates on the assumption that being a lady will protect her, does not seek to get beyond conventional gender roles; she is forced into action because of God's inattention to the situation, not through any apparent dissatisfaction with her sex. However, Drusilla's manliness does, indeed, radically "unsex" her, for her emphasis on her body suggests a more feminized kind of discourse than Granny's textuality. Women stand outside the realm of symbolic discourse as formulated by Lacan, who associates language with the child's move from a presymbolic union with the mother into the realm of the father. Thus Drusilla's use of a kind of bodily discourse represents a particularly feminine response despite its apparent masculinity. Having been objectified by a system which places women on pedestals, Drusilla then transforms that object into a subject by essentially speaking with her body. Her masculine attire speaks what she can barely articulate in language—her dissatisfaction with her gender. Drusilla, like Ringo and, to a lesser extent, Granny, also seeks a third position, one beyond the binaries of race and gender.

But only war offers such possibilities, as by intensifying binaries it also seems to circumvent them. Once the war ends, and the men reestablish control, women must fall back to their gendered positions. More thoroughly defeated than Granny, who at least gets a heroine's funeral and inspires a particularly gruesome form of vengeance, Drusilla ends up back in dresses and marriage. While ostensibly it is the women of community who impose this order, before condemning them too harshly we must remember that the male populace has no intentions of admitting women into its bastion of power; indeed, Drusilla's marriage is delayed while John Sartoris ensures that former slaves are denied their voting rights. Drusilla is tolerated only because she is one, not many, for the lone exceptions do not threaten male dominance. With both men and women trying to reconstruct as much of the antebellum white hegemony as possible, Drusilla stands no chance. Neither man nor lady, she discovers there is no acceptable third position for the likes of her, and must forgo even the costumes through which she had attempted to establish one. Bayard realizes, "But she was beaten, like as soon as she let them put the dress on her she was whipped; like in the dress she could neither fight back nor run away" (201). While this defeat by skirts may seem surprising, given Drusilla's strength of character, it fits with studies of the importance of dress, particularly in defining and protecting femininity for Southern women. In an examination of Southern women's diaries regarding Sherman's march to the sea, Jane E. Shultz remarks that large numbers of women express fear of taking off their clothes, even to sleep, and many more report wearing many layers of garments, both to protect the clothes from theft and to shield their bodies from violation. "Implicitly," says Shultz, "the writers were donning clothing as armor."[21] Drusilla discovers that this armor does more than protect one's body; it determines one's identity. Or rather, it purports to do so, for Drusilla's behavior is not entirely dependent on her attire. After all, she successfully defended her horse against the Yankees while wearing her "Sunday dress" (90). Consequently, once "safely" married and in skirts, Drusilla becomes more threatening and mysterious than she was dressed as a man. She seems to become a femme fatale, sexually tempting her stepson and urging him to murder his father's murderer.

Her body speaks now not visually but sensually, through the verbena which she wears, "the only scent you could smell above

the smell of horses and courage" (220), a smell which transcends
war. In fact, it speaks even when she is absent. As Bayard walks
to confront Redmond, he moves "in a cloud of verbena" (246).
And not only does she speak her own body, she also reads other
bodies, knowing the moment she kisses his hand that Bayard
has eschewed violence. "Because they are wise, women are—a
touch, lips or fingers, and the knowledge, even clairvoyance,
goes straight to the heart without bothering the laggard brain at
all" (238). This body language offers women participation in a
discourse based on the literal rather than the figurative and thus
a different kind of voice. Drusilla thus rewrites gender divisions,
giving women bodies with voices.

Although this "voice" too is silenced, it clearly presents a far
greater threat. As an ersatz man Drusilla can be dismissed as a
freak, but as a sexually charged woman she is firmly ensconced
within the system. As Bayard remarks, "I thought how the War
had tried to stamp all the women of her generation and class in
the South into a type and how it had failed" (228–29). But
Bayard is wrong, as Faulkner's narrators so often are. The war
had not tried to stamp all women into a type; if anything, war
has opened up the possibilities for femininity by its defeat of
masculinity. "And so now Father's troop and all the other men
in Jefferson, and Aunt Louisa and Mrs Habersham and all the
women in Jefferson were actually enemies for the reason that
the men had given in and admitted that they belonged to the
United States but the women had never surrendered" (188).[22]
Neither has Drusilla; she has simply shifted the terms of battle
from clothing to what lurks beneath it, causing consternation
not only for Bayard but for many readers as well. Even the
more sympathetic critics of Faulkner's women have had some
harsh things to say about her. Winifred L. Frazier identifies her
as a "moon-cycled, bloody priestess . . . a symbol of destruction," and David Williams calls her "a vessel of vengeance."[23]
While it is certainly the case that Drusilla urges Bayard to
violence, at other points in the novel violence is not treated
with the same moral outrage. When Bayard not only murders

Grumby but, in a particularly grisly scene, pegs his corpse to the door, cuts off the hand, and lays it on Granny's grave, he meets not shocked horror but communal approbation. It seems apparent, then, that Drusilla's quest for violence is only condemned because of her gender. By using her femininity to urge men to fight, Drusilla seems to violate gender boundaries in an even more deadly way than by riding with the troops.

Why? What makes a womanly woman more threatening than a manly woman? Joan Riviere has suggested that women who wish for masculinity may "put on a mask of womanliness to avert anxiety and the retribution feared from men."[24] Thus, Drusilla's seemingly "put on" femininity may be perfectly consistent with her cross-dressing. Yet whether or not Drusilla seeks masculinity, Faulkner, I would argue, seeks to uncover the precariousness of both masculinity and femininity. In a much glossed passage, Luce Irigaray claims that to find a feminine voice, women must "play with mimesis."

> One must assume the feminine role deliberately. Which means already to convert a form of subordination into an affirmation, and thus to begin to thwart it.
>
> To play with mimesis . . . means to resubmit herself—inasmuch as she is on the side of the "perceptible," of "matter"—to "ideas," in particular to ideas about herself, that are elaborated in/by a masculine logic, but so as to make "visible," by an effect of playful repetition, what was supposed to remain invisible: the cover-up of a possible operation of the feminine in language.[25]

Drusilla certainly makes visible the feminine by her not-so-playful acting out of female sexuality. Having had her gender reimposed upon her, she plays the role with a vengeance, and so uncovers the power of the feminine in language, particularly when juxtaposed to masculine discourse. "I thought then," says Bayard, "of the woman of thirty, the symbol of the ancient and eternal Snake and of the men who have written of her, and I realised then the immitigable chasm between all life and all print—that those who can, do, those who cannot and suffer enough because they cant, write about it" (228). Writing is reduced to mere compensation for lack of experience in a striking reversal of the experience of writing about war, where women are condemned to silence due to lack of firsthand knowledge. But somehow, in sexual matters, one's lack of combat credentials becomes an asset in representation. Yet even this linguistic power falls short, for all the words in the world cannot bridge the "immitagable chasm between all life and all print." At Granny's funeral, Brother Fortinbride preaches, " 'Words are fine in peacetime, when everybody is comfortable and easy. But now I think we can be excused' " (137). War and sex leave words behind. So, in her deadly play with mimesis, Drusilla becomes a far more potent force than through her cross-dressing, revealing the inadequacy of the language with which men attempt to control the world.

In fact, in some ways it seems to me that she is now cross-dressing as a woman, and thus revealing how thin the veneer of femininity can be, as she becomes so powerfully feminine as to seem masculine, urging vengeance and fondling the pistols whose phallic symbolism she understands perfectly. " 'Do you feel them? the long true barrels true as justice, the triggers . . . quick as retribution, the two of them slender and invincible and fatal as the physical shape of love?' " (237). Sherrill Harbison argues that Bayard and Drusilla reverse gender roles here, and that Bayard's appropriation of the feminine succeeds where Drusilla's masculinity fails. "For Bayard, adopting the more 'womanly' attitude toward violence and retribution served to restore his family to good graces with the community. For Drusilla, adopting the masculine, chivalric code of honor, demanding satisfaction for injuries by retaliation, led to the loss of all she had."[26] While these reversals may implicitly privilege the feminine mode by Bayard's triumph, it is the type of triumph Elaine Showalter describes in her famous critique of *Tootsie:* men teaching women how to be better women.[27] Gender has been reconfigured as men now colonize the feminine and incorporate it into a new masculinity, one from which women are as fully excluded as they were from the old one.

Yet a disquieting issue remains: that female sexuality may lead to phallic power. Though Faulkner backs away from this possibility and sends Drusilla packing, he does not erase it altogether. In transferring her power into a phallic gun, a weapon of war, Drusilla also opens up the possibility that war may not be the manly realm it has been assumed to be. As even the Yankees recognize, not only are Southern women not defenseless, they are not even defeated. By shifting the arena of war from the battlefield to the noncombatants, Faulkner privileges a different kind of battle, a more frightening spectacle than bullets and cannons. In fact, the combination of female sexuality and violence proves so threatening that it must be immediately exorcised by Bayard's commitment to nonviolence. For when women play with mimesis to the extent that they uncover a potential phallic power, they also open up the possibility that gender, as Butler argues, can be "performative—that is, constituting the identity it is purported to be."[28] This possibility is beyond even the power of the Civil War to provide. Miriam Cooke has suggested that only postmodern wars successfully challenge gender codes.

> Whereas wars previously codified the binary structure of the world by designating gender-specific tasks and gender-specific areas where these tasks might be executed, today's wars are represented as doing the opposite. Postmodern wars highlight and then parody those very binaries—war/peace, good/evil, front/home front, combatant/noncombatant, friend/foe, victory/defeat, patriotism/pacifism—which war had originally inspired.[29]

I'm not sure she's entirely accurate here, for Faulkner's Civil War literature opens up these possibilities, even if it does not sustain them. Gender may be performative, may be parodied during war, but as Garber points out, "Those who problematize the binary are those who have a great deal invested in it."[30] This is, I would say, as true for Faulkner as it is for Drusilla. Thus, as Roberts says, the "collapsing of hierarchies is intolerable in a cultural narrative that demands [Drusilla's] subordination as feminine, as a lady."[31] This cultural—and Faulknerian—

narrative, I would argue, demands more than her subordination as feminine; it demands her subordination as female.

Ultimately in this novel gender gives way to sex: if you are a woman, it doesn't matter if your behavior is masculine or feminine; eventually your body will catch up to you and neither great Neptune's ocean nor all the verbena in the world will wash it clean of female sexuality and thus subordination. Granting that gender is performative, what does that matter in a novel that keeps coming back to the body itself? And Faulkner, by setting this as a war story, drives home this point all the more forcefully. All the cross-dressing, all the captured uniforms (which Colonel Sartoris seems to specialize in), and all the captured stock will not substitute for human bodies. Victory generally goes to whichever side has the most people alive at the end, regardless of what they're wearing and what gender role they may be enacting. Wars open up all sorts of performative potential, but ultimately the body count determines the outcome. So it is for race and gender. Neither African American nor white women's bodies can long be ignored or masked. Granny is murdered, Ringo abolished, and Drusilla banished as the binaries—in which so much has been invested—are reinscribed. Yet something does remain. Though Drusilla may retire defeated, she leaves behind a sprig of verbena, "filling the room, the dusk, the evening with that odor which she said you could smell alone above the smell of horses" (254). That the odor remains, even after the body has gone, may offer a lingering hope for a system of identity both grounded in the body and independent of it, a system which can operate beyond the upheaval of war, even as the verbena can be smelled "above the smell of horses." A smell, after all, cannot be cross-dressed and may thus offer a fourth term, a term which depends neither on binary logic nor its dissolution.

NOTES

1. William Faulkner, *The Unvanquished* (New York: Vintage International, 1990), 143–44. Subsequent references will be to this edition and will be noted parenthetically within the text.

2. Susan Schweik, *A Gulf So Deeply Cut* (Madison: University of Wisconsin Press, 1991), 3.

3. Anne Goodwyn Jones, "Male Fantasies?: Faulkner's War Stories and the Construction of Gender," *Faulkner and Psychology*, ed. Donald M. Kartiganer and Ann J. Abadie (Jackson: University Press of Mississippi, 1994), 24.

4. I am indebted to Susan Schweik for drawing my attention to the following examples.

5. Jones, 28.

6. *Lion in the Garden*, ed. James Meriwether and Michael Millgate (New York: Random House, 1966), 57–58.

7. Sandra Gilbert and Susan Gubar, *No Man's Land*, vol.2 (New Haven: Yale University Press, 1989), 343.

8. *Essays, Speeches, and Public Letters*, ed. James B. Meriwether (New York: Random House, 1966), 120.

9. Quoted in Edmund Wilson, *Patriotic Gore* (New York: Oxford University Press), 265.

10. Margaret R. Higonnet, "Civil Wars and Sexual Territories," *Arms and the Woman*, ed. Helen Cooper, Adrienne Auslander Munich, Susan Merrill Squier (Chapel Hill: University of North Carolina Press, 1989), 80.

11. Drew Gilpin Faust, "Altars of Sacrifice: Confederate Women and the Narratives of War," in *Divided Houses: Gender and the Civil War*, ed. Catherine Clinton and Nina Silber (New York: Oxford University Press, 1992), 176.

12. Margaret Homans, *Bearing the Word* (Chicago: University of Chicago Press, 1986), 4.

13. Marjorie Garber, *Vested Interests: Cross-Dressing and Cultural Anxiety* (New York: Routledge, 1992), 10–11.

14. Judith Butler, *Bodies That Matter* (New York: Routledge, 1993), 8.

15. William Faulkner, *Absalom, Absalom!* (New York: Vintage Books, 1987), 349.

16. Faust, 194.

17. Diane Roberts, *Faulkner and Southern Womanhood* (Athens: University of Georgia Press, 1994), 16.

18. Faulkner, *Absalom, Absalom!*, 10.

19. Catherine Clinton, *Tara Revisited: Women, War, and the Plantation Legend* (New York: Abbeville Press, 1995), 98.

20. Butler, *Bodies*, 237.

21. Jane E. Schultz, "Mute Fury: Southern Women's Diaries of Sherman's March to the Sea," in *Arms and the Woman*, 64.

22. Drew Faust suggests that, in fact, the Confederacy failed, in part, because women resisted the roles allotted to them and so refused to offer their full support to the war. Faulkner, on the other hand, seems to be indulging in the postbellum rewriting of the myths of the South, including that of the Southern women's unwavering support for the cause. Yet the nature of that support, particularly as demonstrated through Drusilla and Granny, suggests that they were not upholding the Confederacy as much as they were fighting for female power and expression.

23. Winifred L. Frazier, "Faulkner and Womankind—'No Bloody Moon,'" in *Faulkner and Women*, ed. Doreen Fowler and Ann J. Abadie (Jackson: University Press of Mississippi, 1986), 169; David Williams, *Faulkner's Women: The Myth and the Muse* (Montreal : McGill-Queens University Press, 1977), 211.

24. Joan Riviere,"Womanliness as Masquerade," in *Formations of Fantasy*, ed. Victor Burgin, James Donald, Cora Kaplan (New York: Methuen, 1986), 35.

25. Luce Irigaray, *This Sex Which Is Not One*, trans. Catherine Porter (Ithaca: Cornell University Press, 1985), 76.

26. Sherrill Harbison, "Two Sartoris Women: Faulkner, Femininity, and Changing Times," in *Critical Essays on William Faulkner: The Sartoris Family*, ed. Arthur F. Kinney (Boston: G.K. Hall, 1985), 292.

27. See Elaine Showalter, "Critical Cross-Dressing: Male Feminists and The Woman of the Year," *Raritan* 2 (Fall, 1983).

28. Judith Butler, *Gender Trouble* (New York: Routledge, 1990), 25.

29. Miriam Cooke, "WO-man Retelling the War Myth," in *Gendering War Talk*, ed. Miriam Cooke and Angela Woollacott (Princeton: Princeton University Press, 1993), 182.

30. Garber, 110.

31. Roberts, 24.

Faulkner Unplugged:
Abortopoesis and *The Wild Palms*

Joseph R. Urgo

It was a collapsing of the entire body.

1

A current style of performance in the popular music world is for the artist to present himself "unplugged." The term refers to new and to renewed acts by such veteran rock and roll artists as Paul McCartney, who unplugged his electric guitar in a tremendously successful acoustic tour a few years ago. Recordings followed, and unplugged productions became the rage. In addition to McCartney, other rock and rollers have unplugged themselves for public consumption. Pulling the plug aborts the power source, leaving the artist without electrical amplification in a medium that defines itself by electricity. Nonetheless, for many older performers, unplugging the power source represents a means of regaining influence in the music world: Rod Stewart, Neil Young, and Aerosmith, for example, had fallen from the public arena until their return via the unplugged route. Rock and roll performers who became superstars in the 1960s and 1970s *because* they "plugged in" to (and largely defined) electrical music are now returning to prominence because they are unplugging themselves from that same source. McCartney, with The Beatles, set the standard for amplified rock and roll music, moving from his left-handed electric bass guitar to various synthetic creations, all plugged into endless sources of electrified power. Now, thirty years after the electrical revolution in popular music, the old rockers return unplugged, claiming renewed musical relevance through a kind of abdication of surge.

There are clear gains to be had in the masculine act of negating the source of original vitality. However, similar avenues of renewed potency are not open to female artists. The phenomenon of "unplugged" performances has been claimed almost exclusively by males and there are very few veteran female artists who have overtly presented themselves "unplugged." The fact that there is something vaguely ludicrous in the thought of *Bonnie Raitt: Unplugged*, or *Linda Ronstadt: Unplugged*, indicates that there is something particularly male about this phenomenon, and that women are not readily able to participate. Electrified rock and roll has been, traditionally, a male phenomenon, with women operating at the margins. To continue the surge terminology, it may be that female artists are not perceived as being plugged in to begin with. Sexism in popular music has marked the industry from its inception. The female artist without tremendous power is more likely recognized as the *norm* in feminine popular music, with plugged-in acts (such as Janis Joplin's) seen as clear departures. Gender distinctions in rock and roll music are thus brought to the fore in the current phenomenon of unplugged performances. The unplugged female artist is either a redundancy or, even worse, signals the death of the female artist. After all, *k.d.lang: unplugged* would simply disappear. Perhaps a woman cannot unplug a power source to which the culture finds her in dubious connection.[1]

The "unplugged" movement in popular music represents a cultural moment in which the asymmetrical status of the genders can be delineated. What is the qualitative difference between unplugging a male artist and unplugging his female counterpart? When male artists unplug themselves they implicitly claim that the authority of their performance is enhanced by, but not dependent upon, their power source. Unplugged, the artist seems to speak directly to us, aging rock and rollers that we may be. To have had such potency (The Beatles in Shea Sta-

dium, four young men surrounded by such electrical amplification) and then to unplug it: what greater act of intimacy and
strength can there be? Do we not remember how it was, how
close we felt to Paul McCartney thirty years ago? I can almost
imagine the fan's plea to an "unplugged" McCartney: " 'We
cant help it. It's not us now. That's why: don't you see? I want
it to be us again, quick, quick. We have so little time. In twenty
years I cant anymore and in fifty years we'll both be dead.' "[2]

Quoted here, of course, is Charlotte Rittenmeyer's plea to
her lover, Harry Wilbourne, concerning her planned abortion.
Charlotte and Harry, in *The Wild Palms*, attempt to unplug
themselves and their social performances from traditional
sources of gendered power (Harry from his career, Charlotte
from her children) so that it will "be us again," the two lovers,
alone. Harry's cultural potency is based upon his being plugged
into medical school. When he quits, he must rely on his
resources without professional legitimacy. He manages to do
this well enough. The conventional source of female power
flows from the ability to give birth, so Charlotte's attempt to
unplug herself is more dangerous than a simple abdication of
social power. *Harry Wilbourne: Unplugged* is a renegade doctor, an abortionist; but *Charlotte Rittenmeyer: Unplugged* is a
nonentity, a corpse.

What Harry and Charlotte want above all else is to be
disengaged from the sources of power that, initially, have as-
sured their destinies. For Harry, this means quitting school and
assuming an identity based not on a medical degree but on his
learned and discovered talents. Charlotte, on the other hand, is
compelled to abjure motherhood and construct an identity
centered not on procreation but upon the cessation of maternity.
Her final claim to the right of abortion proposes that female
power be based not only in motherhood, being plugged in to
certain biological determinants, but also in the antithesis of
creation, in the act of unplugging the power source itself.
Charlotte's liberation, then, is an assault on an entire system of
patriarchy that is dependent upon the equation of femininity

with maternity. In her traditional definition, the woman is designed to receive what the male produces. Constructed as absence, female sexuality, on such Freudian terms, cannot withstand the willful abdication of what is already understood as an endowed vulnerability. Unplugging Charlotte produces a double negative: the removal of absence. The act, in Faulkner's imagination, is an invitation to disaster, a primal flooding, an overdetermination of consequences. Harry's liberation is a simple walk away from middle-class rewards, with no corresponding loss in his socially defined maleness. Unplugged, Harry is liberated both socially and sexually; but when he tries to unplug Charlotte, he must confront the "tremendous silence which roared down upon him like a wave, a sea" (307). The unplugged man signals life and vitality, but the unplugged woman invites death: she is suicidal.

The Wild Palms provides a useful frame through which to explore the idea of becoming "unplugged" from culturally determined power. The novel's central act of abortion might be cast as *Female: Unplugged,* or the disengaging of the female from the mother. Through abortion the female claims that her potency lies not only in creation but also in a sort of Faulknerian uncreation. And just as the pop artist cannot become "unplugged" unless his musical influence has already based itself upon being plugged in (we can't have James Taylor unplugged), so too does abortion only become a power issue if maternity and pregnancy have been established as primal sources of female potency. Judith Wilt calls contemporary abortion consciousness "the Armageddon of the maternal instinct" because in it she senses "the last days, not of maternity, but of maternity as instinct." Through the choice of abortion, maternity becomes a matter of consciousness, no longer an exclusively natural function.[3] The abortion debate at the end of the twentieth century is a power struggle among women that revolves around the question of where, exactly, female potency originates. When the man is unplugged, a nostalgia for lost power in turn provides him a new source of vitality. When the woman is unplugged, it is not nostalgia that emerges but a kind of natural disaster. A man may give up the signs of his masculinity and become an unplugged male phenomenon, like Harry Wilbourne, who knows that Charlotte is " 'a better man than I am' " (133). He can even dream of lying "passively on his back," achieving the "peace with which a middleaged eunuch might look back upon the dead time before his alteration" (34). But the unplugged female finds no such serenity. Charlotte, unplugged during her abortion, senses "more than just a slackening of joints and muscles," but "a collapsing of the entire body as undammed water collapses" (306). Harry, unplugged, is at peace; he is a "eunuch," a negation of physical masculinity, yes, but also the embodiment of a kind of postsexual tranquility. Charlotte unplugged is "a collapsing," a catastrophic disintegration of both self and, given the consequences, of the social order she has created with Harry. *The Wild Palms* might thus be read as Faulkner's interrogation of the discordant sexual bases of male and female social and cultural autonomy.

The novelty of the unplugged male performer in the 1990s is an emblem of a general trend among men to willingly abdicate traditional sources of power. However, as projected in *The Wild Palms*, the ability of a man to unplug himself from his own masculinity indicates no real loss of cultural dominance, but quite the opposite.[4] When Harry quits medical school to become Charlotte's lover, his masculinity is not reduced, his actions are no affront to nature or to his middle-class "obligations." In fact, both he and Charlotte and the force of the narrative itself argue against any such idea of bourgeois commitment. The only obligation Harry has is to be Charlotte's lover, a particular kind of male fantasy,[5] but also the reversal of a conventional wifely function. Harry is unplugged from any customary masculine duties. Charlotte pulls the plug, as we know, and tries to get Harry to do the same for her. But in Faulkner's imagination (and in ours, too, as a culture that has not achieved consensus on the source of female power) the woman cannot be unplugged without letting loose "the boom

of seas" and "the roar of water" that accompany Charlotte's
death (315).[6]

<h1 style="text-align:center">2</h1>

Abortion, abortion, abortion. Like the oldentime *Be Light*, the
current *Be Still*. Do the creators truly possess the will to
destroy? The modernist has unplugged God and turned to her
own creative powers. *Creativity*. We worship this in ourselves.
We canonize those with creative genius, those who create and
in turn enthrall our critical creativities. *Genius*. Surely William
Faulkner was one. Study him. How did he do it? *Study him*.
Where did he get it? *Study him*. Where did it come from?
Abortion, abortion, abortion. Wouldn't we like to go through
Faulkner's garbage can. What did this man throw away, the
stuff our books are made of? We sing the old Beatles' song:
"Hey, Bungalow Bill: What did you kill, Bungalow Bill?"

<h1 style="text-align:center">3</h1>

The Wild Palms is comprised of a series of narrative abortions.
Every time the text stops and goes either to "Old Man" or to
"Wild Palms" a textual abortion occurs, a stop-narrative of
Faulkner unplugged. Minrose Gwin aligns these narrative inci-
sions with menstrual images: "the novel flows sequentially until
the reader's desire for the story reaches a point of fullness,
beyond which it cannot go without flooding." In Gwin's view
this accounts for the centrality of the Mississippi River, as each
abrupt interruption in the narrative flow is like a "bend" in the
stream.[7] Gwin's interpretation is perfectly valid, but there is
more than one way to deal with fullness. I don't think that *The
Wild Palms* celebrates or even valorizes female fecundity. On
the contrary, I see the novel as one in which creation is inverted,
so that creativity expands to encompass its own cessation. The
novel wants to know what it is like to be unplugged from the

very essence of one's being, to put a stop to the bends and flows of narrative and physical creation.

Certain images are emblematic: Charlotte in her beach chair, the convict in his jail cell, Harry by himself, grieving. We confront these people at points where their own creativity or resourcefulness has left them, ultimately, alone. From the perspective of gender, *The Wild Palms* does suggest a gulf between man and woman that may flood into passion (as Gwin implies); it also suggests that all intergender experience is subject to abortion, to sudden collapse, because each and every one of us is captive to our own sexuality. Abortion, in Faulkner's hands, encompasses gender interaction; it can also stand for the impasse of postfeminist stoppage itself, one of those Faulknerian doors, or barriers, that we cannot pass. The public debate over abortion has crippled the feminist movement in the United States, dividing women, diverting political energies from civil rights. Faulkner draws attention to violent cessation, to impasse, and to the perplexing violations of body and psychic space that are made continually by the Other. When Charlotte discusses her pregnancy with Harry she says that " 'they hurt too much.' " Harry at first mistakes her meaning, thinking "they" are her children: "He was about to say, 'But this will be ours,' when he realised that this was it, this was exactly it" (217). Charlotte means it hurts too much to be plugged in.

The continuity of bodies, from mother to child, denies the autonomy of the female self, and the "hurt" that Charlotte seeks to abort is the pain of this intrusive, unwelcome qualification of her own independence. Charlotte has abandoned everything in her past to assure the complete autonomy of an unplugged self, to create herself and her destiny anew. When she becomes pregnant, she is threatened with the return of her former self, Mother Charlotte. It takes Harry some time, but he eventually realizes what the pregnancy means to this woman. Harry shares Charlotte's desire to be unplugged, and to have the creative freedom of self-renewal and self-construction. But rather than oppose the unborn, Harry initially envies it, thinking about the "wombs into which human beings fled before something of suffering but mostly of terror . . . to become as embryos for a time . . . then to be born again, to emerge renewed" (299). A large portion of our current conception of freedom hinges upon the idea of social construction, of choices, of freely engaged selves. Abortion stares back in negation. Is creative liberty, the freedom to create self and voice, made greater or diminished when adjoined by the freedom to destroy?

The narrative line in *The Wild Palms* is nonlinear; it is abortive. Neither "Wild Palms" nor "Old Man," the twin narratives of Faulkner's text, ever comes to term. The reader is continually wrenched away from one fictional conception and one set of expectations to another setting and another realm of experience. The narrative in *The Wild Palms* is an eternally aborting phenomenon, and it has the potential of repeating itself *ad infinitum, ad abortus*. An abortion, moreover, declares an end not only to an embryo, a potential child, but also aborts a mother and a father, potentialities contained as well within the womb. As readers of *The Wild Palms*, our attention, our expectation of textual fruition, is continually aborted. Many readers have responded (as did editors at Signet[8]) with their own elimination of one or the other of the narratives, reading "Wild Palms" or "Old Man" right through, aborting the other entirely without compunction, even discarding the title Faulkner had given the book initially.[9]

If one begins to create, what is the responsibility to complete that creation? Readers of *The Wild Palms* have often complained, explicitly or implicitly, about Faulkner's series of narrative abortions. Early critics (such as Irving Howe[10] and Joseph Moldenhauer[11]) provided charts and guides to prove the inner logic of the disparate narratives. Thomas McHaney's book-length study of the novel tracks down narrative connections, thematic linkages ("Both the tall convict and the lovers want to evade the realities of life"), and establishes once and for all the holism of the text.[12] Faulkner, of course, claimed the right to provide the story of "Wild Palms" with the counterpoint of "Old

Man."[13] But what is the relation between the creation of Harry and Charlotte and the necessity, or the right, to abort that story with "contrapuntal" action? If the romantic tale of the runaway lovers were not so thoroughly discredited by the botched abortion, Faulkner's method of narrative counterpoint would be, simply, a clever experiment. However, Faulkner's contrapuntal measures are mirrored by the measures taken by the lovers in their attempt to counter Charlotte's pregnancy. Critical measures taken to assure the continuities between the disparate narratives are attempts to naturalize Faulkner's style, to prove that this is, after all, a novel. While the abortion is, in fact, successful (there will be no pregnancy), it comes at the price of Charlotte's own life. And where critical interventions are successful (there will be no separation of these two narratives), it comes at the price of some critical integrity. After all, no matter how many parallels in theme and image we can find, these two stories still have nothing to do with each other. Confronting the novel as a novel, I suggest, means grappling with abortion as narrative contingency. Even though the text makes abortion a deadly business, in other words, its greater significance lies in the dramatic projection of a world in which abortion is a moral dilemma. At one time the power to create held human beings in awe; now it is the power to eliminate life before birth that stops us in our tracks.

Gwin is right: "Charlotte Rittenmeyer bleeds into these pages the unresolvable pleasure and terror of the flooding of self. In the end, Charlotte's *I* floats away like flotsam. We are left to read its indecipherable traces in the dark stain of her woman's blood."[14] But the stain left behind is not entirely indecipherable. Harry can read it, seeing in it the clear choice between memory and eternal obliteration. The community can read also, condemning Harry to prison. No doubt the tall convict reads it as well: his " 'women, - - -t!' " epigraph is one way to decipher the Other. In Charlotte Rittenmeyer's blood, and in her discarded pregnancy, we must read what we mean by self, by *I*, by full subjectivity. When Charlotte becomes pregnant, Harry is aborted as son and empowered as the creator, as father. Aborting that pregnancy, on the other hand, protects the autonomous Harry from qualification. Harry's "botched abortion" puts an end to the pregnancy, to Charlotte, and to his own self as father.

Philosophers and social scientists who have contemplated abortion as an epistemological issue have come to important conclusions which illuminate Faulkner's novel. According to Kristin Luker, "*the debate about abortion is a debate about personhood,*" including the person of the man and woman. Thus, the political debate over abortion concerns whether "*personhood is a 'natural,' inborn, and inherited right, rather than a social, contingent, and assigned right.*"[15] Luker, a social scientist, posits that "pro-life" people find abortion abhorrent because it means that life may be assigned value according to social worth, and that "social worth" may be decided by those in positions of social or economic dominance. On the other hand, "pro-choice" people see the refusal to assume control over human destiny as a kind of cowardice, a failure of will. But the issue will not divide so neatly.

If "pro-choice" people stand for free will, they also have the desire to protect the past, to construct history according to freely made choices in the present. If, in the eyes of choice, nothing is "meant to be," then nothing that has transpired has done so without human intervention. Far from being irresponsible or "anti-life," then, pro-choice people find life itself wrought with human decisions and emotional consequences. On the other hand, "pro-life" people believe in a far more providential, or guided universe, and so they have a logical desire to protect the future from murderous interference, to stand guard over immortality and to assure God of their continued belief. Far from being simpleminded "breeders," pro-life people seek to protect the person from willful destruction. It seems no coincidence that theories of a socially constructed self and sexuality, and especially the rise of gender-based studies, should accompany this era of abortion debate in the United States. The assertive confidence of self-construction is shadowed by the darker question of self-demolition.

Legal philosophy often casts abortion as a privacy issue, leaving aside the social scientist's question of personhood and the literary question of self. Frances Kamm's argument concerning the right of self-defense bears direct relevance to Charlotte's own words about wanting to be alone with Harry. "You have no special obligation to permit your body to be used," according to Kamm, when "an attachment is forced on you."[16] Hence, the right of abortion is akin to the right to defend oneself from unwelcome intrusion. A person must admit that there are limits to what the body can be made to bear, according to Kamm, and the determination of those limits ought to be made by the body in question. Kamm introduces another conundrum into an understanding of abortion that will clarify Faulkner's narrative. The pro-life position, which bases its rhetoric on self-control and willed, physical destiny, hinges upon this issue of limitations. Judith Wilt captures this point when she argues that "the pro-life world-view, so apparently narrow and rigid in practice, so gender structured and hierarchical, prides itself on a philosophical vision of limitlessness—a vision that all possibility may be actuality; while the pro-choice world-view, so multivalent and uncoercive in practice, so committed to the relaxation and crossing of gender and other boundaries, founds itself (pride is not quite the word) on a philosophical vision of human limits—a vision of oscillating losses and gains."[17]

Faulkner's novel cannot be reduced to a dialectic on abortion politics, however. This is because the novel is about abortion more thoroughly and more comprehensively than a simple litmus test would reveal.[18] The Wild Palms raises abortion to the level of narrative trope; it assumes that aborting pregnancy is something human beings can do, and asks what this capacity means in terms of personhood, gender, and human creativity. Abortion imagery plays a central role throughout the novel, even if we leave aside the two surgical abortions that Harry performs. Technically, The Wild Palms contains both its namesake, "Wild Palms," and another narrative, "Old Man," existing in a relation of mother-text to embryo. Whether one has the "right" to abort "Old Man" or "Wild Palms" from *The Wild Palms* raises questions about the integrity of the novel that parallel debates over the rights of women and their unborn children. Beyond this question of structure, the novel is permeated by abortion imagery.

Harry's story begins on his birthday, the recognition and celebration of which he nearly forgoes until he is convinced by his roommate to attend a party, where he meets Charlotte. Had Harry aborted his birthday celebration, none of this would have happened. In order to run away with Charlotte, Harry aborts his medical school internship only a few months before finishing it, or taking it to term. As such, he is a non-doctor, an aborted med-school graduate, with no rights to a job, a career, or to a life as a legitimate doctor. He can, as he says, become an abortionist. The first time that Harry and Charlotte plan to have sex together their lovemaking is aborted because it does not meet Charlotte's romantic expectations. Her language echoes the familiar terminology of abortion: " 'Not like this, Harry. Not back alleys' " (46).

Abortion imagery follows Harry and Charlotte as they attempt to run away together. On the train, still hesitating before leaving with Harry, Charlotte decides to talk to her husband, Rat. She says she must do this in order to "finish" her relationship with him. The terminology, again, casts the deed as an abortion. " 'It's not finished,' " she tells Harry. " 'It will have to be cut' " (59). The "monthly" letters sent back to Charlotte's husband are meant to assure him that Harry has not aborted Charlotte, that she is still being taken care of and may eventually emerge once again in her husband's life. The one time she and Harry don't write (when they "miss" their monthly obligation), detectives come and Harry loses his job. He loses his job because his employer finds out that as a doctor he does not really exist, that Harry is an abortion.

The peaceful, edenic existence that Harry and Charlotte

enjoy after Bradley leaves them alone is also broken by abortion
allusions. Charlotte calls Harry "Adam," and he assures her
that "they had always been alone" (109). After Bradley leaves,
Charlotte swims naked every morning while Harry lies in bed
"existing in a drowsy and foetuslike state, passive and almost
unsentient in the womb of solitude and peace. . . . Then one
day something happened to him" (110). What happens is Time.
Harry realizes that they will soon run out of food; it is time to
come to terms, so to speak, with their predicament. Harry
thinks of his relationship with Charlotte and their life together
in birth imagery. Before birth " 'you are never alone' " because
" 'you are secure and companioned in a myriad and inextricable
anonymity.' " It is after birth that " 'you are going to be alone,' "
Harry says. And as he tells McCord, " 'you can bear just so
much solitude and still live' " (138). According to this logic,
abortion returns the embryo to a community that pre- and
postdates life itself. Alone together, Harry and Charlotte exist
in a womb of self-sufficiency. They are aborted by Time itself, a
sort of romantic miscarriage.

Finally, in the realm of the contrapuntal, the tall convict is
suddenly removed from the society of prisoners into the world
in which he is both alone and a free man. He is born into the
world of civil freedoms as he rides the flood where a literal birth
takes place. He is then sent back into the foetal-state of the
"unborn" or "unfree" prison population. The reappearance of
the tall convict is troubling because he is already technically (or,
bureaucratically) dead. The guard has reported that " 'the body
of the prisoner was no longer in his possession' " (330), that he
had, in a sense, aborted the prisoner. Like an embryo that will
not be extinguished, the tall convict forces the Warden to
declare him in violation of the law, extending his term, forcing
him back into the prison-womb.

The list could well continue and be brought to completion,
but it can also stop here. Others have noted the "foetal and
maternal images"[19] that saturate the novel, and have pointed out
the way that "the birth metaphor limits narrative possibilities for

Charlotte."[20] Janet Carey Eldred cites "still life" imagery in the novel, and points out that critics have largely avoided the centrality of Charlotte's abortion, or have seen it as "unnatural, immoral, unethical, in short, not fit subject matter" for fiction.[21] Recently, Gary Harrington has seen the abortion as emblematic of artistic and personal failure: Harry's professional decline ("hack-work as a doctor") and Charlotte's "attempt to escape the cost in suffering involved in being a parent."[22] But we are dealing here with characters in a novel, not real people (although Faulkner reminds us of a collective fantasy: "*It should be the books, the people in the books inventing and reading about us*" [52; italics in original]). As such, Charlotte's guilt or innocence is not, finally, as important as the way that Faulkner projects the idea of abortion, the narrative means by which he incorporates it into his aesthetics, and the way that those aesthetics, in turn, speak to our own confusion, as a culture, on this matter.

In *The Wild Palms*, abortion is a trope of human existence, one possible response to immanent meaning. Barbara Johnson has asked, "How might the plot of human subjectivity be reconceived (so to speak) if pregnancy rather than autonomy is what raises the question of deliberateness?"[23] The question is a good one to put to *The Wild Palms*, since its conception of human subjectivity is tied inextricably to "all pregnant and female life" (153). Johnson finds "encoded into male poetic conventions" the substitution of creativity for the literal act of giving birth. If "male writing" has been cast as "by nature procreative," Johnson provocatively suspects the implication that "female writing is somehow by nature infanticidal."[24] In *The Wild Palms*, the artistry of Charlotte is under scrutiny, and both she and Harry are, at alternate times, productive in their respective crafts. Gail Mortimer points out as well that it is only when "Charlotte's role as a mother threatens to reassert itself" that her relationship to Harry (and her artistry) falls apart. To Mortimer, the pregnancy and Harry's reaction to it "symbolizes the boundary confusion that is the ultimate threat from women."[25] This reading is sensible especially if we consider the logic by which Charlotte is destroyed. She wishes to be alone with Harry and attempts to stop her pregnancy in order to secure that isolation. She also wishes to capture, in her art, the quality of " 'motion, the speed' " (100) rather than the moving image itself. Her abortion stops her own life as well as that of the embryo inside her, returning Charlotte to the dimension of potentiality along with the unborn, a place of "boundary confusion" where her art is certainly aligned with infanticide, and suicide. As a woman unplugged, disengaged from the known source of her being, there is no place for Charlotte on earth.

It can only be this subconscious realization, the alignment of her creativity with aborted lives and with her own death, that inspires in Charlotte a truly novel term for the feminine experience of sexual intercourse: bitching. To "bitch" is to complain as only a woman can complain. There is no male counterpoint to this term. When she bitches, a woman faces the prospect of hysteria, of becoming unplugged. To "bitch" is to protest with female vigor and in excess of civility. Against what does Charlotte bitch when she bitches with Harry? Heterosexual lovemaking may be a kind of Faulknerian No to death, with Charlotte bitching against her own mortality and the suicidal predicament of female creativity. She says she likes to bitch, and by the evidence in the text, she speaks truthfully. " 'I like bitching, and making things with my hands' " (88). If both of Charlotte's favorite acts are potentially creative, the products of either her hands or her bitching can be aborted. Nonetheless, neither bitching nor making things grants autonomy to the subject; on the contrary, both court danger, not stemming from the acts themselves, but from the painful processes of pregnancy and artistry. Both also stem from desire, and for this Charlotte's term is most appropriate. She bitches against the natural fact that the object of her desire is also the source of her eventual obliteration. Harry kills her, but only after she talks him into risking it. " 'We've done this lots of ways but not with knives, have we?' " (221). She bitches; he botches.

Karen Ramsay Johnson has argued that, throughout his fiction, Faulkner transgresses "traditional male and female sex roles" and "rejects stable categories of self-definition to participate in the re-creative process of narration." As a result, sexual deviance, or departure, signals creativity in much of Faulkner's apocryphal world. Hence Charlotte Rittenmeyer, who "stubbornly refuses to fit any category," also "cannot give up her femaleness," and so she is trapped. "For Charlotte, as for other of Faulkner's female rebels, there is no room"[26] Duvall echoes and expands upon the threat to "traditional gender distinctions" represented by "Charlotte's quest for subjectivity."[27] Charlotte's desire for autonomy will not be compromised by pregnancy or by motherhood. Moreover, Charlotte bitches against the equation of her body and its desires with the loss of subjectivity. She seeks, in a sense, to stop the inevitability of that loss by aborting it every time it appears. " 'I dont think that's too much to be permitted to like, to want to have and keep,' " she tells Harry. (88). If such desires signal a deviant creativity, Charlotte is constructing, in *The Wild Palms*, an alternative femininity; but she ends up martyring herself to that alternative. And as martyr, any feminine alternative represented by Charlotte Rittenmeyer is aborted.

"While on the surface it is the embryo's fate that seems to be at stake," Kristin Luker writes, "the abortion debate is actually about the meanings of women's lives."[28] Critics have attempted to assign meaning to Charlotte's character, given the choices she makes. We may agree that "the plot punishes Charlotte's individualism,"[29] or that "both lovers are to blame for what happens,"[30] but either way, we have the trope of abortion surging through the text. Both Charlotte and Harry attempt to become unplugged from their time and place—Harry from his career as a doctor, Charlotte from her artistic calling and the call of her husband and daughters. Harry articulates the danger involved: " *'You are born submerged in anonymous lockstep with the teeming anonymous myriads of your time and generation; you get out of step once, falter once, and you are trampled to death'* " (54). To Harry the "death" here is figurative. He has killed his chances to become a doctor. Abortion is an abstract issue for males, involving the beginning of life, the power to create and to destroy. But for Charlotte, as portrayed in *The Wild Palms*, it is the very source of her creative vitality that hinges upon her abortion.

4

" 'None of us are androgynous' " (129), quips Harry, a sentiment that might serve as the golden rule in gender studies. Much in the way that "Wild Palms" stands separate from and yet entwined with "Old Man," female and male cannot be collapsed as texts or as genders, although the prospects for intertextual linkages are endless. Placing the parallel narratives together results in interpretations that may be aborted or allowed to mature. In any case, the novel is, as the saying goes, "very pregnant" with critical possibilities. The way the convict sees his pregnant companion is the way I see the novel as a whole, substituting the text for the woman's body: "When he looked upon the swelling and unmanageable body before him it seemed to him that it was not the woman at all but rather a separate demanding threatening inert yet living mass of which both he and she were equally victims" (154). We become the victims of this novel when we see that it compels us to recognize the Age of Abortion as one in which we must confront the implications of our quest for creative freedom, individual license, and autonomy.

There is much in *The Wild Palms* to suggest that gender itself, as a critical category, represents an analytical incongruity. McHaney has commented on how "almost everyone is depicted in androgynous terms" in the novel, suggesting "the oneness of life beneath the apparent diversity of individuality."[31] Duvall even says we should reverse Harry's quip and recognize that the novel presents a case in which "all of us are androgynous."[32] But in the intellectual climate of the present age, "oneness" and "androgyny" simply don't pay as well as diversity and the study of gender difference. Ours is an individualist culture, in which differentiated existence is prized highly and what we have in common simply is not very interesting. The "androgynous couple,"[33] Charlotte and Harry, are an affront to everyone. Again, Harry sees the danger he is entering: " 'So I am afraid,' " he confesses to McCord. " 'Because They are smart, shrewd, They will have to be; if They were to let us beat Them, it would be like unchecked murder and robbery' " (140). Faulkner's scarlet letter stands for Abortion, and beating Them means achieving a state of unplugged self-sufficiency and clean perfection.

No conventionally moral interpretation will suffice for this novel. It is not pro-life and it is not pro-choice; Charlotte and Harry are neither good nor evil; the convict is neither victim nor culprit. *The Wild Palms* is *Faulkner: Unplugged,* and abortion is its chief symbol of the age. In Faulkner's hands, the issue incorporates far more than rights and freedoms; but also in Faulkner's hands, it all comes down, finally, to women's lives. Abortion represents the deadend of modern individualism as much as the death of the maternal instinct. To be unplugged from the cultural significance of her body means that Charlotte must be prepared to die for the abdication of her maternal powers.[34]

Pro-choice contemporaries are often appalled when abortion demonstrations turn violent, seeing a contradiction in pro-life activists who will kill to stop abortions. Faulkner's novel makes clear that this is, indeed, a life and death issue, and it is not only the life of the embryo that is at stake. Men have already died for the freedoms Harry takes for granted: the freedom to walk away from a job, the freedom to run away with another man's wife (and in his case, be provided an insurance policy for it). For males, the freedom to become "unplugged" may indicate that men are not quite so divided amongst themselves over the meaning of their bodies in the public realm.[35] Women, however, have yet to completely negotiate the terms of their own physical freedom. Charlotte takes all the risks in *The Wild Palms*. The abortion performed on her body is only the most dramatic example of the danger in which she places herself when she gets out of step, falters once and is "trampled to death." Harry unplugged is a free man. Charlotte unplugged is a dead woman, leaving Harry convicted of complicity in the botched attempt at her liberation. The act of unplugging, like the act of abortion itself, may signal the exhaustion of modernist freedoms. We would all like to be Unplugged: no complicity in power relations, nothing but our self and what we love, and our audience. It is a suicidal desire. Harry has his famous choice between grief and nothing; Charlotte is not so fortunate. "Between grief and nothing?" Shit.

NOTES

1. Even Watkins locates a parallel discontinuity between male and female roles in soap operas, where men can "depart" from sanctioned male roles (to the extent of being criminals, even rapists) and then reform themselves via penitent sympathy for their victims, eventually rejoining the community as renewed males. Women lack this power: once a bad girl, always a bad girl; no penitence or gender-reversal is allowed female characters. "That such an option never really appears [for women] is a good clue to who actually benefits from the modalities of performance," according to Watkins. "The destabilization of gender-identified roles facilitates what nevertheless remains a primarily *masculine* power of behaving differently. Men, again, can act differently as men; women can act differently only by somehow appearing 'beyond gender.' " *Throwaways: Work Culture and Consumer Education* (Stanford: Stanford University Press, 1993), 154–55. In the language of MTV, males can unplug themselves far more meaningfully (and profitably) than females.

2. William Faulkner, *The Wild Palms* (New York: Vintage, 1966; orig. published 1939), 210. Subsequent references to this text are made parenthetically.

3. Judith Wilt, *Abortion, Choice, and Contemporary Fiction: The Armageddon of the Maternal Instinct* (Chicago: University of Chicago Press, 1992), 34.

4. Faulkner took advantage of this male prerogative in the 1950s when he presented himself "unplugged" in the public arena, claiming no literary authority and identifying himself as a Mississippi mule farmer. Jay Watson, in *Forensic Fictions: The Lawyer Figure in Faulkner* (Athens: University of Georgia Press, 1993), identifies this role as that of the American Cincinnatus and traces its origins to George Washington's return to farming after serving two terms as President. "For Faulkner discovered, just as Washington had, that he could legitimate and even strengthen his authority as a leading citizen and public spokesman precisely by appearing to renounce his authority. By retiring to his farming duties, his ostensible first love, he sought to whet as much as to escape public interest in his political views" (36). Can we turnabout and imagine Toni Morrison making the claim, after winning the Nobel Prize for Literature in 1993, that she is no literary woman but a simple farmer, or perhaps a quilter? The consequences of Morrison's unplugging would not result in an increase in her authority, but would probably invite ridicule.

5. On the status of the novel as "a masculine popular romance plot," see Anne
Goodwyn Jones, " 'The Kotex Age': Women, Popular Culture, and *The Wild Palms*," in
Faulkner and Popular Culture, ed. Doreen Fowler and Ann J. Abadie (Jackson:
University Press of Mississippi, 1990), 142–62.

6. Faulkner experienced a similar "roar" of reaction when he would attempt, later
in his life, to unplug himself from the South by his more moderate public statements
during the Civil Rights era. I thank Robert Hamblin for pointing this out to me. Perhaps
the culture has not achieved a consensus on the source of the writer's power either.

7. Minrose C. Gwin, *The Feminine and Faulkner: Reading (Beyond) Sexual Difference* (Knoxville: University of Tennessee Press, 1990), 136, 137.

8. *The Wild Palms and The Old Man* (New York: Signet/New American Library,
1954). Malcolm Cowley preceded Signet, however, when he printed "Old Man" in *The
Portable Faulkner* (New York: The Viking Press, 1946), claiming that it was "more
effective" than "Wild Palms" and that "it gains by standing alone," a kind of paradoxical
right to life through narrative abortion.

9. I thank Noel Polk for pointing out that the very first abortion performed on the
text eliminated the title Faulkner had intended for the novel, "If I Forget Thee,
Jerusalem." Faulkner's Random House editors considered the reference to the 137th
Psalm too biblical, too Jewish, to sell. According to Polk, who has edited a Corrected
Text of the novel restoring its embryonic title, Faulkner was furious with the placement
of *The Wild Palms* on the title page (electronic correspondence with me, 24 August
1994). Judging by reactions at the 1994 Faulkner and Yoknapatawpha Conference to the
restoration of *If I Forget Thee, Jerusalem*, the handling of this text continues to be
controversial. I have chosen, in this paper, to cite the abortion, not the restoration, and
thus I would hope that my cunning not be concealed by either hand.

10. Irving Howe, *William Faulkner: A Critical Study*, 2nd ed. (New York: Vintage
Books, 1952), 233–43.

11. Joseph J. Moldenhauer, "The Edge of Yoknapatawpha: Unity of Theme and
Structure in *The Wild Palms*," in *William Faulkner: Three Decades of Criticism*, ed.
Frederick J. Hoffman and Olga W. Vickery (New York: Harcourt, Brace & World,
1960), 305–21.

12. Thomas L. McHaney, *William Faulkner's "The Wild Palms": A Study* (Jackson:
University Press of Mississippi, 1975), 118.

13. "I decided that ["Wild Palms"] needed a contrapuntal quality like music. And so
I wrote the other story simply to underline the story of Charlotte and Harry." *Faulkner
in the University: Class Conferences at the University of Virginia, 1957–1958*, ed.
Frederick L. Gwynn and Joseph L. Blotner, 2nd ed. (New York: Vintage, 1965), 171.

14. Gwin, 151.

15. Kristin Luker, *Abortion and the Politics of Motherhood* (Berkeley: University of
California Press, 1984), 5, 157. Emphasis in original.

16. Frances Myrna Kamm, *Creation and Abortion: A Study in Legal Philosophy*
(New York: Oxford University Press, 1992), 42.

17. Wilt, 6–7.

18. John N. Duvall, *Faulkner's Marginal Couple: Invisible, Outlaw, and Unspeakable
Communities* (Austin: University of Texas Press, 1990), puts this issue to rest: "The
presence of the Buckners . . . works against those critics who wish to read 'Wild Palms'
as Faulkner's antiabortion tract. That line of reasoning claims: Charlotte has an abortion
and dies; therefore, Faulkner did not approve of Charlotte and Charlotte is aligned with
the forces of death. But Billie has an abortion too and lives through it, so apparently
Faulkner felt no need to kill off women who have abortions" (49).

19. François Pitavy, "Forgetting Jerusalem: An Ironical Chart for *The Wild Palms*,"
ed. Michel Gresset and Noel Polk, *Intertextuality in Faulkner* (Jackson: University
Press of Mississippi, 1985), 124.

20. Janet Carey Eldred,"Faulkner's Still Life: Art and Abortion in *The Wild Palms*,"
Faulkner Journal 6:1&2 (Fall 1988/Spring 1989): 151. Eldred places Charlotte's abortion
within the historical context of "the liberalization of abortion law during and after the

Great Depression" (143 and *passim*) and argues that Charlotte's primary threat to orthodoxy is her "rejection of the role of motherhood" (154).

21. Eldred, 140. Eldred thoroughly reviews the critical history surrounding *The Wild Palms*. The question of what is and is not "fit subject matter" is problematic, to say the least. If the Western literary canon begins with ancient myth and drama, worse things than abortion lie at its core.

22. Gary Harrington, *Faulkner's Fables of Creativity: The Non-Yoknapatawpha Novels* (Athens: University of Georgia Press, 1990), 82, 71.

23. Barbara Johnson, "Apostrophe, Animation, and Abortion," *Diacritics* 16 (Spring 1986): 33.

24. Ibid., 38.

25. Gail L. Mortimer, "The Ironies of Transcendent Love in Faulkner's *The Wild Palms*," *Faulkner Journal* 1:2 (Spring 1986): 34. The "boundary confusion" that Harry experiences is "the blurred sense of self and hence, of control, that is the essential danger of closeness to women (in Faulkner's view)" (35).

26. Karen Ramsay Johnson, "Gender, Sexuality, and the Artist in Faulkner's Novels," *American Literature* 61:1 (March 1989): 1, 6, 7.

27. Duvall, 46.

28. Luker, 194.

29. Claire Crabtree, "Plots of Punishment and Faulkner's Injured Women: Charlotte Rittenmeyer and Linda Snopes," *Michigan Academician* 24:4 (Summer 1992): 532.

30. Dieter Meindl, "Romantic Idealism in *The Wild Palms*," in Michel Gresset and Patrick Samway, SJ, *Faulkner and Idealism: Perspectives from Paris* (Jackson: University Press of Mississippi, 1983), 91.

31. McHaney, 147.

32. Duvall, 55.

33. Ibid.

34. A figure who tries to remain racially disconnected from his time and place, Joe Christmas, is physically unplugged by his brutal executioner in *Light in August*. Charlotte's ambition is no less tragic. I don't want to push this image too far, but Faulkner creates a number of characters whose attempts to unplug themselves result in physical disaster: Temple Drake, Quentin Compson, the mutinous regiment in *A Fable*, Flem Snopes in *The Mansion*. On the other hand, empowerment awaits some via the same act: the corporal, the reporter, Anse Bundren, Bayard Sartoris in *The Unvanquished*.

35. I do not wish to overstate this point, but only to suggest the unevenness of the parallel. Men are certainly divided on issues of male sexuality, from their reactions to homoeroticism through various manifestations and definitions of sexual deviance. Compulsory male participation in armed services, furthermore, has divided men concerning the relation of their bodies to the state. But none of these issues has reached the social thoroughness of the abortion question, an issue over which males divide as vehemently as do females.

Mister: The Drama of Black Manhood in Faulkner and Morrison

PHILIP M. WEINSTEIN

I wish to begin at what appears to be a certain distance from my topic—"Mister"—by reflecting on what it means to come back to this conference, for the fifth time to be standing on this podium. No one does it for the money, and the weather in August can be downright uncomfortable. Nevertheless, when I arrive, usually a few days before my talk, I find myself helplessly acting out a Faulknerian scenario. Deep in *Go Down, Moses*, I am on the threshold of yet another hunt—male and female this time—wondering who's going to be here, how many familiar faces, how many new ones, whether this will be the year we catch him once and for all. And I say to myself what a laconic Sam Fathers says to the eager Ike McCaslin: "We aint got the dog yet."[1]

"We aint got the dog yet": this won't be the year we catch up with, gain possession over, the writer who is both our beloved and our prey. He'll escape once again. However indelibly this year's talks may (or may not) capture Faulkner's meanings, he'll elude our chase; we'll regroup next summer and begin again. Indeed, what would it mean to capture him? Could we ever have the dog that secures a final grasp upon our desired object? Would we want this even if we could achieve it?

We continue to participate in the *Go Down, Moses* hunt, seeking less to capture him than to invoke him, wanting this event in time—a week in August—to partake as well in something that has happened often enough to seem timeless: "the old bear absolved of mortality and himself who shared a little of it" (*GDM* 195). As with a love affair, it may be the radiance of encounter rather than penetration or possession that we're after. Our entries into the beloved's textual body leave him fabulously unmarked: "forever wilt thou love and she be fair."

In his name we foregather, and there would be no pursuit if he were not its object, yet this ritual is as much about the hunters as the hunted. He is the unifying occasion in whose name we play out "the best game of all, the best of all breathing and forever the best of all listening, the voices quiet and weighty and deliberate for retrospection and recollection and exactitude. . . . There was always a bottle present" (*GDM* 184). "We aint got the dog yet." We don't want the dog; we would refuse him if we had him. We come for refreshment (in its several senses), we come to encounter rather than to penetrate: a good hunt is one that makes us look forward to the next one next year. The name for this activity, for why I've been coming to Oxford in August since 1985, is not possession but identification.

The boundedness of possession (of self and of the other) versus the fluidity of identification (of self with the other): between these two extremes we may begin to conceptualize a more flexible poetics of identity. At the one extreme, identity— one's own, that of others—is imagined as a possessible property. At the other extreme it is an aleatory, interpenetrable, and frighteningly vulnerable resource. The one is solid, with the strengths and weaknesses that attach to solidity. The other is liquid, with the strengths and weaknesses that attach to liquidity. Treating them both as psychological propensities, Freud distinguishes possession and identification as the desire to *have* the other versus the desire to *be* the other. Though he also stresses that "identification . . . is ambivalent from the very first; it can turn into an expression of tenderness as easily as into a wish for someone's removal," he makes it clear that possession accesses the other as object while identification seeks (impossibly) to access the other as subject.[2] These opening remarks, I hope, no longer seem so distant from my topic, for the terms of possession and identification not only describe our commerce with Faulkner and each other, but also take me to "Mister: The Drama of Black Manhood in Faulkner and Morrison."

*   *   *

Years after the [Civil] war white Southerners sighed with relief when Booker T. Washington received a doctorate. They had too much respect for him to call him "Booker" and could not call any black man "Mr."; but "Dr. Washington" presented no problem.
—EUGENE D. GENOVESE, *Roll, Jordan, Roll:*
The World the Slaves Made

Mister: the term articulates two specific moments of racial/gender crisis in Faulkner's *Go Down, Moses* and Morrison's *Beloved*. More broadly, it puts before us, as in this early twentieth-century white dilemma over how to address Booker T. Washington, a host of racial/gender norms. Descended from "master," Mister performs as an address of respect. Whatever ironic inflections it may take on notwithstanding, the term acknowledges a sustained distance between self and other, a minimal space surrounding the male designated Mister that keeps him, so to speak, intact within a field of address. Children are not yet Misters, not yet inserted into the social network securely enough to receive this deference. Thus Mr. both betokens male adulthood as achieved insertion within the symbolic order—one can only be Mr. within a larger community of Misters—and simultaneously declares a certain measure of autonomy. To be addressed as Mr. is to be addressed properly, with propriety, with the implication of property. All three of these notions—property, propriety, the proper—are intertwined components of the mastery that stands behind Mister, and they point to those aspects of manhood reserved for the white Master, denied explicitly to the black male slave and implicitly to the black freedman.[3]

Mister may further imply, I want to argue, a completed negotiation of the Oedipal crisis itself. All Misters are deemed to have passed through the crucible of potentially crippling infantile confusions and to be credentialed as fully individuated human beings within the social order. They have internalized the father's authority (in the form of the superego), become capable of policing themselves, achieved adult identity. Propertied or not, Misters are assumed to be self-owning and entitled to larger ownership; fathers or not, they may occupy paternal terrain.[4] The refusal of Southern white culture to call Booker T. Washington "Mr." is a refusal to grant him manhood within that culture's registers of property, propriety, and the proper: the potential property of goods and land that define the birthright of white post-Enlightenment males, the propriety of membership within a community of white Misters, and the proper (the *propre*, "one's own") of achieved masculinity itself. These are the larger stakes at issue in the drama of black manhood.

* * *

Property, propriety, the proper: perhaps the greatest of these is property. Before moving forward to the specific resonance of these terms in Faulkner's and Morrison's texts, I want briefly to rehearse the larger American claim for property as a defining attribute of free men. That claim, of course, derives from the European Enlightenment; its best-known source is probably John Locke's "Second Essay Concerning Civil Government" (1690).[5] Seeking (in the wake of a century of religious war) to shore up England's 1688 bloodless revolution, proposing an argument of natural law that would supersede any monarchical constraint upon the subject, Locke writes: "The *natural liberty* of man is to be free from any superior power on earth, and not to be under the will or legislative authority of man, but to have only the law of Nature for his rule" (283). Deeper than any covenant imposed by church or king, Locke argues, is our natural, inalienable liberty. This liberty acquires focus and grounding through the concept of property: "Though the earth, and all inferior creatures be common to all men, yet every man has a *property* in his own *person*. This nobody has any right to but himself. The *labour* of his body and the *work* of his hands, we may say, are properly his. Whatsoever, then, he removes out of the state that Nature hath provided, and left it in, he hath mixed his *labour* with, and joined to it something that is his own, and thereby makes it his *property*" (287–88). Given these convictions, Locke has no difficulty in assigning to government its foremost purpose: "The great and *chief end,* therefore, of men uniting into commonwealths, and putting themselves under government, *is the preservation of their property*" (350–51).

It would be hard to overestimate the appeal of this argument to our Founding Fathers. Louis Hartz, seeking to characterize this country's liberal tradition, calls Locke "America's philosopher" as he could never have been Europe's: "When Locke came to America . . . a change appeared. Because the basic feudal oppressions of Europe had not taken root, the fundamental social norm of Locke ceased in large part to look like a norm and began, of all things, to look like a sober description of fact. . . . History was on a lark, out to tease men, not by shattering their dreams, but by fulfilling them with a sort of satiric accuracy."[6] Our labor, the activation of our own personal resources, the goods we individually gather through such expenditure of energy: these are to be thought of (with a literalism inconceivable in the Old World) as our inalienable property, central to our unfettered identity. British refusal to recognize—through appropriate representation—this American right to property led to a justified war of independence. The individual possession of property is not only what we will go to war to protect, it is also what most securely keeps the peace. "Government, thought the Fathers, is based on property," Richard Hofstadter writes. "Men who have no property lack the necessary stake in an orderly society to make stable or reliable citizens."[7] Noah Webster extends this view in a 1787 commentary on the Constitution, seeing in the maintenance of property rights the very basis of freedom:

> Wherever we cast our eyes, we see this truth, that *property* is the basis of *power;* and this, being established as a cardinal point, directs us to the means of preserving our freedom. Make laws, irrevocable laws in every state, destroying and barring entailments;

leave real estates to revolve from hand to hand, as time and accident may direct; and no family influence can be acquired and established for a series of generations—no man can obtain dominion over a large territory—the laborious and saving, who are generally the best citizens, will possess each his share of property and power, and thus the balance of wealth and power will continue where it is, in *the body of the people. A general and tolerably equal distribution of landed property is the whole basis of national freedom.*[8]

If property is proposed as the grounding concept of both peace and freedom, we might begin to note the anxieties and omissions that hedge this claim even in Locke and Webster, and that have bedevilled it ever since.[9] Suppose that each did not possess his share, that property were not spread through "the body of the people . . . [with] tolerably equal distribution," that one man did take more than he could actually make use of? Suppose he did obtain "dominion over a large territory"? Locke feebly argues that "He was only to look that he used them [the goods that make up his property] before they spoiled, else he took more than his share, and robbed others. And, indeed, it was a foolish thing, as well as dishonest, to hoard up more than he could make use of" (300). But this rejoinder had no more force in 1690 than the following one penned 245 years later and put into the mind of young Thomas Sutpen: "and as for objects, nobody had any more of them than you did because everybody had just what he was strong enough or energetic enough to take and keep, and only that crazy man would go to the trouble to take or even want more than he could eat or swap for powder and whiskey."[10]

But somebody always does have more than you do, and Sutpen stumbles down from the mountain upon a Tidewater drama that sharply subverts Locke: the spectacle of a white man so engorged with property that his power is revealed not in his labor—Locke's crucial justificatory term—but in his indolence: a man whom others fan and feed, who lords it over "a country all divided and fixed and neat with a people living on it all divided and fixed and neat because of what color their skins happened to be and what they happened to own" (*AA* 179). Here the defects of the property schema leap into visibility. Far from a natural right of every human being, it is always selectively distributed, first to industrious white males who underwrote England's bloodless revolution of 1688 and our bloody one of 1776, thereafter to white males (even those originating from the Old Bailey) cunning or hungry enough to acquire it. Propertied white men not only may grow greedy for more property, but there are other, gaping omissions on the American scene: poor whites who lack property; women who both lack property and are property; slaves who are nothing but property; their offspring still in search of property. History only seemed to be on a lark, for what beckoned as a manageable fact—the effective accumulation of property—would for many Americans never be more than a dream. Founded on a premise destined to implode from within—to make of class, gender, and race the very factors that will cause the dream of identity-as-property to collapse—American culture comes into being, it seems, as a white male drama with its tragic exclusions already inseparable from its intoxicating promises. Faulkner and Morrison were conceived centuries before they were born. Before turning specifically to Lucas Beauchamp and Paul D, I would like briefly to probe the larger "repercussion" of property and self-ownership in both writers.

*   *   *

Faulkner becomes Faulkner, paradoxically, by finding his way into the drama of radically failed self-ownership. The voices of Benjy and Quentin Compson testify eloquently to the collapse of the American dream of identity-as-property. Rather than the Lockean premise of successful labor, of a thrusting male will that subdues and shapes an estate in its own image—that knows itself through what it possesses—Faulkner gives us the drama of interior dispossession. Caught up within a stream-of-consciousness technique that produces them not as subjects with a coherent project but as cacophonous sites of cultural interference, Benjy and Quentin never do or own anything. Instead, they are done to, they suffer the consequences of previous cultural designs gone awry: the burden of generations of Compson dysfunction comes to rest upon their ineffectual minds and bodies. "I was trying to say" is the hallmark of Faulknerian voice, and it can find utterance only when a culture's known forms of saying—of articulating social possibility as an achievable personal project—have failed. Early Faulknerian voice is an unforgettable way of saying No after a host of conventional ways of saying Yes have proved bankrupt.[11]

Benjy, Quentin, Darl, Joe Christmas: these are the subjectivities the early Faulkner most brilliantly produced; each signals the unavailingness of cultural designs as maps for achievable selfhood. If in Western culture the Oedipal crisis is the ordeal the male child must go through in order to emerge as a candidate for paternity and its perquisites—property, propriety, the proper—then each of these figures remains arrested on the threshold of that journey, dancing around a wound that precedes the Oedipal. Damaged by defective or disappeared mothers, insufficiently birthed into the culture's symbolic orders (or birthed into the culture's insufficient symbolic orders), they cannot manage the simplest tasks of self-ownership. Insecurely gendered, incapable of separating internal from external, resolutely untrainable, these boychildren career across the Faulknerian canvas, revealing fissure and contradiction wherever they touch down. Desiring their mother or their sister or their brother, they are hopelessly enmeshed in incest schemas, and such schemas only deepen as scandal if the sibling turns out to be black as well. Indeed, Faulkner found his way into the ordeal of race through the ordeal of family, and in a certain sense he never ceased to view racial torment as an epiphenomenon of family torment. Incest and miscegenation are the prime motives fueling his narrative, guaranteeing its subversion of Lockean proprieties by contaminating all definitions of the proper. If there is one thing his most memorable characters share, it is the knowledge that they do not possess themselves. Is it too much to say that a fear of contamination—an all but hysterical sensitivity to odors and touches that have already invaded and deformed before they are even recorded by consciousness—coils at the core of Faulknerian sensibility? Or should we say that this fear of contamination registers simultaneously an impossible (because ideologically taboo) longing—a desire to cross illicit boundaries (incestuous, miscegenous) in which successful transgression could only mean the death of the "proper" subject? At any rate, from Donald Mahan to the reporter in *Pylon* to Chick Mallison, a characteristic male note is to be moved beyond control, overwhelmed: hardly traits on which a fiction committed to the masculine pursuit of identity through attainment of fixed property could be built.

Even if we grant that Faulkner's work is invested in such a critique of identity-as-property, we might also concede his work's yearning for achieved selfhood, attained project, the successful maturation of child into property-bearing adult. *Go Down, Moses* manages in its portrait of Ike McCaslin to attend with equal generosity to why he must repudiate and what social price he pays in repudiating. Who better than Faulkner could understand a refusal to take on the guilt attaching to propertied Southern adulthood, even as he shows both that property repudiated remains property someone else will accept and abuse, and that the undeviating pursuit of property could be an epic male undertaking, however disastrous its consequences?

As for Morrison, her texts likewise recognize that while identity as self-contained property might foreclose one's emotional resources, on the one hand—think of Macon Dead Jr. in *Song of Solomon*—identity as unchecked identification threatens to run rampant over the fragile boundaries of one's selfhood, on the other. No one who has imagined the damage done to individual identity by the institution of slavery—the attack on sustaining psychic boundaries, the undoing of one's own self-possession—will discount the power of the freed Baby Suggs's discovery: "But suddenly she saw her hands and thought with a clarity as simple as it was dazzling, 'These hands belong to me. These *my* hands.' "[12] Hers to own, to make plans for, take charge of: the text's most lyrical passage rehearses Baby Suggs's sermon of self-ownership, of reclaiming your body from the institution that had controlled it. "Claim" is a term that punctuates Morrison's text: "Freeing yourself was one thing; claiming ownership of that freed self was another" (B 95). The radically unclaimed self—unable to count on its free labor as its own property—is rudderless, a creature of others' will, what Locke quite deliberately calls a slave.[13]

Beloved both endorses and provocatively calls into question this model of achieved self-ownership—calls it into question not least because no people who had experienced three centuries of enslavement could afford to envisage their subjectivity in such immaculate terms of self-management. If you had to own yourself to be yourself, and if this model could actually be realized only for a certain class of white males, then what goes on inside the mind and heart of all those others—unpropertied white males, women, slaves—for whom such a definition of who they are is only a mockery of what they are? This is exactly the question I want now to pursue, more deliberately, through Faulkner's and Morrison's black males. Unable to be a Mister, how does an unpropertied black male negotiate his manhood? I turn to Lucas Beauchamp in a scene from "The Fire and the Hearth" in *Go Down, Moses*.

> "Are you the husband?" the Chancellor said.
> "That's right," Lucas said.
> "Say sir to the court!" the clerk said. Lucas glanced at the clerk.
> "What?" he said. "I dont want no court. I done changed my—"
> "Why you uppity—" the clerk began. . . .
> "Not now," Lucas said. "We don't want no voce. Roth Edmonds knows what I mean."
> "What? Who does?"
> "Why, the uppity—" the clerk said. "Your Honor—" Again the Chancellor raised his hand slightly toward the clerk. He still looked at Lucas.
> "Mister Roth Edmonds," Lucas said . . . (GDM 124)

"Are you the husband?" The question resonates in the mind, inasmuch as the deepest crisis Lucas Beauchamp undergoes in this novel revolves around his status as Molly's husband. If he were Molly's husband as a white man is husband of a white woman, Zack would never have presumed upon Molly as his own property (a presumption the text produces as normative more than as transgressive). And Lucas would never have needed to wonder, " 'How to God . . . can a black man ask a white man to please not lay down with his black wife?' " (*GDM* 58) "Please": the word betokens not personal timidity but a structured nonmastery, a pleading with the master to abrogate a right that is his in some way deeper than the law itself. Of course it was until 1865 the law itself: during slavery there were no legal black marriages.[14] Despite the overwhelming reliance of black families upon this ceremony, it was for obvious reasons illegal: in the eyes of the law the offspring of slaves belong to the white master. "Are you the husband?" Earlier in the South he would not have been, and Faulkner saturates this 1940s court scene with Lucas's continued eccentricity to legal norms. We have here a Chancellor, a clerk, a Mister—and Lucas. Each of these white titles conveys entitlement within the social system, and the scandal Faulkner delights in is Lucas's nevertheless insisting on agency. Pressured as to juridical identity, menaced as to courtroom manners, Lucas insinuates his own purpose into the scene: " 'Roth Edmonds knows what I mean,' " and Roth does. The price Lucas pays registers not in his checkbook—Edmonds pays court costs—but in that required term of respect he must utter yet can never himself receive from the lips of white men: "Mister."

Faulkner dramatizes Lucas's pursuit of an independent identity as an ongoing struggle with the white Symbolic implicit in "Mister." His origin, announced in "The Bear" as already white-bestowed, "ledgered," is what he seeks to rewrite:

not *Lucius Quintus* @c @c @c, but *Lucas Quintus*, not refusing to be called Lucius, because he simply eliminated that word from the name; not denying, declining the name itself, because he used three quarters of it; but simply taking the name and changing, altering it, making it no longer the white man's but his own, by

himself composed, himself selfprogenitive and nominate, by himself
ancestored . . . (*GDM* 269)

We should note the desperate illogic of this premise: how can a
man change his name from inherited Lucius to invented Lucas
and be imagined as therefore free, self-progenitive, and nominate? The old man, the original Lucius Quintus Carothers
McCaslin, dominates Lucas's psychic life; all alterations relate
to this white origin.[15] But Lucas strives to relate to it on equal
terms—Lucas to Lucius—whereas Isaac's very name places him
in a structure of Biblical sonship, his moves limited to support
of or withdrawal from the parental narrative.

Lucas, by contrast, would step into the entitlements of that
narrative; this requires, however, taking on its originary white
male terms. Put starkly, Faulkner redresses Lucas's race and
gender marginality—his lack of entitlement, of land, of secured
wife—not by immersing him within the living resources of a
native black culture, but by phantasmatically aligning him with
the authority of his white male soul-mates. Locked in an embrace that harbors this text's deepest yearning, Lucas is dramatized in unforgettable encounter with Zack across the marriage
bed and with Old Carothers over the upholding of masculine
honor, just as in *Intruder in the Dust* he will be dramatized in
charged relation to Chick, his childlike suitor, and to Gavin, his
garrulous and frustrated brother. White to black, male to male,
each of these pairings figures the bond that Faulkner has
invested in, and each represses from view its excluded other:
black to black, male to female. "Are you the husband?" is the
surface question—are you capable of enforcing your claim to
your wife?—but the underlying question is different: "Are you
the man?"—can you hold your own with Old Carothers?

Thus when Lucas makes his way through Zack's challenge to
his manhood by a ritual encounter of honor-bound moves,
advantages offered first by one and then by the other and
accepted by neither, the enemy cherished even as he is pursued
(all of this enacted over the wife-empty bridal bed)—when

Lucas terminates this love scene to his own satisfaction, he thinks: *"Old Carothers . . . I needed him and he come and spoke for me"* (*GDM* 57). This suturing moment locates Lucas's self-possession within the fantasy of a white male structure of subjectivity. He becomes himself by being spoken/spoken for by Old Carothers. Defiantly risking his own life and Zack's, Lucas answers—as no one else in *Go Down, Moses* does answer—the old man's original challenge. That challenge was shaped, precisely, by the American property-model: simply to take all you wanted and could get, to bend your will to no man's rejoinder, to map the world and name its creatures as though you were indeed your own ancestor and all others your progeny or property. *Go Down, Moses* eloquently testifies to the inhumanity of this project, but perhaps we have overlooked the text's covert longing for it nevertheless. Old Carothers, Du Homme, Sam Fathers, Old Ben, Lion: these impenetrable male icons brook no quarter, absorb no insult. Figures of imaginary wholeness, they are archaic or marginal within the realm of the ongoing social—a solution at one level that is a collapse at another. Is there any doubt that Lucas reincarnates these figures when he silences Roth by saying: " 'I'm the man here' " (*GDM* 116)? In my reading, *Intruder in the Dust* continues this phantasmatic project, suturing Lucas into a monument of fixed manhood, a phallus without the complications of interiority, pure, immovable, impervious: imprisoned in the social yet unbroken in the imaginary. It is as though, by 1948, the only Man Faulkner could envisage among the puling boys and men he gazed upon—the only figure beyond social cooptation and therefore capable of genuine self-possession—would have to be black, immolated, and unconquerable. I turn to Paul D in *Beloved*.

> "Mister, he looked so . . . free. Better than me. Stronger, tougher. Son a bitch couldn't even get out the shell by hisself but he was still king and I was . . ." Paul D stopped and squeezed his left hand with his right. He held it that way long enough for it and the world to quiet down and let him go on.

285

"Mister was allowed to be and stay what he was. But I wasn't allowed to be and stay what I was. Even if you cooked him you'd be cooking a rooster named Mister. But wasn't no way I'd ever be Paul D again, living or dead. Schoolteacher changed me. I was something else and that something was less than a chicken sitting in the sun on a tub." (B 72)

Like Faulkner's totem animals that radiate an imaginary integrity, Mister impresses Paul D as immovably centered, and therefore free. Even eaten, Mister stays what he is, remains intact, a feat beyond Paul D's capacity. Paul D has lost his proper, his own; owned and invaded by Schoolteacher, he has been remade into a being he can no longer subjectify as himself. Why has his identity project failed and how does Morrison propose its recovery?

We begin again with names. Garner named them all, bestowing both their names and their manhood. Others' slaves were treated as boys; Garner's were trained as men:

"Beg to differ, Garner. Ain't no nigger men."
"Not if you scared, they ain't." Garner's smile was wide. "But if you a man yourself, you'll want your niggers to be men too."
"I wouldn't have no nigger men around my wife."
It was the reaction Garner loved and waited for. "Neither would I," he said. "Neither would I," and there was always a pause before the neighbor . . . got the meaning. Then a fierce argument, sometimes a fight, and Garner came home bruised and pleased, having demonstrated one more time what a real Kentuckian was: one tough enough and smart enough to make and call his own niggers men. (B 11)

Garner performs exactly the definition of manhood he pretends to offer his slaves: the maintenance of physical integrity, the capacity to make good on your word, to prove it through bodily prowess. White manhood is the maintaining of self-possession, the adequation of one's behavior to one's will, the ability to patrol one's property—one's self at all times, one's wife in this instance—and guarantee that she remains one's own. The fights break out over just this, the other men's realization that Garner has insulted their capacity to patrol their wives in the presence of nigger men, not boys. A "real Kentuckian" looks remarkably like Old Carothers: he makes people do his bidding, assigns their names and object-status in relation to his subject-control, remains inalterably himself.

Paul D's crisis stems from his having been trained to believe himself such a man.[16] Choices had been made available to him, he was never forced. Rather, he had subjectified the proffered model, assented to the hailing, imagined himself in charge of himself. Only later, after Morrison has exposed him to the full brunt of slavery, does Paul D see that on this model he can never be a man: the black experience of slavery simply disallows the equation of male identity with male will. In Genovese's words, "The slaveholders deprived black men of the role of provider; refused to dignify their marriages or legitimize their issue; compelled them to submit to physical abuse in the presence of their women and children; made them choose between remaining silent while their wives and daughters were raped or seduced and risking death."[17] The list continues. Paul D's experience of such impotence is harrowing.

The text produces him as a man invaded, treated like an abusable woman. Things are put into male slaves: a bit in their mouths, a penis in their mouths, irons upon their legs. If manhood means self-ownership, Paul D is owned by others, raped repeatedly. He ceases to be a single entity: his body shakes uncontrollably (as Temple Drake's does after her rape in *Sanctuary*). He becomes a site of overrun boundaries: "Paul D thought he was screaming; his mouth was open and there was this loud throat-splitting sound—but it may have been somebody else. Then he thought he was crying. Something was running down his cheeks. He lifted his hands to wipe away the tears and saw dark brown slime" (*B* 110). Liquids pour out of him, over him, into him; his own, those of others, those of nature. Out of control, venting without knowing it just as Sethe's urine breaks without her consent, Paul D undergoes a self-undoing that grotesquely reverses the Oedipal crisis. Rather than struggle with taboo desires and succeed in imposing a boundary upon them—a boundary enabling eventual entry into language, individuation, manhood, paternity, and property— Paul D reverts, under such pressure, to a chaotic, prehuman economy of liquids. At the extreme, when a male slave is confronted with the utter incapacity of his will to affect his reality, forced to watch impotently while his wife is beaten and milked, he becomes—like Halle—simultaneously not-male and insane (his identity no longer his own), a creature smeared in butter, undone by a liquid economy erasing all boundaries, disfiguring a face and a mind once male.

This critique of the Oedipal seems as profoundly Morrison's intention as the re-imagining of the Oedipal seems Faulkner's. As the grounding norm of white society, the Oedipal stabilizes patriarchy itself.[18] It does so by providing Western culture's central paradigm for justifying the male child's endurance of (rather than rebellion against) libidinal repression imposed by authority: justified because in time that child will achieve the individuation of centered selfhood, will take on the structural position of the vacated father, and will inherit his authority and his possessions. To become properly oneself, to move from infantile polymorphous perversity to adult conventionality, is to discipline desire and to enter the genealogical field of property-descent. Morrison shows that this gender economy—geared to the patriarchal notions of propriety, property, and the proper— must be reconceived if it is to nourish disenfranchised black subjectivity. *Beloved* contributes in a number of ways to just such a reconception.[19]

There is, first, the tension between loving small and loving large. Morrison's commitment to the Margaret Garner materials radiates from a slave woman's refusal to love small. A sentimental writer would have exonerated such large love, a lesser writer would have criticized it: Morrison explores both its cost and its necessity.[20] She shows that for black slaves to love large is to enact an identification that risks insanity when the loved ones are abused: "He saw a witless coloredwoman jailed and hanged for stealing ducks she believed were her own babies" (*B* 66). At the same time Morrison shows us that Paul D's heart cannot be confined within that rusted tin can. So long as he believes this, Paul D is on the run, unwilling to invest his feelings where he cannot, manlike, maintain his will. Indeed, his initial indictment of Sethe—"You got two feet, Sethe, not four" (B 165)—follows from a sense of manhood in which the proper still reigns: her behavior is hers to patrol, there is a right and a wrong choice, she has made the wrong one.

Our judicial system is founded in certain ways on such distinctions; its notions of right and wrong are largely calibrated according to the male criterion of self-responsibility before the law. We are assumed individually responsible for patrolling our territory, maintaining our proper/property. *Beloved* recurrently undermines this model, perhaps most eloquently in those intense passages in part 2 where we cannot responsibly assign utterance to speaker, say what belongs to whom. This collapse of boundaries is writ with equal power in Sethe's act itself— "This here new Sethe didn't know where the world stopped and she began" (B 164)—an act in which self and world are inextricably intertwined. The murder of the child explodes the boundaries without which there can be no proper itself: it is her act and yet not hers, her fault and yet not her fault. The weight of an entire institution—the institution of slavery—must be brought to bear, if we would understand how a mother might kill a child out of love and be both right and wrong in doing so. If the law is useless for sorting this out, if the law incites to violence rather than to self-possession, if the law proposes no credible paternal model for normative behavior, how is Oedipus to oversee our maturation by laying down and legitimizing our categories of gender difference? Paul D eventually comes to see—in washing Sethe's feet rather than counting them, in nursing rather than judging—that male and female are massively interdependent realms, and that a black man cannot sustain a model of white manhood. As Hortense Spillers puts it, "the black American male embodies the only American community of males which has had the specific occasion to learn who the female is within itself."[21] This female-within-male calls into question gender categories in ways that go beyond the ken of all impenetrable Misters.

*   *   *

I would close speculatively. Both writers know—how could they not?—that the central damage done by slavery to black manhood was to cripple individual agency. Unable to equate self with will, black men were wounded in their own proper, their capacity to own themselves, to become full-fledged Misters. "A man without force," Frederick Douglass had written as early as 1855, "is without the essential dignity of humanity. Human nature is so constituted that it cannot *honor* a helpless man, although it can *pity* him; and even that it cannot do long, if the signs of power do not arise."[22] The blow dealt by such impotence to the pride that sustains identity fuels Faulkner's intricate exploration of Lucas Beauchamp and accounts for *Intruder in the Dust*'s suturing of Lucas's authority. Morrison, by contrast, does not so much restore Paul D's manhood as reconceive it. The reconception calls into question the Oedipal economy of the achieved proper itself.

In her work—especially her theoretical work—we find, foregrounded, what we may be learning to recognize in Faulkner's as well (though against the grain), that identity of every sort is differential rather than "properly" achieved. Self-owning is rarely innocent. Men too often know who they are, they ratify their self-image, through repudiating the other: they are not women, they are not blacks. "I aint a nigger," little Jason says in "That Evening Sun."[23] In this casual paradigm we see the fantasy of a pure identity being constituted by a juxtaposition against contaminating others. Morrison powerfully explicates the drama, acted out in countless scenes in American history, in which the meaning of white freedom requires for its salient unfolding an immovable black silhouette. I quote from *Playing in the Dark:*

> The need to establish difference stemmed not only from the Old World but from a difference in the New. What was distinctive in

the New was, first of all, its claim to freedom and, second, the presence of the unfree within the heart of the democratic experiment—the critical absence of democracy, its echo, shadow, and silent force in the political and intellectual activity of some not-Americans. The distinguishing features of the not-Americans were their slave status, their social status—and their color.

It is conceivable that the first would have self-destructed in a variety of ways had it not been for the last. These slaves, unlike many others in the world's history, were visible to a fault. And they had inherited, among other things, a long history on the meaning of color. It was not simply that this slave population had a distinctive color; it was that this color "meant" something. That meaning had been named and deployed by scholars from at least the moment, in the eighteenth century, when other and sometimes the same scholars started to investigate both the natural history and the inalienable rights of man—that is to say, human freedom.[24]

Here we return to Locke and the Enlightenment with a darker awareness that freedom and unfreedom, like male and female, white and black, are inextricably interdependent terms—that selfhood as achieved property plays itself out differentially, against a backdrop of dispossession. "Before slavery," Orlando Patterson argues, "people simply could not have conceived of the thing we call freedom."[25] Surely it is because Faulkner's characters so yearn for self-sufficiency that his texts dramatize their discovery of internal rupture—their incapacity to maintain identity as a self-patrolled property—as a tragic burden. To be rudely ejected from the sanctuary of one's imaginary self-possession is to be involuntarily invaded by others, to be othered:

But after that I seemed to see them [black people] for the first time not as people, but as a thing, a shadow in which I lived, we lived, all white people, all other people. I thought of all the children coming forever and ever into the world, white, with the black shadow already falling upon them before they drew breath. And I seemed to see the black shadow in the shape of a cross. And it seemed like the white babies were struggling, even before they drew breath, to escape from the shadow that was not only upon them but beneath them too, flung out like their arms were flung out, as if they were nailed to the cross. I saw all the little babies

that would ever be in the world, the ones not yet even born—a long
line of them with their arms spread, on the black crosses.[26]

The speaker is Joanna in *Light in August*, but the burden she
carries here is more generally Faulknerian. It is the awareness
that those of us who are white are both orphaned and multiply
possessed, both abandoned and penetrated by our parents and
by the larger culture's unwanted arrangements. Women not
only show men that they are, satisfyingly, men, but women also
live within men uninvited, disturbing the propriety of male
norms. And blacks, because of what those of us who are white
did to them in the South before we were even born, will forever
live inside us, owed a reparation beyond our capacity to repress
or repay. Insofar as the property model of identity may nevertheless operate in Faulkner's work—requiring the other's disenfranchisement to know itself as free—it does so outside the
comforts of innocence, in the form of an overdetermined and
internalized debt, an accumulating cultural mortgage—a property with insurmountable liens upon it—one of those checks we
somehow co-signed before exiting from our mother's womb and
which will be called in for cashing any day now.

Morrison, by contrast, seems to register the penetrability of
identity as both burden and promise. Whites may know themselves as not-black, yes, but her best work goes past this
oppositional frame, opening into a complex embrace of the
mutuality that funds all identity.[27] Identity as patrolled property
too easily slips into figurative ossification of self or literal enslavement of others. *Beloved* shows, instead, the irresistible
need to live in others, to know self through identificatory
investment in others. You could be reduced to insanity by the
damage done to your loved ones, but you could also survive
disaster by identifying—as Sethe does in her flight to freedom—
with those beings who came from your body but who are not
you. They call to that in you that exceeds you, that is not your
property to patrol. Sethe's breasts are not her own; they and
the milk they carry link her to her offspring. The text's most

terrifying image is of white boys enclosing those breasts as their own property. What is for Faulkner our human tragedy—that we are never our own, are always trying to say, always inadequate to and in excess of ourselves—is for Morrison our human possibility.

NOTES

1. Others have said it too. Jim Carrothers said it to me at the American Literature Association in San Diego (June 1994) when I brought up the *Go Down, Moses* analogy for our ritual regrouping to discuss Faulkner. This and subsequent citations are from *Go Down, Moses* (New York: Vintage International, 1990).

2. Sigmund Freud, *Group Psychology and the Analysis of the Ego* (1921), in *The Standard Edition of the Complete Psychological Works of Sigmund Freud*, ed. and trans. James Strachey (London: Hogarth Press, 1953–74), 18:105. In the 7th chapter of this text, Freud undertakes his fullest exploration of the dynamic of "identification," which he generalizes as "the earliest expression of an emotional tie with another person" (105). This tie may or may not be libidinal, and it can later occur significantly among members of a group who share "an important emotional common quality . . [which] lies in the nature of the tie with the leader" (108). This last description seems clearly to implicate the odd bonding—affectional and rivalrous—that unites scholars mutually attached to a single author: like Faulknerians.

Laplanche and Pontalis characterize Freudian "Identification" as the "psychological process whereby the subject assimilates an aspect, property, or attitude of the other and is transformed, wholly or partially, after the model the other provides. It is by means of a series of identifications that the personality is constituted and specified" (*The Language of Psycho-Analysis*, trans. Donald Nicholson Smith [New York: Norton, 1973], 205). Such transformative dynamics may well be the core psychic resource enabling subject-other interaction, in both life and literature. It is therefore fascinating that Freud has, on the whole, so little to say about "identification," and one may speculate that Freud's own anxiety about "identification"—e.g., his sustained silence about Nietzche's influence, his neurotic response to Jung's brilliance, his insistence on his own priority—is pertinent to his reticence. Freud's insistence on the successful negotiation of the Oedipal complex as achieved individuation may shed light on why he only late in his career considered the radically "unindividuated" condition of the pre-Oedipal. Jim Swan speculates that, for Freud, "Maturity (that is, *masculine* maturity) means being well-defended against one's past, which amounts to the same thing as having a strong capacity for resisting identification. . . . In effect, Freud's picture of maturity is of a man driven to outrun . . . identification with the body of his mother, the original unity of mother and infant" ("Mater and Nanny: Freud's Two Mothers and the Discovery of the Oedipus Complex," *American Imago* 31 [1974]: 9–10).

"Transference" may seem to be a rough synonym for "identification," but Freudian analysis differentiates sharply between them. Rather than relating transference to that larger and continuing intersubjective process whereby one invests another with one's own psychic structures—or becomes oneself reshaped by the perceived structures of the other—Freudians understand transference as primitive, neurotically charged, and more narrowly enacted within the psychoanalytic encounter itself. "For psycho-analysis," Laplanche and Pontalis write, transference is blindly projective, "a process of actualization of unconscious wishes. Transference uses specific objects and operates in the framework of a specific relationship established with these objects. Its context *par excellence* is the analytic situation. . . . Classically, the transference is acknowledged to be the terrain on which all the basic problems of a given analysis play themselves out" (455). Since the interactive model of identity that I am pursuing in this essay is potentially reciprocal and enabling, I shall speak more of "identification" than of "transference."

3. The *OED* gives twenty-three different definitions for "master" as a noun. Most of them circulate around the notion of control over something (or someone) else, and the seventh definition is typical: "One who has the power to control, use, or dispose of something at will." As early as the sixteenth century, British children in well-off families were addressed by servants as "master" or "young master." (The *OED's* twenty-second definition identifies "master" as "the usual prefix to the names of a young gentlemen not considered old enough to be entitled to be called Mr.") Remove the constitutive relation between possessor and person/thing/concept being possessed, and the term loses its conceptual core. (*The Compact Edition of the Oxford English Dictionary* [Oxford: Oxford University Press, 1971], 2: 1738.)

4. It should be clear that I am describing in an ideal or normative fashion the frame of assumptions that attach to "Mister." Actual usage varies enormously, yet the normative frame (diminished since the Civil Rights activity of the 1950s and 1960s but not eradicated) affects that usage.

5. John Locke, *An Essay Concerning the True Original, Extent, and End of Civil Government*, in *John Locke, The Two Treatises of Government*, ed. Peter Laslett (Cambridge: Cambridge University Press, 1988), 265–428. Subsequent citation from Locke refers to this edition. For useful discussion of Locke's importance to the Founding Fathers' notions of American politics and appropriate norms, see Bernard Bailyn, *The Ideological Origins of the American Revolution* (Cambridge: Harvard University Press, 1967), Richard Hofstadter, *The American Political Tradition* (New York: Random House, 1948), Thomas Pangle, *The Spirit of Modern Republicanism: The Moral Vision of the American Founders and the Philosophy of Locke* (Chicago: University of Chicago Press, 1988), and James Tully, *An Approach to Political Philosophy: Locke in Contexts* (Cambridge: Cambridge University Press, 1993).

6. Louis Hartz, *The Liberal Tradition in America: An Interpretation of American Political Thought since the Revolution* (New York: Harcourt Brace, 1955), 60.

7. Richard Hofstadter, *The American Political Tradition* (New York: Random House, 1948), 13.

8. Noah Webster, "A Citizen of America," *The Debate on the Constitution*, Part One, ed. Bernard Bailyn (New York: The Library of America, 1993), 157–58.

9. Pangle (among others) notes this problem: "Locke's conception of the natural law of property . . . imposes no effective, intrinsic restriction on acquisitiveness" (161). Indeed, this abuse remains unavoidable so long as inventive labor remains, in Locke's world view, a primary good. Subscribing to an Enlightenment project that has its source paradoxically in both Bacon and Genesis, Locke sees the scientific progress of civilization as founded on a limitless transformation of the brute, natural world. In Pangle's words, "The sum of Locke's message, then, is this: so barren is nature, so difficult is it for mankind to wrest from nature's materials a comfortable existence, that there is no ascertainable limit to the necessary growth in the productivity of human labor" (166).

10. *Absalom, Absalom!* (New York: Vintage International, 1990), 179. Subsequent citation from *Absalom* refers to this edition.

11. I have developed this argument more fully in *Faulkner's Subject: A Cosmos No One Owns* (New York: Cambridge University Press, 1992), 82–109. For a rigorous classification of the different registers of Faulknerian voice, see Stephen Ross, *Fiction's Inexhaustible Voice: Speech and Writing in Faulkner* (Athens: University of Georgia Press, 1989).

12. *Beloved* (New York: New American Library, 1987), 141. Subsequent citation from *Beloved* refers to this edition.

13. Locke writes: "But there is another sort of servants which by a peculiar name we call *slaves*, who being captives taken in a just war are, by the right of Nature, subjected to the absolute dominion and arbitrary power of their masters. These men having, as I

say, forfeited their lives and, with it their liberties, and lost their estates, and being in the *state of slavery*, not capable of any property, cannot in that state be considered as any part of *civil society*, the chief end whereof is the preservation of property" (322–23). Locke's justificatory phrase—"taken in a just war"—may have made sense within an Athenian frame, but its impertinence to the American scene was not lost on eighteenth-century Americans. According to Bailyn, "The contrast between what political leaders in the colonies sought for themselves and what they imposed on, or at least tolerated in, others became too glaring to be ignored and could not be lightened by appeals to the Lockean justification of slavery as the favorable fate of people who "by some act that deserves death" had forfeited their lives and had been spared by the generosity of their captors. The reality of plantation life was too harsh for such fictions" (235).

14. Herbert Gutman's *The Black Family in Slavery and Freedom, 1750–1925* (New York: Pantheon, 1976) establishes in detail the cultural reality of black marriage during a period in which it did not legally exist. He warns against a confusion of the two realms of "law and culture" (52).

15. For a fuller reading of Lucas's overdetermined relationship to Old Carothers, see *Faulkner's Subject*, 64–81.

16. Deborah Sitter comments on Paul D's model of manhood in related terms: "Although Sixo is his [Paul D's] model of a manly man, the qualities Paul D associates with manliness originate in the dominant culture of the white slaveholder Mr. Garner. These qualities include strength, courage, and endurance—all of which Sixo possesses—but they are directed toward maximizing the power of the individual to dominate weaker beings" ("The Making of a Man: Dialogic Meaning in *Beloved*," *African-American Review* 26 [1992]: 24).

17. Eugene Genovese, *Roll, Jordan, Roll: The World the Slaves Made* (New York: Random House, 1972), 490.

18. See Carolyn Porter's reading of *Absalom, Absalom!*'s diagnostic engagement with the patriarchy/Oedipal ("[Un]making the Father: *Absalom, Absalom!*," in *The Cambridge Companion to William Faulkner*, ed. Philip M. Weinstein [New York: Cambridge University Press, 1995], 168–96). Porter argues that *Absalom* most disturbingly reveals what carnage occurs not when, as Bleikasten and others claim, the father fails, but rather when, in classic patriarchal fashion, he succeeds. By the time of *Intruder in the Dust*, I argue, Faulkner was seeking to dignify Lucas by immersing him within an Oedipal structure as phantasmatically intact as it was materially nonexistent (no actual father: no land, no goods, no descent—except at the level of the spirit).

19. Probably no novelist in America today is the subject of more academic commentary than Morrison. For a useful general introduction to Morrison studies, see *Toni Morrison: Critical Perspectives Past and Present*, ed. Henry Louis Gates and K. A. Appiah (New York: Amistad, 1993). For specific readings of *Beloved* that probe (through both form and theme) the idea of the masculine "proper," see Barbara Christian, "Fixing Methodologies: *Beloved*," *Cultural Critique*, 24 (1993): 5–15, Karla Holloway, "*Beloved*: A Spiritual," *Callaloo* 13 (Summer 1990): 516–25, Deborah Horwitz, "Nameless Ghosts: Possession and Dispossession in *Beloved*," *Studies in American Fiction* 17 (1989): 157–67, David Lawrence, "Fleshly Ghosts and Ghostly Flesh: The Word and the Body in *Beloved*," *Studies in American Fiction* 19 (1991): 189–201, Satya Mohany, "The Epistemic Status of Cultural Identity: On *Beloved* and the Postcolonial Condition," *Cultural Critique* 24 (1993): 41–80, and Jean Wyatt, "Giving Body to the Word: The Maternal Symbolic in Toni Morrison's *Beloved*," *PMLA* 208 (May 1993): 474–88.

20. Maggie Sale, having studied contemporary reactions to Margaret Garner's deed, reinforces this claim: "The abolitionist press . . . represented Margaret Garner's infanticide as in the heroic tradition of the American fight for liberty . . . . [but] this polemical interpretation erases the emotional cost of Garner's decision" ("Call and Response as Critical Method: African-American Oral Traditions and *Beloved*," in *African-American Review* 26 [1992]: 44). The proslavery press predictably read Garner's behavior as simply monstrous.

21. Hortense Spillers, "Mama's Baby, Papa's Maybe: An American Grammar Book," *diacritics* 17 (1987): 80.

22. Frederick Douglass, *My Bondage and My Freedom*, in *Frederick Douglass: Autobiographies* (New York: The Library of America, 1994), 286.

23. *Collected Stories of William Faulkner* (New York: Random House, 1950), 297.

24. *Playing in the Dark: Whiteness and the Literary Imagination* (New York: Random House, 1993), 48–49. A few pages earlier in the same essay, Morrison draws on Bernard Bailyn's *Voyagers to the West* to develop her most haunting vignette of American freedom enacted upon the body of the black slaves. Silhouetted by figures of unfreedom over whom he has (and exercises) absolute control, William Dunbar of Scotland systematically beats his American slave and then thinks of himself as somehow magically transformed within the new American landscape: "Once he has moved into that [new] position, he is resurrected as a new man, a distinctive man—a different man. And whatever his social status in London, in the New World he is a gentleman. More gentle, more man. The site of his transformation is within rawness; he is backgrounded by savagery" (*PD* 44).

25. Orlando Patterson, *Slavery and Social Death* (Cambridge: Harvard University Press, 1982), 340.

26. *Light in August* (New York: Vintage International, 1990), 253.

27. It does not detract from Morrison's remarkable imagination to note that the mutuality she represents occurs less between whites and blacks than among blacks themselves—and most memorably among black women. Yet Paul D shows a similar resourcefulness in his capacity to enter the subjectivity of those other chain-bound slaves in Alfred, Georgia. Their effective mutuality transforms that chain from bind to bond, and they escape enslavement the only way they can: together.

Contributors

Deborah Clarke is associate professor of English and Women's Studies at The Pennsylvania State University. She has published several essays on Faulkner, Toni Morrison, and Albert Camus, as well as *Robbing the Mother: Women in Faulkner*. She has received the George W. Atherton Award for Distinguished Teaching.

Andrea Dimino is associate professor of literature in the division of Humanities at New College of the University of South Florida. She has published essays on *Absalom, Absalom!*, the Sartoris family, and *The Hamlet*. She recently completed a book, *Faulkner's Hunt for the Present: Reading Faulknerian Time*.

John N. Duvall did his doctoral work at the University of Illinois and is currently Professor of English at the University of Memphis. At the 1985 Faulkner and Yoknapatawpha Conference, he presented "Faulkner's Critics and Women" and subsequently published *Faulkner's Marginal Couple: Invisible, Outlaw, and Unspeakable Communities*. He is also a contributor to the newly released *Approaches to Teaching "The Sound and the Fury"* published by the Modern Language Association. In addition to his work on Faulkner, he has published numerous articles on modernist and contemporary American literature in journals such as *Novel, Modern Fiction Studies, Arizona Quarterly*, and *College Literature*.

Doreen Fowler, professor of English at the University of Mississippi, has coedited twelve volumes of proceedings of the annual Faulkner and Yoknapatawpha Conference. She is the author of *Faulkner's Changing Vision: From Outrage to Affirmation* and has published articles in *American Literature, Journal of Modern Literature, Studies in American Fiction, The*

Faulkner Journal, and others. Her new book-length study of Faulkner will be published by University of Virginia Press.

Minrose C. Gwin is professor of English at the University of New Mexico. She is author of *Black and White Women of the Old South: The Peculiar Sisterhood in American Literature* and *The Feminine and Faulkner: Reading (Beyond) Sexual Difference,* as well as articles on reading as "space travel," African American women's spaces in *Go Down, Moses,* and father-daughter incest in contemporary Southern women's fiction. She is working on a book entitled "Space Travel: Feminism and Reading."

Michael E. Lahey recently received his Ph.D. in English from the University of Alberta in Edmonton, Canada. His dissertation, "Constructing Justice: Faulkner and Law," was conducted under an interdisciplinary committee of professors of English and law. He teaches several courses in the Department of English and has recently delivered papers on Charles Chesnutt at the Thirtieth Annual Canadian Association of American Studies Conference in Ottawa and on *Beloved* and *Song of Solomon* at the First National Toni Morrison Conference in Louisville, Kentucky.

Robert Dale Parker is professor of English at the University of Illinois at Urbana-Champaign and the author of *Faulkner and the Novelistic Imagination, The Unbeliever: The Poetry of Elizabeth Bishop, "Absalom, Absalom!": The Questioning of Fictions,* and articles on Faulkner and other topics in American literature in such journals as *American Literary History, The Arizona Quarterly,* and *Studies in American Fiction.*

James Polchin has studied at the University of Maryland, American University, Drew University and is currently completing a Ph.D. in American Studies at New York University. His work focuses on the relationship between twentieth century literatures and the development of sexual identities.

Noel Polk is professor of English at the University of Southern Mississippi. He is the author of numerous publications on Faulkner, including *William Faulkner's "Requiem for a Nun": A Critical Study,* and has edited *The Marionettes, Sanctuary:*

The Original Text, and many other Faulkner works. His most recent book is *Children of the Dark House: Text and Context in Faulkner,* published by University Press of Mississippi.

David Rogers is principal lecturer and course director of English at Kingston University, London, having earned his Ph.D. at Rutgers in 1991. He has published essays on Faulkner in England and the United States and recently provided introductions for Wordsworth editions of *Dracula* and the poetry of Walt Whitman. He is currently in the final stages of a book-length manuscript entitled "Articulating the Flesh: The Paradox of Form and Gender in the Novels of William Faulkner."

Joseph R. Urgo is associate professor and Chair of English and Humanities at Bryant College in Rhode Island. He was a Fulbright Lecturer in Spain in 1992. His publications include *Willa Cather and the Myth of American Migration, Novel Frames: Literature as Guide to Race, Sex, and History in American Culture, Faulkner's Apocrypha: "A Fable," Snopes, and the Spirit of Human Rebellion,* and numerous journal articles, including "*Absalom, Absalom!:* The Movie" and "Faulkner's Real Estate: Land and Literary Speculation in *The Hamlet.*"

Philip M. Weinstein is Alexander Griswold Cummins Professor of English at Swarthmore College. His publications include *Henry James and the Requirements of the Imagination, The Semantics of Desire: Changing Modes of Identity from Dickens to Joyce,* and *Faulkner's Subject: A Cosmos No One Owns.* Recently he edited the *Cambridge Companion to William Faulkner,* and the essay in this volume is part of his forthcoming book, *What Else But Love? The Ordeal of Race in Faulkner and Morrison,* published by Columbia University Press.

Patricia Yaeger is associate professor of English, University of Michigan. Coeditor of *Nationalisms and Sexualities* and *Refiguring the Father: New Feminist Readings of Patriarchy,* she is the author of *Honey-Mad Women: Emancipatory Strategies in Women's Writing.* She is presently at work on two books: "Dirt and Desire: The Grotesque in Southern Women's Fiction" and "The Poetics of Birth."

Index

301